Feeding The K

At first, the attempt to be a stay-at-island dad was a failed experiment. I blame biological evolution. My wife points to me losing the kids in a jungle on the side of a mountain. Sink or swim, however, is an especially apropos idiom on an island, and on the open seas of parenthood I learned to swim fast. Over the course of two years I managed to cook and clean, cajole and console, correct and, most importantly, connect with the kids. For a man, even a modern-day man, this is saying a lot. Yes, it's the 21st century. Yes, we've come a long way baby. No, we still don't see the irony in yelling at our kids to stop yelling.

Praise For
Feeding The Kids To The Sharks

"If I didn't know the island of Pohnpei exists, I'd think it was all a fever dream, conjured by someone utterly exhausted by a doom-scrolling, over-achieving, corporate-climbing existence in dystopian 21st-century America. *"Feeding the Kids to the Sharks"* is the antidote to everything we've gone through in the past year. It's a gorgeous, insightful, laugh-out-loud trip into the mind of a guy who dove head-first into life on a remote Pacific island, embracing a ragtag band of local characters, housework, boat repairs, memorable gecko/insect wars and, especially, his kids. I plan to read it again and again, just because."

~ Diane Carman, The Colorado Sun

"This is one of the funniest books I've read in years. JJ Martin writes with a wit and style that will make you laugh out loud. Take a ride with him and his family as they navigate the ups and downs of making a new life in exotic Micronesia. You'll have the time of your life."

~ Mark Eddy, former Denver Post reporter

"Thanks to Martin's keen sense of observation and humor, I missed the following: several critical appointments that ended up costing me my career, a lottery ticket purchase with my secret numbers I have played for 6 years that came up on the one day I was reading his bloody book, and my child's wedding. But those sacrifices were a small price to pay for the hilarity of Martin's chronicling of his parental ineptitude and his unique perspective of the American male in the early 21st Century. If you are averse to laughing and feeling good, do not read this book."

~ Frank Scandale, The Journal News

"*Feeding The Kids To The Sharks* is a delightful, sometimes harrowing journey of a stay-at-home Peace Corp dad's 2 ½ year-odyssey to a tropical island in the middle of nowhere. Martin, a PR specialist from DC, struggles to keep his house clean and his two young daughters from killing each other, but finds himself strangely at home with a zany cast of island characters and bizarre island customs that include regular hallucinogenic trips with a sludgy drink made from a pepper plant. JJ Martin's memoir will make you laugh, squirm, consider leaving your big-city life behind … and maybe think twice about having kids."

~ Dave McKibben, former LA Times reporter

In memory of Bill Raynor and Dr. Lois Engleberger – the banana lady.

Acknowledgments

I want to thank the people of Micronesia, and especially those on Pohnpei, for graciously accepting an invasion of loud and obnoxious interlopers with the warmth and hospitality one reserves for family. Speaking of loud and obnoxious, I also want to thank the expats (yes, I'm particularly looking at you, Aussies) for showing us the unwritten guidelines of living on an island and filling our lives with laughter, love, and an almost lethal amount of booze.

To Ken Friedland and Frank Scandale for actually reading and editing the rambling, inane, over-written refuse of a rough draft and telling me it was rambling, inane, over-written refuse. They helped shape the direction of the book even though I accepted not one single word of their advice.

Most of all, to Bette, whose wanderlust equates traveling to Zambia with going to the corner store for milk, but led us on journeys over the edge of this flat earth and on adventures many have only dreamed of. And to Devon and Tess … my mind, my heart, my soul … and an incredible pain in the ass.

NO THANKS

To

Simon & Schuster

Knopf

Harcourt

The Knight Agency

Viking Press

Equinox Press

Dutton

Harper's

The Ahearn Agency

Fresh Books, Inc.

Marsal Lyon Literary

Dystel, Goderich & Bourret

Corvisiero Literary Agency

The Stringer Literary Agency LLC

Andrea Hurst Literary

Diana Finch Literary

TriadaUS Literary

DeFiore

Rosenkrantz

Lisa Dawson Associates

Etc.

Etc.

Etc..

"Pirakih me I pwahpwa"

(What I have spoken is crooked. A person never
knows if he has found the whole truth.)
~ Pohnpeian proverb

A Good Fish

*Twenty years from now you will be more disappointed by
the things that you didn't do than by the ones you did do. So
throw off the bowlines. Sail away from the safe harbor.
Catch the trade winds in your sails. Explore. Dream.
Discover.*

~ Mark Twain

Bette climbed into the small, weathered boat and scanned the vast ocean, intently focusing on the distant horizon as if attempting to draw Pakin closer. The sooner they reached the tiny Pacific atoll the better. Ominous storm clouds had gathered in the late afternoon sky and the waves were beginning to jump and snap in the prevailing wind. She was determined, however, and would not be deterred, for she had promises to keep. The driver jumped in, gave her a reassuring smile through blood-red teeth stained from betel nut, the sloppy, chewy stimulant favored by locals throughout the area, then launched the boat into the surf.

Professionally, my wife goes by Elizabeth. It is the name given on her birth certificate, passport and other official documents. Unprofessionally – no, that's not right. Domestically – good god, that's even worse. Amongst friends and family – much better – she simply goes by Bette. Not Liz, not Beth and definitely not Betty, which ironically, is what she is called by the two people in the whole world who should know better.

"You don't go by Betty?" her mother will ask incredulously, the revelation hitting her for the umpteenth time.

"Mahhhh," Elizabeth will say in the New York City accent she inevitably slips into whenever her parents are around. "How many times I gotta tell ya? No!"

"Since when?"

"Since my entire life."

"What's wrong with Betty?"

"It's a great name … if you're a gum-chewing, 1950's waitress on roller skates."

"Well, excuse me." Her mother will then whack her father on the shoulder with the back of her hand and ask, "Are you listening to this? So now it's Bette, not Betty."

It's like an old black and white movie with the same black and white dialogue every time we go to see them.

A devout Catholic of Spanish/Italian heritage, her mother will handle the situation the only way it can be handled when a daughter completely changes her God given name and the nickname endorsed by the very woman who gave her birth and sacrificed for her lo these many years – by crossing herself three times and looking up to the Lord Almighty for an answer. When it doesn't come, she'll wave both hands at us in an attempt to clear the air and change the conversation.

"So, Betty, where are you off to now?"

Ah, there it is – THE question. The one Betty, er, Bette gets from everyone; asked as casually as one might inquire about the weather or the time of day.

Some people are born blessed; others are born bad to the bone. Some are born to be wild, some are born to run, and some are born free … as free as the wind blows. Bette was born to travel. As a small child, while others her age snuggled teddy bears and dreamed of going to Disneyland, she fell asleep cradling an Atlas and dreamed of Mauritania. At age three she could spell Kyrgyzstan. In the third grade she took second place in her class writing contest with her essay, "Degenerative tract infections in developing countries: global impact and priorities for women's reproductive health." "Fritzy the Rainbow Unicorn," took first place.

With a natural propensity for papers and policies, she went on to receive a Master's degree in Latin American Studies and quickly immersed herself in the noble field of development work. That meant she was forever destined to heroically labor in the nonprofit world helping the tired, the poor and the huddled masses yearning to breathe free and that, eventually, given her nonprofit salary, she would become one of them.

Which brings us back to her name, her professional name. A Bette can't save the world (and certainly not a Betty); an Elizabeth can. Valiant causes deserve valiant names.

Bette likes Elizabeth. There's a sense of competence and a certain sophistication that goes with it. It is a proper period piece name that harkens back to an era of refinement, elegance and culture, evoking the graceful character out of *Pride & Prejudice* that would easily suit Bette if only Elizabeth Bennet was from the Bronx.

On that blustery day, however, in that rather unrefined patch of the Pacific, it was a name oddly out of place as she struggled to sit Elizabethan and lady-like while the boat slammed against the waves, sending a continuous spray of salt water over her business white blouse and long floral print Pohnpeian skirt. As Peace Corps' deputy director for Micronesia, she was headed to Pakin Atoll to visit a volunteer and the small, concrete and corrugated tin school where he taught.

Suddenly, the driver swerved the boat wildly to the right and gunned the engine. Off in the distance, a frenzy of frigate birds clamored just above the shimmering ocean surface. The boat finally arrived and it wasn't long before the driver's hand-held fishing line was taut in the water.

"Oh, this is a good fish," he said, patiently pulling and yanking on the line hand over hand. He struggled as it reached the side of the boat, wildly flipping back and forth in a vicious fight for freedom. It was a Skip Jack tuna and a good sized one at that. "Grab the line and help me," he shouted to Elizabeth, throwing a ragged right-handed glove toward her.

3

She put the glove on and, as instructed, grabbed the line close to its gnashing mouth while he snatched the tail and hoisted it into the boat. The fish flopped about for several moments and then, accepting its fate, lay still. The driver released his hook and quickly surmised the fish was too big for his small cooler. Whack! His machete lopped off the head, sending a wave of blood splattering against Elizabeth. Nope, still too big. Smack! He chopped the tail off and more blood sprayed across her.

"Ah, just right," he said smiling up at my wife.

"I'm really happy for you," she replied surveying the damage to her blouse and skirt. "That's a good fish."

The engine again roared to life and Elizabeth raised her feet as the red water sloshed to the back of the boat. Sensibly, she decided against wearing her dress flip-flops. After another two hours of crashing through the waves they arrived at the atoll. The boat weaved its way through the vibrant green and yellow coral reef to a small opening surrounded by swaying palm trees where the volunteer and the entire school stood waiting on the shore. The local principal approached waded in from the shoreline, then stopped and looked my wife up and down.

"Fish?" he asked, pointing to the bloodstains. The driver held up the headless Skip Jack. "Oh, that is a good fish," the principal said, assisting Elizabeth out of the boat and into the knee-deep water. "Here, let me introduce you to the teachers and the children."

Later that night on the atoll, Elizabeth lay awake on a bamboo woven mat, listening to the wind howl and the metal roof ring with rain. The storm had arrived. She wondered if it hit the section of sea where I was and if I was alright.

It had and I was not.

Does anyone know where the love of God goes
when the waves turn the minutes to hours.
~ Gordon Lightfoot
The Wreck of the Edmund Fitzgerald

The black silhouette of the monster wave, at least the faint outline you could see through the driving rain, rose menacingly in the night and thundered down onto the deck of the boat. Despite its powerful twin 150 Evinrude engines, the 32-foot Penga-Marine was no match for this storm in this sea. I wrapped my arms around the back railing, shook the water off and watched helplessly as moments later the next 15-foot wall of water leapt from the darkness and descended upon us. Thirteen hours into our four-hour excursion, it was becoming frighteningly apparent we weren't going to make the Sapwauhfik Atoll where a Peace Corps volunteer and a local friend awaited my visit.

The islanders on board braced themselves, gripping the handles of their large coolers to remain stable, but I had a notion they were also readying them to be used as flotation devices. Although they remained stoic, the fear was palpable whenever we made eye contact and a nonverbal "Please God, get us through this" would pass between us. I'm not a deeply religious person, but you know what they say – there are no atheists in a boat at night in a tropical storm in the middle of the Pacific Ocean 43 miles off the island of Pohnpei, 158°15'E, 6°55'N.

The storm increased in ferocity and the barrage of water, fresh from above, salt from below, continued to pound the boat. Our only hope was to push it full throttle and head directly into the gathering swells, then shift into neutral to ride them out and keep from capsizing. An eerie silence enveloped the boat as we pointed straight up, crested the wave, and then quickly, nauseatingly, plummeted back down before gunning the engines again to meet another mountain of water.

Suddenly a particularly large wave engulfed us, not a rogue wave, but certainly an impolite one as it arrived several seconds ahead of the swells we had been timing, sending passengers and their coolers crashing into the back of the boat and causing me to smack my mouth against the railing. It was beginning to dawn on me that, perhaps, this trip might have been a bad decision, but bad decisions often lead to good stories. The trick is surviving them. I turned and spit a mouthful of blood and seawater out just as the next wave descended.

A man by the name of Philip Dunne once said, "I didn't lead a very wise life, myself, but it was a full one and a grown-up one. You come of age very quickly through shipwreck and disaster."

I think anyone who knows me would agree I didn't lead a very wise life, and there would be little debate as to whether or not it was a grown-up one, but as the boat continued to struggle against the roiling black sea, I had the sinking feeling I was about to "come of age very quickly."

Chapter 1

ADRIFT

Life is a zoo in a jungle.
~ Peter De Vries

"MAYBE YOU AND MOMMY SHOULD HAVE THOUGHT A
LITTLE MORE BEFORE YOU HAD US KIDS," our insightful seven-year-
old daughter Devon screamed from the top of the stairs after being punished
for not listening. Our beautiful, robin's egg blue aluminum sided home in the
quiet, suburban neighborhood of Silver Spring, Maryland, was filled with
love, laughter, and an inordinate amount of yelling.

"Honey, ain't that the truth," I screamed right back. "Back in your
room!"

Devon always had a good grasp of the obvious and a perceptive
logic all her own. At age four, the day after the World Trade Centers
collapsed and with the Pentagon still smoldering nearby, she asked who did
it.

"Bad guys," we said, driving home through Washington, D.C.

Safely strapped in her little car seat, she thought for a moment and then asked, "Do their mommies know?"

"I'm sure they do now."

She reflected on this a little more before digging deeper.

"Do bad guys wear underwear?" she asked.

"Why no, no they don't," I said with a bemused smile. "Why do you ask?"

"I heard they don't," she said definitively.

"Who told you that?" Bette asked.

"Nobody," she said. "My brain told me. My brain is smart and tells me lots of things. It's going to go to college.

She looked out of the car window, nodded her head knowingly and added, "Brain College."

Brain College? It sounded awfully expensive. I tried to shift the conversation to the advantages of attending the local community college or smart investments in the lottery, but to no avail. Brain College it was.

Ah, children, they're priceless. Well, not really. According to the latest study by the Center for Nutrition Policy and Promotion, a division of the U.S. Department of Agriculture, the estimated cost of raising a child from birth through age 17 is $233,610 – or as much as almost $14,000 annually. Families in the urban Northeast face the highest child-rearing tab with an average of $253,770. And remember, this is before they even enter Brain College.

The solution if you already have a child? Don't have a second one. Of course, we did, and Tess was born two-and-a-half years after Devon. The two couldn't have been more different physically, Devon's dark brown hair and eyes (Bette's side of the family) in stark contrast to Tess's blonde tresses and vivid blue eyes. That would be my side of the family although I really couldn't be sure. While my mom's lineage, typical of the English, traced back to the Garden of Eden, my dad's side (part Scottish, part German, part who knows) only traced back to the Garden State, and not very far at that. Having grown up on the streets of New Jersey, he'd merely shrug his shoulders whenever I asked about whether he had any aunts, uncles or cousins. Not one mention of either set of his grandparents, ever. The family twig on his side only went back as far as – him.

Whatever the lineage, we at least had ourselves a typical nuclear family, defined by sociologists as "a group of people who are united by ties of partnership and parenthood and a tremendous amount of yelling." Stress became the norm in our typical dual-income, dual-car, dual-kid household. Our family life had come to resemble a major corporation with appointments, time cards, pick up/drop off schedules, memos tacked on a bulletin board no one read, a cafeteria no one wanted to eat in and, every so often, my wife threatening to fire me.

Chaos was king. Each morning lunches were made and the kids dressed before we bolted out the door and into the car where we'd rush to drop them off at school by 8 a.m. My thrill-seeking wife preferred to drive to work, maniacally honking and weaving in and out of the cars on 16th Street while listening to the calming, melodic voice of Corey Flintoff on NPR. To save our marriage, we decided it would be best if we didn't drive in together and I was dropped off at what was for us the Air-Kiss & Ride section of the Metro station where, after waving away the smoke from her screeching tires, I walked down to the trains.

After a long day doing the Lord's work in the nonprofit field we'd rush to get the kids from "aftercare" before the 6 p.m. deadline. Latecomers were charged $1 for every belated minute past the hour, and yes, they'd heard every car accident on Connecticut Avenue/Metro train breakdown sob story imaginable. We'd find Devon and Tess amongst the mob of students (in DC it seems every kid has dual-income parents and stays for aftercare) and, with them changing into dance costumes in the car, make it just in time for lessons on Monday; no wait, Monday meant soccer, or was it piano lessons on

9

Mondays and Wednesdays with soccer on Tuesdays and Thursdays, and dance lessons on … when the hell were dance lessons? "Just keep the tutus on, girls, and go and kick the soccer ball anyway," I'd say.

Weekends, though, meant quality family time as we rushed to get the kids to their respective soccer matches and dance recitals and then over to the birthday parties which took place … every … single … Saturday afternoon (25 classmates at school + 15 soccer teammates + 12 friends/acquaintances outside of school = 52 weeks out of the year. Do the math).

When Bette was on a work trip in another country, I had to shift from our normal man-to-man defense and drop back into zone coverage or worse, the "prevent" defense, which, as any follower of American football knows, prevents nothing. I bathed, fed, and clothed; parried, praised and punished; cooked, cleaned and coached, mostly with little, if any sense of progress.

This is insane, I thought. Yes, it is, I was told by other parents. This isn't normal. Oh, this is normal, I was told. This can't be. Oh, it be, they said, it be. Insanity was the new normal. (I checked, by the way, and health insurance covers neither insanity nor parenting). Bette was of no help, having slid down the slippery slope of parental madness years earlier. I discovered this when "Greenie," Devon's lizard, had died. So as not to upset Devon and distract her from a fourth-grade history test which, in Bette's mind, would either make or break Devon's application for Brain College, Bette moved the lizard around in its terrarium all week long to make it appear alive. She even got creative, once putting its head in a hole as if looking for food. This, of course, was the very definition of insanity.

Stress fractures were forming throughout our suburban stressed lives. Something had to give. I was a mess, mentally and physically and my job as a media relations director at a nonprofit certainly wasn't helping matters.

Our organization, like so many others, was a ship adrift in the uncertain sea of 2007 when a new energetic CEO was brought on board to steer us back to the golden shores of prosperity. He was one of us, he said. He was going to listen to us, his door forever open. He was going to be a "change agent;" a "thought leader" who would lead us in a bold and new direction. He was ... a former congressman. The organization was decimated into a skeleton within two years.

Being neither DC driven nor razor sharp smart, I never really fit in at the political center of the universe anyway. My older brother could have told me that decades earlier and saved me the trouble.

"What does this say?" he asked when we were teenagers, holding up the cover of the latest Foghat album. It was a picture of a stone, followed by a plus sign, and then a photo of a piece of bread in the shape of a bun.

"Stone ... plus ... bun," I said slowly. "Stone & bun!"

He smacked the back of my head. "It's a picture of a rock plus a roll you idiot. It's rock & roll." Outwitted by the cover of a Foghat album; you really can't sink lower than that.

My wife, however, who would never confuse rock 'n roll with a stone and a bun, fit in perfectly. After working several years at Peace Corps' headquarters, she served as the senior technical advisor for reproductive health in developing countries at CEDPA, the Center for Development and Population Activities. If you have to take a deep breath before mentioning your job title, the acronym of the organization you work for and what it stands for, you are officially in Washington, D.C.

While I may have been the breadwinner of the household, my job was going nowhere fast. Meanwhile, Bette's job at CEDPA was taking her to the Philippines, Romania, Ethiopia, Ghana, Nigeria, Mali, Rwanda, Tanzania, Kenya, Zambia, Thailand, and Peru.

Travel was in our blood, and having served as Peace Corps volunteers in Papua New Guinea and then alternating jobs within the

11

organization over the years (Bette as program officer, me as a public affairs specialist), the agency served as both family and travel agent. Soon after floating her name back into the realm of overseas Peace Corps possibilities the call came for Bette to be interviewed for the programming and training officer position in Kiribati (oddly pronounced kihr-eh-bas), a horribly hot strip of sand straddling the equator in the middle of the Pacific Ocean. Not our first choice but, hey, it was somewhere else.

The job was hers but quickly derailed when we learned that I would have to homeschool the children. Negotiators call that a "nonstarter." Not that we have anything against it. Home schooling is a viable alternative to formal schooling and can provide children with a wonderfully enriching learning environment, especially if you are a parent who is nurturing, persistent and, most importantly, patient. I had the persistent part down; the other two, not so much. When asked by her children why they weren't home schooled, a friend of ours who, like me, wasn't exactly blessed with patience answered, "Because I love you, that's why."

Anxiety was reaching a crescendo at home as well. Bette was in Rwanda but I had little sympathy for her. If she wanted to see a war zone and destitute children she could have just stayed home. I was the lone soldier on the home front and gunfire erupted daily.

By week's end I had had it. Racing out the door one morning, late again as usual, I found Tess lying naked on the floor, sucking her thumb and twirling her hair. "My clothes are itchy," she said. I yanked her itchy clothes back on, but the battle wasn't over when, for the 127th day in a row (breaking her record of 126 days the previous year), we couldn't find her sneakers. I yanked on a pair of old, undersized sneakers and out the door we went.

Luckily, things were beginning to pop over at the Peace Corps in a roundabout way that only a Peace Corps veteran would understand. There was a vacancy announcement for the Eastern Caribbean that was posted internally only a week after being posted externally which meant it was

12

already wired for someone else. However, Bette also received a call from the chief of programming who was in Kyrgyzstan asking about a programming and training officer position in Mongolia. Would Bette be interested? After hanging up from that phone call, she checked her messages and found there was also a call from the country director in Pohnpei, Micronesia. Somewhere deep in the geographical labyrinth of the Peace Corps mindset, this country-to-country game of Scrabble made sense. After a successful interview, Bette was offered, and accepted, the position in Pohnpei.

"Didn't, like, a volcano destroy a whole civilization there," I asked?

Bette rolled her eyes. I have never been entirely up on my geography. Whenever Bette mentioned a country I always figured it was best to say Africa. She'd bring up, say, Guyana in a conversation. "That's in Africa, right?" I'd offer. Or she'd mention Suriname during a dinner conversation with guests. "Well, you know how hot it can get in Africa," I'd say. Or she'd try to trick me with French Guiana, which, we all know, is right next to France, which is just above Africa.

"The volcano was in Pompeii, Italy," she said, emphasizing the "m." "We are headed to the island of Pohnpei," she added, this time emphasizing the "n," "which is in Micronesia."

"Ah, Micronesia," I said, nodding my head, not knowing what the hell that meant. Our friends and relatives were even more skeptical with some doubting its existence at all.

"Nah, that's not right," my friend said, looking at where my finger was pointing on the map.

"What do you mean, not right? It's a map. What, I just made it up?"

"You might have, knowing the things that go on in your head," he said with his hands swirling around in the air. The argument was over and the battle lost when I couldn't logically explain why Micronesia wasn't featured in Epcot Center.

It also didn't help when I found that Micronesia lay within the sub region of Oceania, a name that sounded like the title of a Disney animated kids movie. I checked the map to see if Barbie's Fairytopia Mermadia was also listed. It wasn't, but Ulithi, one of the largest atolls in the world, was.

"There are Ulithians in Oceania," I said, still pouring over the map.

"Now I know you're making it up," my friend said.

For those who believe at least in the possibility of its existence, Micronesia is a vast two-million-square-mile expanse of the Western Pacific Ocean just north of the Equator, with Palau marking its western boundaries, and the Marshall Islands anchoring the east. Within Micronesia lies the Federated States of Micronesia (FSM), a nation of roughly 107,000 people on 607 islands scattered across one-million-square-miles of the ocean. The entire land area of the small island state (huge ocean state might be more apt), accounts for only 271 square miles but includes more than one-quarter of the world's atolls. The majority of the FSM population is on the four largest islands, Chuuk, Yap, Kosrae and, our new home, Pohnpei, the capital of Micronesia.

This was it, we were accepted and heading overseas, about as far away from the chaotic life we led as you could get, both mentally and physically – San Francisco, the closest point in the continental United States, was still more than 4,600 miles away. It worked on so many levels. Peace Corps would pay for our transportation costs and, once there, our overall (and rather moderate) lifestyle including schooling, health insurance and housing as well as all electricity, water and maintenance bills. Financially, it pretty much bought us the same opportunities we had with a dual income in D.C. We were set – as long as they didn't have piano lessons, dance lessons, soccer, summer camps or birthdays on the island.

We were officially in the Peace Corps and leaving the world we knew entirely. It was one of those seminal moments that stay forever burned in your memory, like where you were when John Lennon was shot or Pee

Wee's Playhouse was canceled. Our dream of living overseas was flying high again, albeit with a 10-year-old and a seven-year-old as additional carry-on.

Bette sat me down to review, yet again, the rules of order while we served overseas. "This isn't a vacation," she admonished. "While I am working, and there is quite a bit of travel involved, you are going to have to take care of the kids and the overall housework."

She continued, now sounding more like a product liability lawyer than a happy, cheerful Peace Corps worker.

"This includes, but is not limited to, cleaning the house, and yes that means the bathrooms as well, taking care of the yard, doing the laundry, getting the kids ready for school, making breakfast, lunch and dinner and doing the dishes after each meal, reviewing homework with the kids and then getting them to bed."

There was more, lots more. I decided to cut her off rather than continue reviewing this death by a thousand chores contract. "Right," I said. "I'm Mr. Mom. Got it. Piece of cake.

"I have a bad feeling about this," I murmured to myself as I left the room.

"I have a bad feeling about this," Bette murmured to herself simultaneously.

Chapter 2

Separation Anxiety

You may find yourself living in a shotgun shack
And you may find yourself in another part of the world,
... And you may ask yourself, well, how did I get here?
~ Talking Heads
Once In A Lifetime

Consider the clove. Once valued as the rarest of exotic spices in the ancient Orient, this tiny aromatic flower bud, not more than two centimeters in length, became the catalyst in a clash of cultures that helped shift the shape of our world, giving rise to a new trade and unfortunately, centuries later, the Spice Girls.

The clove quickly became THE hot commodity amongst the European citizenry, making its way into medicines and perfumes and bringing forth new flavor to their meals and (often spoiled) meats. It was the clove, this diminutive bud, that sent armadas of Spanish and Portuguese ships over the edge of the then square Earth and, ultimately, brought to an end the

17

seclusion of a people who lived for thousands of years on the remote islands now known as Micronesia.

Daybreak, 6 March, 1521. The inhabitants of Guam peered from behind the bushes and trees along the beach and murmured quietly amongst themselves, trying to comprehend the aliens hovering in the blue waters just beyond the reef. They had been up since the first fishermen spotted the strange vessel in the predawn hours and anxiety no doubt was running high throughout the village as they contemplated what they should do with this new entity.

Meanwhile, aboard the *Trinidad*, the dazed and starving crew was experiencing a different sort of anxiety as they gaped at the breadfruit, bananas, coconuts and lush green vegetation covering the island. It had been more than three months since Ferdinand Magellan and his crew had seen land after entering the sea Magellan himself first called the Pacific. According to *The First Taint of Civilization*, by Francis X. Hezel, "the crew had been reduced to eating worm-ridden biscuits and, when this ran out, gulping down sawdust and chewing on rawhide to ease their hunger. Even rats were a commodity, selling for half a ducat apiece as the days wore on."

Soon, the villagers manned a fleet of outrigger canoes and, in what had to take a tremendous amount of courage, headed out to confront the aliens in their behemoth ship. For the first time in history, the Pacific Islanders stood face to face with Europeans, and apparently decided to make themselves at home. Without even so much as bringing a cheap bottle of wine or a frozen dessert, they swarmed all over Magellan's flagship, taking whatever caught their fancy, including cloth, bits of rope and, especially, iron. Now viewing the islanders as just one step above having in-laws visiting, Magellan ordered his crew to take aim with crossbows and the islanders left, but not before stealing the captain's skiff from under the stern of the ship.

18

The next morning, Magellan and 40 crew members came ashore to gather food, water and other supplies. Provisions, however, were not the only item on his mind. Intent on avenging the injustice from the previous day, he had his crew burn down the village and fired their muskets into the crowd, killing seven men. Adding insult to injury, not to mention testing the limits of even ancient medicine, the crew then filled buckets with the intestines of the slain islanders to be used by the sick onboard the ship as a cure for scurvy.

And thus, the Europeans introduced "civilization and culture" to Micronesia.

Daybreak, 1 September, 2007. The dazed and starving Martin crew aboard the airship *Continental* gaped at the pretzels and peanuts being offered by a band of friendly flight attendants. It had been more than three hours since they ate and more than 24 hours since they left their homeland, entering the sea Tess herself called the "Specific Ocean." The Martin crew had been reduced to eating granola bars which, according to Tess, "tasted like cardboard" and, when this ran out, chewing on empty bags of Skittles to assuage their hunger. Tensions were high and almost came to a head between the kids and the flight attendants when it was announced they were all out of Sprite.

"There it is, I see it," Devon shouted from the window seat as we flew over the waters surrounding Pohnpei, whereupon Tess, banished to the "boring" middle seat, snapped off her seatbelt and proceeded to climb over Devon for a view. Pushing, shoving and rude words were exchanged. For the first time in history, Pacific Islanders came in contact with the Martins when an elderly Pohnpeian woman calmly advised that Tess really should have her seat belt fastened. I nodded then, summoning all of my parenting skills, turned to the kids and yelled "KNOCK IT OFF!" Every single passenger turned and stared.

And thus, the Martins introduced American "civilization and culture" to Micronesia.

To be fair, Devon and Tess did their best to behave themselves and hardly complained during the entire trip, made all the more difficult as we were sans Bette who landed in Pohnpei a month earlier to get us settled.

However, separation anxiety had taken hold of Tess and as we made our way through the various airports I made sure to keep her close as my taking two steps in any direction was quickly followed by a worried, "dad, where are you going?"

During a short layover at the Minneapolis-St. Paul International Airport, I realized I still hadn't canceled our Verizon landline phone. This was important, as it would officially end our connection, both symbolically and literally, with our life in D.C. I looked down the hallway and saw the phone booths only 50 yards away. It would be risky, but Devon would have to stay with our mountain of suitcases and duffle bags while Tess and I made the phone call.

"I'm not staying here by myself," Devon exclaimed.

I turned desperately to Tess. "Can you be a big girl and stay with Devon while Daddy makes a quick, brief, short, five-minute phone call?" I begged. "I'll just be right there," I added, pointing to the phone booths.

With Tess temporarily placated, I dashed for the phone and plunked in the coins. The brief five-minute call quickly turned into 15 minutes as I was transferred through a number of computerized voices before finally getting a real person who then directed me to another number where I was forced to meet the demands of yet another computerized voice. My head swirled and at one point I could've sworn I heard my name mentioned. Back on the phone, the computer voices assured me how important I was as a customer in between stints of Burt Bacharach singing "This Guy's In Love With You" while on hold. Suddenly I heard my name again, only this time much louder and with an urgent emphasis. "Jeff Martin. Paging Jeff Martin to gate F14. Jeff Martin, please come to gate F14."

Oh my God … Tess! I hung up and flew back down to the gate where I was met by two flight attendants, an angry Devon and a crying Tess. "I was just," I stammered, pointing to the phone booths. "I had to … just …" I took the kids and settled into the corner in a futile attempt to avoid the glares of the flight attendants and everyone else in the waiting area. What kind of a monster would leave a seven-year-old and a ten-year-old alone in an airport?

The Mr. Mom thing was obviously going to be tougher than I thought. Even the name didn't sit right with me. "Mr. Mom" was so last Century (the movie came out in 1983). To be honest though, I actually got a lot more respect as "Mr. Mom" than I ever did in any of my professional positions. When I told an acquaintance, who was a third-degree black belt and a vet with two tours in Iraq, that I was going to take care of the house and the kids and asked if he ever thought of trying it, he put his hands up and backed away as if I were holding a gun. "No fucking way, man," he said.

So, do we even need a title anymore? Couldn't I just be "dad?" Of course not. We are a market savvy society that requires logos, slogans and, especially, labels. What I needed was a new title for the role I was about to play, something flashy, yet respectable; something that would immediately project successful parenthood. I gave it some thought. "Stay At Home Dad?" No, too confining. "Family Man?" Too conservative. "Child Rearing Man?" Definitely not as I'd be arrested within five minutes and forced to stay at least 150 feet away from elementary schools. None of those worked. No, the title had to be visionary. It had to be a title that would broaden society's standards for acceptable male behavior and redefine modern masculinity in the 21st Century.

Home Daddy. That's it! It covered the who, what and where aspects of the position. Best of all, it had street cred. Men would greet each other with a "What up, home daddy," while bumping fists. Women would ... hate it, but that's a given for anything we come up with. Home Daddy it was. Respect and admiration would be mine.

This, of course, was fantasy and became apparent while at our hotel in Hawaii after Tess went to the bathroom and, having used three rolls of toilet paper, flushed, sending a tsunami of soiled water into our room. I once interviewed Kent Haruf, author of the best-selling novel *Plainsongs*, for the Peace Corps newsletter since he also served as a Peace Corps volunteer in his younger days. When I asked him what it was like helping to raise his three daughters, he seemed to fall into a trance and, looking off into the distance, whispered, "Oh, the toilet paper."

The incident became a catalyst in yet another psychological battle as Tess would spend the next year in a state of flush avoidance, much to the dismay of the rest of us.

Our flights to the other side of the world continued. After interminable stopovers on Kwajalein Atoll (proud home of the Ronald Reagan Ballistic Missile Defense Test Site), Majuro Atoll, and the island of Kosrae, we finally saw the jungle-covered mountains and steep volcanic slopes of Pohnpei rising out of the ocean. We zoomed in low, past Sokehs Rock, a 662-foot cliff and the most recognizable landmark on the island, then dropped even lower and hurtled toward a rapidly approaching spit of asphalt.

"Uh, dad?" Devon asked, squeezing my arm. "Don't you think we're coming in a little too fast?"

The engines screamed and I watched the water speeding past us only a few yards below the window. I had flown hundreds of times but I had to admit, landing on a runway about the size of your average driveway was more than a little unnerving. The asphalt came up fast and we dropped down on it with a loud THUNK! Everyone let out a gasp as the plane shuddered left and then right. The pilot immediately thrust the engines into reverse. We sped toward the end of the runway and could hear the loud squeal of the brakes clamping down hard, finally bringing the plane to a halt literally only a few yards away from the deep blue bay beyond.

"Ok, that was exciting," I said, prying Devon's nails out of my arm, as the plane spun around, then taxied to the terminal. We descended the staircase into a stifling wall of heat and humidity, which bent the air, causing the horizon to wave and dance before us. Sweat dripped from our bodies and sizzled on the cracked black tarmac beneath us. Tess's first words on the island spoke volumes.

"It's hot."

We shielded our eyes from the blazing sun and saw a beaming Bette waving from behind the fence. David Reside, the Peace Corps country director, was also there to greet us with his wife, Alison, and their two daughters, Sarah, 7, and Anya, 5. *Mwar mwars*, beautifully scented wreaths of yellow and white flowers, were placed on our heads and the two sets of kids became instant friends, talking and holding hands. It was a wonderful introduction to the island. Damian, the Peace Corps administrative officer, and his wife, Mary, who also lived only two doors away from our new house, rounded out the welcoming committee.

We then headed to our house, cutting through the outskirts of Kolonia, the small town and heart of Pohnpei, which garnered little praise from scribes visiting only a few decades earlier:

"Kolonia is anything but beautiful: a cluster of weathering wood and rusting corrugated buildings strung anyhow along a wide street ... Kolonia, indeed, reminds me of nothing so much as an American frontier town."
> Georgia Hess
> San Francisco Examiner

"Downtown Kolonia ... looks like a small, seedy western town, with a ramshackle mix of wood and corrugated tin."
> George Cruys
> Pacific Travel News

The western frontier town, however, had since given way to more than a few modern western amenities. We were surprised to see professionally paved roads, a few local restaurants, an Ace Commercial grocery store directly across the street from an Ace hardware store, and even a movie cinema. "Yay, Harry Potter and The Order of the Phoenix," the kids shouted.

Just beyond Kolonia, we turned down a short, crater filled dirt road and came to our house, a small two-story white concrete structure with tiled floors and a corrugated tin roof. Modest by conventional standards, the house was huge compared to most other dwellings on the island and came equipped with the modern conveniences of a washer/dryer, a barbeque grill and, be still my beating heart, air conditioning which, in order to better acclimate to the heat, we used only at night to sleep. It even had an outdoor deck known as a *nahs*, a traditional open-aired meeting area with a thatch roof, attached to it. Best of all it was located right on the banks of the Nett River (pronounced "nech" as Pohnpeians use "ch" when articulating their "t's") whose dark waters, some 75 yards wide, ambled slowly back and forth from the ocean, only a quarter of a mile away. The back of the house was comprised almost entirely of glass, allowing us a wonderful view of the river and, rising up from the opposite bank, a steep, lush volcanic ridge, some 200 feet high.

The vibrant, green jungle erupted in every direction all along the dirt road in front of the house. Thick ropes of vines twisted around the trees, then dangled from the broad canopy of palm fronds all the way back down to the razor-sharp grass that shot upwards, sideways and every which way. The morning and early evening air offered the sweet scents of orchids, frangipani, jasmine, honeysuckle, and the beautiful yellow flowers of the Ylang Ylang tree.

24

To the right of us, where the dirt road ended, lived the Mallarmes, the local family who owned all of the property up to the main road. That evening, with true Pohnpeian hospitality, Mely Mallarme, the matriarch of the family, welcomed us with a basket woven from palm leaves and filled with breadfruit and coconut shavings. "Breadfruit" was supposedly coined by the famous Captain Cook while on a trip to the Pacific with none other than the infamous William Bligh, future captain of the HMS *Bounty*. It is dry, starchy and tasteless, and while there are 78 varieties of this "bread growing like fruit from the trees" recorded, the only way I could eat any of it was if it was fried, salted and sliced thin like potato chips or cooked in coconut oil. My first culinary tip on the island was that breadfruit, hell anything, cooked in coconut oil turned into a sweet delicacy.

Mrs. Mallarme who, like most on the island, spoke perfect English, then invited us over to her place next door. After walking past a few rusted, abandoned cars and trucks lining the entrance, the area opened up considerably, giving it the appearance of a compound, with friends and relatives sitting outside conversing above the din of barking dogs and squealing pigs. The majority of Mallarme activities took place in the back corner of the property under a huge tree, some 50 feet high and almost equally as wide at the top. White plastic chairs sat under a blue tarp stretched between the branches, providing further protection from both the sun and rain. We sat down and, after being offered *pwaht* (coconut leaf plates) overflowing with yams, taro, bananas and papaya, were introduced to the Mallarme clan.

In addition to Mrs. Mallarme there was Maxson, the eldest, and only, son, followed by Melyann, Melinda, and Merlinda, who went by the nickname of *Pwo Hpwo* (baby). The kids included Maryann (who would soon become our babysitter); Maxson's kids, Anfernee and Ferleen; Melyann's son Kai Logan; and Melinda's kids, Benjamin, Tia Lana and Arthisha. Nohno Pe, Mrs. Mallarme's elderly mother, and Hilario Bermanis, better known as HB, a cousin, were also regulars on the compound as were a number of unrelated children at any given time.

The Mallarme kids

In the communal society of Pohnpei, child rearing was remarkably uncomplicated simply because everyone took care of everyone else's kids. Children never lacked for an adult lap to sit on or a shoulder to sleep on. Older children watched over the younger ones, even when they were barely old enough themselves. It wasn't at all uncommon to see a four-year-old lugging a one-year-old around on his or her hip. Safety concerns were minimal and with few, if any, repercussions. Babies played with machetes while young girls started the cooking fires and young boys shimmied 60-feet up a palm tree to send coconuts hurtling down to the crowd of children below.

Clans on the island were matrilineal with clanship inherited through the female line. In explaining the family line and the rights extended to each member, Gene Ashby wrote in *Pohnpei: An Island Argosy*:

"In addition to a traditional "kingdom," each native Pohnpeian is born into two kinship units, the extended family and the clan. While the extended family consists of several generations held together through the patrilineal line, the larger kinship unit, the clan, consists of a number of extended families who consider themselves descendants of a common female ancestor or the matrilineal line. Clans have no overall chiefs. However, they are divided into sub-clans and ranked by seniority, the highest being the sub-clan that had the first descendant from the common female ancestor."

As in much of the rest of the world, however, the men of Pohnpei were reluctant to accept this fact. The island culture, it appeared, was matriarchal in lineage only. According to Ashby, on Pohnpei the father dominated the nuclear family and the mother was usually subservient to him (a local saying went "No man is afraid of a woman and a man should not let his wife rule his life"). I had a hint Bette would be slow in adapting to this new culture.

We bid goodnight to the Mallarmes and were told that we were welcome to stop by anytime as sharing was an integral part of Pohnpeian life. True to form, we quickly found there was barely a village we could walk by without being invited over for something to eat or drink.

Later that night, we strolled down to the small bridge that crossed the river just past our house. The tide was up and the black water rolled in underneath us from the ocean. Above us, the sky was ablaze with stars, brilliantly twinkling from end to end, even those just above the horizon. I had trouble finding Orion, the hunter, always my first reference point high in the sky, until I saw him sinking low in the southwest with the tip of his arrow pointing down into the dark jungle. The Southern Cross hung just above us and it seemed as though we were on a completely different planet.

We got back to the house and began to settle in when the phone rang. It was only a matter of time. They found us.

27

"Don't answer it," I hollered. "It's work. They probably found out I never replaced the paper tray in the copier or that I rounded up the numbers on my timesheet."

Bette shook her head and picked up the phone. It was Damian and Mary asking how we were and if we needed anything. Later, as we crawled into bed with the warm trade winds blowing through our open windows and the pitch-black darkness enveloping us, a wonderful feeling of well-being came over me and I soon fell into a deep and satisfying sleep.

THWAK! I bolted upright. What the hell was that? Something huge had hit our tin roof. Moments later, two more landed. THWAK, THWAK!

"It's these blue acorn thingies falling from the trees above us," Bette said, not even opening her eyes. "You'll get used to it."

Used to it? My God, it sounded like mortar shells exploding. Eventually, I managed to fall back asleep but not for long. Only hours later I was again awakened by the sound of an ear-piercing scream. Some animal, some "thing" of considerable size was just outside our bedroom.

"Ok, now what the hell was that?" I asked, certain that it was a Chupacabra or some other demon of the darkness.

"The Mallarme's roosters," Bette said, again not opening her eyes and only barely moving her mouth.

"It's still dark out. I thought they only crowed at dawn." I quickly learned a fun fact of nature – roosters actually do crow at dawn ... and at 9 a.m., noon, dusk, 10 p.m., 2 a.m. and every minute in between.

"You'll get used to it," Bette said.

Morning arrived and the animal parade continued. I opened the front screen door and was immediately trampled by a pack of wild, frothing, yelping dogs.

"That's Mali and Jamaica, Damian and Mary's dogs," Bette said. "The third is Yoshi, the Mallarme's dog. I don't know who the fourth one belongs to."

"Well, they're not staying here," I said. I was wrong.

"Awwww, look at the cute doggies," the girls screamed as they rolled on the ground with them. Despite what their owners thought, the dogs became ours right then and there. To make matters worse, Mali figured out how to clamp his claw onto our front screen door and open it, sending the pack stampeding through our living room on a daily basis.

The curiosities continued. As I drove up a dirt path after dropping Bette off at work, a camouflaged tank suddenly pulled out of the brush forcing me to jam on my brakes. Having successfully blocked my path, the turret turned and pointed its cannon at me. Boy, they sure are touchy about trespassing, I thought.

"Sorry about that, mate" said a man popping out of the bush wearing army fatigue shorts and an olive green short-sleeved shirt. "We're testing her out." He then waved his hands at the tank and shouted in an Aussie accent, "Ok, let's back her up." It jolted in reverse for a second but then came to a grinding stop when its caterpillar track came undone. The man just shook his head. "Dammit." He had already put in some 2,000 hours restoring the two-man, WWII Japanese tankette. Other than the engine, an Atlas 4-cylinder diesel, all of its parts were original. The 7.7 mm cannon and the tank's machine gun, with the original magazine still in it, were also in working order.

"It's the only operating one of any Japanese make in the world," he said proudly before adding a caveat, "at least as far as I know."

I soon discovered World War II artifacts were easy to find as navy battles raged from island to island and Japanese Zero's crashed in taro patches throughout Micronesia. Kolonia and much of Pohnpei were pummeled during the course of some 250 air strikes by U.S. B-24 bombers. The island received its most punishing attack on May Day, 1944, when it was bombarded by no less than six battleships: the U.S.S. *Iowa*, U.S.S. *Alabama*, U.S.S. *New Jersey*, U.S.S. *Massachusetts*, U.S.S. *North Carolina*, and the

U.S.S. *South Carolina*. The hike up Sokehs Rock became a favorite of ours and a living history lesson as the kids played in the bunkers and on the rusting anti-aircraft guns.

That weekend we were invited over to David and Alison's for a barbeque welcoming us to the island. There we met several of the expats or *men wai* (literally, white men, but used to describe anyone not Pohnpeian), living on Pohnpei. There was Joanna and Ben from Australia; Helen, a Canadian; and Chip, an American. There was also Simon from England and his American wife, Eileen, both environmentalists. Later we'd meet Uta from East Germany, her American husband, Steve, as well as people from Japan, China, the Philippines, and throughout Europe. A veritable United Nations of beachcombers from all over the world, the *men wai* would prove to be every bit as interesting as the Pohnpeians.

As the evening faded, I leaned on the railing of the concrete patio overlooking the ocean and watched David throw bloody chicken scraps into the water. Suddenly a fin appeared and then another.

"Here they come," he said smiling.

"Um, your kids swim in this water?" I asked, watching the chicken chunks being yanked under the water's surface.

"Sure," he said, waving his hand at the water. "Just not during the evening. Besides, look at 'em. They're small reef sharks and more afraid of us than we are of them. You'll get used to them."

Sharks, WWII tanks, and purple acorn thingies throttling our tin roof every night – and that was only the beginning. Apparently, there would be a lot to get used to on the island.

Chapter 3

The Storms Within

And you may ask yourself
Am I right?...Am I wrong?
And you may tell yourself
MY GOD!...WHAT HAVE I DONE?
~ Talking Heads
Once In A Lifetime

In its Emergency Action Plan for Micronesia, the Peace Corps casually points out the islands are "subject at all times of the year to natural disasters such as tropical cyclones or typhoons, storm surges, floods and landslides, lost at sea incidents, earthquakes, tsunamis or seismic sea waves, droughts, wild fires, epidemics (including a cholera outbreak on Pohnpei in 2000 and a dengue fever epidemic on the island of Yap just as we arrived in 2007), environmental pollution, oil and chemical spills, and other natural and man-made causes."

It sounded like the Book of Revelations and my guess was that the four horsemen of the apocalypse were listed somewhere under 'man-made causes.' It also sounded like the Peace Corps was being litigation-ready. That way, in the event we were swept away by a seismic sea wave, they could shake their finger at the horizon in our general direction and say, "we told you so."

Leprosy also used to abound in Micronesia, which at one point in the 1980's had the highest per capita incidence in the world. I could just see us explaining that one to the grandparents.

"…and oh, by the way, the kids have leprosy. No need for concern as we're giving them Tylenol. Listen, though, don't bother sending rings or anything for their fingers as they really won't be needing them. Likewise, regarding shoes."

The government completed an eradication program in the late 1990's, however, and the actual probability of contracting the disease when we arrived was next to nil.

We quickly learned to ignore the less serious maladies. Bites and rashes covered our bodies at any given moment and tiny alien inhabitants marched freely in and out of our pores, but that was to be expected. My feet were perpetually covered with white pustules and red insect bites. During our first Christmas, pink eye hit the island and poor Tess could only dab gingerly with a tissue at the slits where her eyes used to be. It wasn't long before Bette caught it too, her face contorted into an odd shape with one eye about three times larger and five inches lower than the other. It was like living with a Picasso painting.

Unfortunately, due to her constant traveling, Bette bore the brunt of more than a few interesting ailments. On one of her first trips, two weeks on the outer islands surrounding Yap, she came back with Giardia (intestinal amoebas). There would soon be other islands and other maladies. It was just another thing we had to get used to – or not.

32

Often, marriage counselors will advise you not to use disease as a weapon. Someone should have told Bette when, yet again, she came home from some micro island bearing a micro bug as yet unmapped by the CDC. As was our usual custom when she had been away for a while, she climbed on top of me while I lay on the couch. After a warm embrace and a wonderfully wet, sensuous kiss, she whispered, "I think I have dengue."

"WHAT!" I jumped up, ran to the cupboard underneath the sink and began spraying Clorox Base, Tub & Tile cleaner into my mouth. "You know if I die from dengue fever it will be considered premeditated murder on your part." Bette let loose a sinister laugh.

She didn't have dengue but we still had to forever be on guard. Water borne illnesses were a problem and the water piped in from town, while supposedly safe to drink, was not recommended. Toward that end, just outside of our house stood a huge 500-gallon container, which caught the waterfall of rain flowing from our tin roof. Rainwater was fresher and we would use it for showers and washing dishes but, again, I'd like to point out it came from the roof of our house. After seeing all of the bugs and dirt floating around in the container, we opted to use bottled water for drinking and for brushing our teeth.

While it was awfully inviting as it gently lapped the steep shore of our yard, the Nett River was also verboten as it more than likely contained any number of diseases, not the least of which was leptospirosis, a potentially serious bacterial illness which could lead to organ system damage and, in rare cases, death. When we learned the disease was borne from the feces and urine of the pigs kept along its banks, we decided to pull afternoon swims in the Nett from our list of family activities.

Stray swine aside, there wasn't anything to fear from the animal kingdom. No wolves, coyotes or cougars. No cheetahs or hyenas or anything that roamed the Serengeti. And while huge fruit bats screeched and soared overhead in the evenings, at least there were no snakes, thank God, slithering underneath. The snakes, however, would have at least eaten the rats, which scurried in and out of our pantry as if it were a delicatessen, complete with numbered tickets and a little counter bell that was rung when an order was up. This was remedied through the rather delicious innovation of Peanut Butter Mouse & Rat Bait Block. How clever, although it's a little discomforting to know that somewhere some corporate marketer thought, "hey, you know what would be great? Peanut Butter poison," and then they mass-produced it. It worked on the rats, though. After a few dead carcasses, the rats visited the delicatessen less and less although, in hindsight, I probably shouldn't have placed the package of peanut butter poison next to the kid's jar of grape jelly.

Also, and this may surprise you, I discovered there are a tremendous number of bugs in the jungle. At our house, the ubiquitous bugs were the bane of our existence. Back in the U.S., while talking to someone, one might scratch their arm without looking because it's just an itch. On the island, there was a reason for that itch; it was more of a tingly feeling and yes, it was ALWAYS a bug. Centipedes and millipedes, some with an awfully painful bite, and spiders of all shapes and sizes cruised our corridors day and night. Once, we left the car windows open and within a short time a huge spider had woven an enormous web that stretched across the entire backseat.

Ants, the infantry of the insect regime, were also everywhere. We bought special ant traps with Borax as the active ingredient which, according to the directions on the box, sterilizes them – not as fun as the peanut butter poison but, supposedly, more thorough. The ants, however, were only one of several insect armies occupying our house.

Every morning I'd come downstairs to find the remnants of the horrible bug battles that occurred during the night, the signs of death and carnage everywhere. Insect arms, wings and antennas -- some still moving -- were strewn across the kitchen counter. Beetles, minus their heads, lay scattered across the stove. The most intense battles, however, were between the geckos and the cockroaches. They ruled the kitchen kingdom and often

34

battled each other for supremacy. Hanging out on the ceiling in their laid back, nonchalant sort of way, the geckos were definitely the bad boy reptiles in the hood. They had attitude. I learned they clean their eyes by licking them with their tongues. That's badass in any society. Best of all, they ate bugs, millions of them. They were our hero house pets and we actually enjoyed their constant clacking calls and their scurrying across the walls.

The huge cockroaches, on the other hand, could also be quite formidable. We had one particularly large cockroach that was about three inches in both length and width and weighed in at, I'd say, a full pound; one round mound of cockroach. The Charles Barkley of bugs.

Barkley scared me. Unlike the other cockroaches, which scattered as soon as the light went on, he would just sit there and stare me down. He became my nemesis. Late one night I saw him in the kitchen, which, after midnight, was basically his turf. Hoping to end it once and for all, I picked up a boot and brought it down with a SLAM. When I lifted it again he was gone. He was that fast.

I knew I wouldn't be the alpha male of the household as long as Barkley was around. I needed protection. That's when I heard Devon scream from the bathroom and I ran up to find him – the largest gecko I'd ever seen; over ten inches of green death. I called him Gordon and yes, I had recited the "greed is good" *Wall Street* movie inspirational speech to him several times over. Each time he would look at me, flick his tongue knowingly, and then lumber off to hunt cockroaches.

The only problem was that whenever I saw Barkley in the kitchen, Gordon was in the bathroom or vice versa. At some point they had to meet. It was inevitable, and it would be awesome to behold – Ali vs. Frazier, the Yankees vs. the Red Sox; a battle for the ages and I was making sure I had a ringside seat.

Bugs and disease aside, while there was a lot that could happen in Pohnpei, it rarely, if ever, did. Epidemics were few and far between and

35

earthquakes proved to be a non-issue. Typhoons or cyclones were also scarce since they merely developed near the island before quickly moving west with the full brunt of their force. This was good for Pohnpei, not as good for Yap and Guam as they lay in the direct path of the storms.

In fact, as harsh and formidable as they were, the insects and elements would only play a relatively small part in our island adventure. In the end, it was neither wind nor rain, nor gloom of night that truly threatened us. No, something else lurked in the shadows of the jungle, something menacing and wicked. Ever opportunistic, it prowled both day and night, entering unseen through the walls of our house, but leaving rather visibly and, often, all too noisily. It hovered over our family's sense of wellbeing and had the genuine potential to tear us apart. Looking back, the breach came not from the squalls outside, but from the angry storms within.

"YOU SHOULDN'T YELL AT US SO EARLY IN THE MORNING," Devon yelled at me over her bowl of Fruit Loops. "IT RUINS OUR DAY."

"YEAH, WELL I GOT NEWS FOR YOU," I shot back. "IT RUINS MINE TOO."

Again with the yelling. Looking back I have to ask myself, did we yell too much? I knew this made us an atypical Pohnpeian family, but did it also make us an atypical American family? Probably not.

I still have a note written by Devon when she was just seven years old.

"Tuseday, Dec. 27, 2004. I had the worst time driving over to grandma's house. Tess and I were playing in the car and my dad yelled because he had a head ace. Well actually, he yelled because we

36

where to loud and he turned the music
down because he thought it was the music
but he still had a head ace. That's when
he yelled. So after a few minutes I yelled
MAYBY WE WHERE BOARD! That's
when he said sorry. I said its okay. Well
actually what started everything was that
Tess was trieing to wipe her ear wacks on
me."

The note was rolled up and I believe she was going to throw it out
the window at the first police car she saw for help.

Apparently, nervous breakdowns run in my family. My mother
claims she had one when she was just 27 years old. Of course, having three
boys (the first one at 19) and all that entails, she was too busy running after us
to know it at the time but, she still assures me every chance she gets, it was a
nervous breakdown. "Didn't have time to take care of me," she says. "It was
you damn kids 24/7."

Actually, I do take care of me. I am a firm believer in what I call the
oxygen mask theory whereby, as is customary on all flights, you are told to
please be sure your oxygen mask is fastened securely before assisting your
children and those around you. According to the safety video you are required
to watch, even amidst the panic of a free-falling airplane the adult puts his
mask on first and THEN proceeds to help the child next to him. That adult
would be me. The point is that if you are not happy, or in this case breathing
oxygen, then you really can't be of much help to your children or those
around you. Provide for yourself and you can then provide for others. Ah, the
wisdom of flight attendants.

Lest you think I'm being selfish, know that by working 24/7 on
securing my needs, my wants, my oxygenated happiness, I still only end up
with a tiny sliver of the family pie. The kids get the rest, which they then

accidentally flip over onto the floor along with their full glass of milk (while I'm throwing analogies and metaphors around know that the glass is never half empty when a child spills it … NEVER!).

Bette's travel schedule didn't help as she was off Peace Corpsing on the outer islands. I didn't need to remind myself, however, that we had been forewarned of her travel schedule and that it was the whole reason we were allowed this crazy adventure in the first place. I also knew she was working hard preparing a mid-year conference for the volunteers and was up to her ears in handling the arrival and placement of the new batch of volunteers. And while her itinerary of wandering off to exotic islands sounded like an adventurer's dream, it was often more like traveling with your kids – all 50+ of them ("I don't like my site." I can't eat the food." "My host family doesn't talk much." "I didn't know there'd be bugs."). Still, her being away for five of the first six weeks we were on the island was a baptism by fire I didn't need.

It began the night I made what I thought was a beautiful dinner – corn, baked potato and pork chops rolled in breadcrumbs. Vegetables, protein, starch, all of the food groups I was supposed to have on the table every night. This was a huge victory for me as in the past I believed you only needed to have your meat group and your cold beverage group represented for it to be considered a complete meal; oh yeah, and your dessert group.

Midway through the meal their pork chops lay only half eaten, the corn was spread over the entire plate to look as if it was eaten, and the baked potato wasn't eaten at all. Excuse me, but I thought the whole point of eating dinner was to EAT! I laid down the law and told them no one was leaving the table until their plates were clean. Of course, thirty minutes later and with maybe only five kernels of corn eaten, I had the girls clear the table but added, "you can forget about dessert" to at least give the appearance that I had won the battle.

Later, I noticed Tess scratching her head. I checked – lice. LICE! Forget the cockroaches, it's the lice that will survive the nuclear holocaust. Luckily we had a few extra bottles of prescription lice shampoo, but everyone on the island assured us the lice would be a constant companion; item #27 in the "you'll get used to it" category.

After washing her hair with the lice shampoo (containing benzyl alcohol, isoparaffin, polyoxymethylene, and phenyl ether – and these were only the "inactive" ingredients), we played games, I read to them in bed and then it was lights out. Victory.

However, as the days passed my patience decreased in direct proportion to the amount of fighting, chaos and "quality family time" the kids spent alone with me (our babysitter, a multi-cultural, multi-lingual, quality educator with a 32-inch screen, was still months away from arriving). Pandemonium usually hit its stride during supper amidst the kids sophisticated dinner table conversation.

"I hate your punk butt!"

"Fine. Die."

"Watch this, I can drink through a chip," Tess said one evening as she took a curled Dorito (the Doritos being the "bread" part of our dinner) and proceeded to slurp her milk through it. She then burped while sipping through the chip and, because this was THE funniest thing that had happened or ever will happen in her life, laughed, spewing milk everywhere.

By the end of the third week my patience had been wrung out of me and I felt as if I would never, ever get it back. At one point I even wrote down on a yellow sticky note, "have doctor check the kids for attention deficit disorder."

After a long day, finally, mercifully, night would fall and the kids would settle down with a nice shower before putting on their pajamas and heading off to bed. If only. As soon as the kids closed the door and turned the shower on, the bathroom became a water theme park, complete with slides, an

39

Olympic pool with both a deep and shallow end, water baseball where the object was to slide headfirst into home plate, and swirly toilet rides for their dolls. Tip for kids: a bunched up, waterlogged towel makes for a great log flume ride.

The fun came to an end one night when, surprise, they began fighting yet again (apparently Devon instituted a "you must be at least this tall" policy on certain rides). On top of this, the shower curtain was outside the tub and the showerhead, instead of pointing downward, was facing sideways toward the opening in the curtain and directly onto the floor. The shampoo bottle then came flying out and, still open, drained its contents onto the floor, which soon became a bubbly, mango/guava fragrant lake.

During better times I might have been reminded of the foamy fountains at the Bellagio Hotel in Las Vegas, rhythmically spraying water high into the air while classical music played wistfully in the background. During better times I'm sure we'd all laugh and laugh about how the water leaked through the ceiling and onto the kitchen floor below. During better times it would have been a teachable moment. It wasn't. When my brothers and I were young and misbehaved my mother would scream, "Jesus, Mary and Joseph and all the bald-headed apostles." This would help her keep her composure. This wouldn't even come close to helping me keep mine. I lost it and began speaking in a maniacal language not officially recognized by the Linguistic Society of America. Cursing and screaming and with arms flailing, I went on a tirade before giving them both a good spank on the rear. The fooling around stopped and the wailing began. Suddenly, Devon got a determined look on her face and boldly stepped out of the tub and right up to me.

"Violence is NOT the answer," she said jabbing her finger in the air at me. "This is EXACTLY why Abraham Lincoln freed the slaves. And now YOU are bringing it right back to our generation. Well, I won't stand for it!"

Now I can't say for certain that spanking wasn't a part of the Civil War atrocities, nor that it was ever brought up somewhere in one of Lincoln's historic addresses, but I can tell you I felt chagrined, and more than just a little amused at the nude theater being played out before me. She was absolutely right.

"You're absolutely right," I told her. "Daddy shouldn't have lost his temper."

"It ... was ... just ... water," she sobbed. Her crying had stopped but she was still gasping for air between every word. My whole being was crushed. The sobbing and gasping for air will forever be a complete heartbreaker for me. She was right again. I would do anything to keep anyone from hurting them, and yet I hurt them with my yelling (ok, and spanking).

I knelt down to their level, looked them in the eyes, and again told them how sorry I was. Knowing they just may have snatched victory out of sure defeat, both the crying and sobbing stopped immediately and with the innocence and unconditional forgiveness only little children can bestow, they added "that's alright daddy."

"But you can see why I might get angry," I said, pointing to the floor and the shampoo bubbles floating upward all around us. "You need to listen to daddy the first time. If you did what I asked it wouldn't have to come to all of this AND there wouldn't be this mess."

Psychologists call this deflection. I call it parenting 101.

"Ok, let's get this all cleaned up," I said, adding, "If you didn't wash your hair yet, just mop the floor with it and it'll be clean."

Lesson learned all around, we jumped into Devon's bed. I read a few Pohnpeian folktales with one child on each side of me before turning the light off and drifting off to sleep, still holding both kids in a firm embrace as if protecting them from ... me.

41

Chapter 4

Nahs Life

How inappropriate to call this place 'Earth,'
when it is clearly 'Ocean.'
~ Arthur C. Clarke

It was one of those dark, moonless nights and the entire world seemed to end in the black void just outside our open air, thatch roofed *nahs* or deck. If we squinted hard enough, though, we could see the outline of the Nett River lapping at the bank behind our house, its ripples flashing pale silver then disappearing in a slow, shadowy surge toward the ocean.

We sensed it before it even began. The stars on the horizon, brassy and bright, were the first to go, initially one at a time and then, quickly, several vanished as if being swallowed whole. The jungle also took notice as the insects' continuous choir abruptly stopped and the air became deafeningly still. The flame from the candles flickered and an eerie silence enveloped the entire island. All within knew – a storm approached.

The loud rumble of rain drew closer and finally cascaded down over the ridge just on the other side of the river. In the daytime we could actually see the charcoal grey clouds, thick with water, settling into the palm trees at the top of the hill across the way and the sheets of rain pummeling first the opposite bank, then the river and finally....us. But at night, with the visual completely gone, there was just the sound of the approaching waterfall, which only heightened the anticipation.

Suddenly, the air was sucked out of the *nahs*. It then quickly re-entered as a gust so strong it knocked bottles off the table. Within moments, the gusts became monsoon-like winds as we scrambled to get whatever we could inside. With a roar, the storm arrived, sending the rain sideways through the open *nahs* drenching everything. To us, it was loud and energizing, more of an event, like a rock concert, than just a typical tropical storm. The rain crashed, the wind howled, and I stayed in my front row seat on the deck as long as I could, broad smile across my saturated face, until eventually going in to dry off.

Water, water everywhere... above, below and all around. It was the one element that ruled all other elements on the island. It dripped from the trees and lapped our shores. It gurgled in the creeks and streams that twisted through the tropical forests. It hovered in the air and poured forth from our bodies. Never have I sweat so much just standing still. It trickled and it bubbled, it whipped vertically across the road and sprang up from the ground. But mostly, it came down.

Rain was the one constant you could count on with the sky heaving its entire supply of water downward almost every day, if only for brief moments at a time, and certainly every night. The island didn't care for the word precipitation, something that merely moistened the leaves and dampened the earth. No, this was an angry rain whose loud roar let you know it was personal, a veritable wall of water deluging an already drowning jungle. As a result, Pohnpei is one of the wettest places on earth, averaging

44

almost 16 feet of rain annually along the coast and more than 30 feet of rain in the upper highlands. To give you some perspective on just how much and how hard it rains, while the average annual rainfall for the "wet" Seattle area is 38.80 inches, Pohnpei once had a record setting torrent of 22.48 inches of rain in just a 24-hour period.

With only two seasons, wet and wetter, it was interesting to note that virtually no one owned an umbrella, although the huge, green banana leaves came in handy during the downpours. The rain, like all of the water in and around the island, was just something you accepted (like we had a choice) and it wasn't uncommon to see children strolling through a downpour on their way to school as if it were just another sunny day.

While the temperature in Pohnpei was usually in the 80's (Fahrenheit), the humidity seemed to perpetually hover at close to 100 percent, leaving everything sticky and forever damp. Mold thrived. I'm not just talking about your normal everyday household mold. This stuff lived and breathed, engulfing everything in its path. Any opened food item that wasn't stored in the freezer was wearing a fuzzy green coat within a few days. Even the kid's Flintstone Vitamins were covered. I mean, what chance did we have if the Flintstone Vitamins couldn't fight it off.

Although the rain ruled the island, it was merely a subject of the sun, which appeared just as nice as could be after every storm and, apologizing for the rude disruption, immediately began to withdraw the water back up to the sky.

The give-and-take of the weather, and Pohnpei itself, struck me as I hung the laundry out to dry following a typically intense rain. One minute it was ominously overcast and the next the sun was shining with a slow, steady breeze blowing across the stark blue sky. Good or bad, nothing lasted for long on the island.

Even the laundry was particularly colorful that morning. This, however, was not good as they were all originally white. My initial duty as

Home Daddy had been subverted when Tess slipped six new crayons into her shorts pocket just before I threw them into the wash. My first load of laundry on the island produced pants, underwear and T-shirts with an array of designs and colors that resembled a psychedelic 1960's Peter Max poster. I was off to a bad start.

As I was hanging the psychedelic clothes out to dry, Melyann Mallarme passed by and curiously nodded at me. I nodded a hello back. She again looked at me, and then the palm tree I was standing under, this time with a more pronounced nod. I would soon come to learn that Pohnpeians, easily the most laid-back culture on the planet, rarely spoke out, instead opting to use their eyes to communicate. A subtle rising of the eyebrows could mean yes or, cast slightly downward, no. A faint flash of the eyes could mean both the salutary 'how are you,' and its answer, 'I am fine.' Particularly wide eyes could express shock or sorrow. Eyes spoke volumes. There were times when an entire conversation would go by without anyone ever speaking to me.

"Hi Melinda."

Her eyes would flash a hello.

"Is Maxson around?"

Her eyes cast downward meant no.

"Do you know where he is?"

She would again flash her eyes and nod with a slight turn of her head towards town.

"Let him know I need to speak with him, will ya?"

"Will do, bro," she'd reply as I walked away.

On this occasion, since we were new to the island and she probably felt sorry for me as I stood there with tiny tie-died shorts in hand, Melyann dispensed with the subtlety of the eyes and, stopping to dramatically point at the palm tree above me, said "watch … out … for … the … coconuts." This was no idle comment. When they ripened, coconuts dropped from as high as

46

40 to 60 feet and landed with a crashing THUD. Countless windshields were smashed on the island and news reports cited that worldwide as many as 150 people per year died from head injuries due to falling coconuts. I looked up and noticed they were indeed ripe and just waiting for me to move another six inches to the right. It was best to leave that side of the clothesline empty.

Culture, customs, coconuts; there was a lot to learn. Clearly, though, I first needed to comprehend what was being said locally. Many languages are spoken in Micronesia, but the nine central languages are Chuukese, Kosraean, Kapingamarangi, Noukuoran, Pohnpeian, Mortlockese, Ulithian, Woleaian, and Yapese. It would be a lot tougher than I thought as I couldn't even pronounce Kapingamarangi, let alone speak their language, and Ulithian and Woleaian were clearly made up from an episode of Star Trek. Luckily, since most of the languages were completely dissimilar, English was the language spoken by almost everyone although, not being from New Jersey, most still didn't understand when I asked them what exit they were from.

I quickly learned the basic Pohnpeian words needed for me to get along.

- *Kaselehlia mehng* - the general greeting to one person.
- *Kaselehlia mehngo* - the general greeting to a group of people.
- *Kalahngan* or *menlau* - thank you.
- *Ya irum* - an informal 'how are you.'
- *Kay lyle* - the response to '*ya irum*,' literally meaning 'I am strong.'

I also learned the local informal response to *ya irum* which is *kay lyle son koch*, meaning, 'I am as strong as a cat.' On Pohnpei, since a cat has nine lives, this is strong indeed. The *kay lyle son koch* response never failed to illicit shouts of laughter from the Pohnpeians. Laughter also came whenever I said *mehnseng mau*, or good morning. I would later find out that *mau*, spoken as if it had a "w" in it (mwau) meant "good" and that *mau*,

47

spoken without the "w," meant fish. I therefore spent the first few months on the island smiling and bidding everyone a "fish morning."

The Mallarmes were extremely helpful in our cultural crossover. Melyann, an attractive woman in her mid 30's who worked with the local Red Cross and taught a hula dancing class our girls soon joined, was instrumental in helping us learn all things Pohnpeian.

"The four common, most important things a family should have are yams, breadfruit, pigs and sakau," she told me one day as I stood picturing her hula dancing instead of actually listening to her. She snapped her fingers in front of my face. "Hello, Jeff, are you listening?" I shook my head and became more attentive to the conversation at hand.

"If you have those you are rich," she continued. "Money is not important. Those four items are needed to ask one's hand in marriage, to apologize, for funerals and just about any local gathering."

Of the four, sakau held the most interest for me. A derivative from the root of the pepper plant, sakau was an intoxicating, mildly narcotic drink commonly used throughout Micronesia.

"When do I get to try the sakau?" I asked.

"Don't worry," she said, patting my hand. "There will be plenty of time for that."

She took me around to the side of our house and we began my first agricultural lesson.

"There," she said, pointing to a small, gnarled tree. "There is your breadfruit tree. You need to plant your yams under the breadfruit tree. The yam is a root, but when it matures it climbs like a vine."

We moved along. "That's a *tebwuk* tree which can be used for medicine," she said before coming to a halt. "Ah, you have a *noni* tree. It has a smelly fruit that few people eat, but its medicine is very good. Its strong smell is used to chase bad spirits out of the body, and it can be used for headaches, fevers and stuffy noses. It also settles the stomach.

"More importantly," she whispered, "if you take the leaves and put it over a grave, then press your ear against it, you can hear the dead speak."

"What do they say?" I whispered back.

"That is between you and the dead," she again whispered

We moved on and came to a tall, sturdy tree down by the river.

"This is what we call the *wih* tree as it is always close to the sea," she said. "It comes from *wih en sed*, meaning 'we of the ocean.' The nuts and beautiful white flowers are crushed and used as oil for rashes. It gives you healthier, cleaner skin and thicker, darker hair."

We continued to walk around the yard which seemed to have more nourishing trees and plants than your average city's entire botanical garden. There were papayas, tea leaves, star fruit and sour sap. There were avocados, bananas, and guava and betelnut trees aplenty. There were plants that helped your eyesight and plants used to harden the soft spot on a baby's head. It was the coconut bearing palm tree, however, which stood first and foremost in the eyes of the Pohnpeians.

"We call it the tree of life," Melyann said. "The roots, the bark, the leaves, everything is used to provide us with food, clothing, shelter and all of the essentials we need. Not an inch of it goes to waste."

Just then Maxson joined us, smiling through blood red teeth, the result of chewing betelnut, yet another mildly intoxicating product of the jungle. "We use everything, see," he said looking around and spreading his arms wide. "From the coconut to the breadfruit to the guava to the betelnut, everything, even the flowers. There is nothing that we can't obtain from the jungle."

I pointed to a betelnut bunch hanging about 60 feet up in a palm tree.

"Nah, too high," he said.

"Ok, one more question," I said, picking up the walnut-sized purple thingy that pounded our tin roof every night. "What's the name of this?"

Melyann and Maxson looked at each other and shrugged their shoulders simultaneously. "You can't eat it or do anything with it," Maxson said. "So we don't really have a name for it."

Damn. The greatest threat to our survival on the island and there wasn't even a name for it. For the time being the purple thingies would have to remain ... the purple thingies.

While Melyann helped us with the local ins and outs, Alison, the Peace Corps country director's wife, took us under her wing as the expat mentor and offered much needed advice.

"You can get beer almost anywhere," she said as we drove into Kolonia, "and it's cheaper if you buy it by the case."

I liked her already. We were talking not of six-packs, but cases of beer, which foreshadowed the social atmosphere of the island.

"Also," she continued, "the container ship arrives every couple of months or so with food and supplies. The produce is usually crappy and already wilted by the time it arrives, but sometimes you can get lucky."

Ah, the container ship, that life sustaining bridge to the western world. The shelves in most of the smaller stores would be threadbare for weeks before it arrived except, of course, for the Spam aisle which spread far and wide with bacon Spam, liver and onion Spam, garlic Spam, barbecue Spam, and any other flavored spam you could think of (I couldn't help but think of the Monty Python spam skit every time I walked past that aisle). Whatever the island didn't have, which was a lot, the container ship brought, which wasn't much. Still, the expat phone tree would ring out as soon as the ship was sited on the horizon.

"Hello, Jeff? This is Alison...it's in."

"Hello, Kristen? This is Jeff...it's in."

"Hello, Uta? This is Kristen...oh, you already heard?"

We'd all rush down to the grocery store and laugh as we mobbed the produce section. "Ooh, peppers, they have peppers." Then we'd hear someone call out from the frozen food section, "DiGiorno Pizza! They have DiGiorno Pizza," and we'd make a mad dash to procure as many as we could. Island etiquette called for taking only what you needed, ok maybe slightly more, but leaving some for the later expat arrivals.

The only milk available was the shelf milk in a box from Australia, Ultra High Temperature (UHT) processed to stay fresh with or without refrigeration for up to nine months. The UHT process partially sterilizes a product by heating it for a short time, just one or two seconds, at a temperature exceeding 275°F (135°C), which is the temperature required to kill spores in milk. I wasn't crazy about drinking boxed, dead spore shelf milk and expected it to taste like a cross between breast milk and Ovaltine, but to my surprise it was actually quite good.

Most importantly, wine was readily available at the grocery store although, with Boone's Farm, Night Train, MD 20-20, Mateus Rose, Lancer's and Liebfraumilch Blue Nun lining the shelves, I had a hunch that the island's wine buyer was a teenager.

Since everything had to be either flown or shipped in, the price of groceries was exorbitant and easily three to four times the price of the same items back in the States. Using alcohol as an example, a bottle of Charles Shaw or "Two Buck Chuck," wine that literally sold for $2 a bottle back in the United States, went for $10 (the U.S. dollar was the currency used on the island).

Of course, the price and amount of food available mattered not since I knew little, if anything, about preparing food. Yes, yes I knew cooking was one of the stipulations Bette pushed for while we sat at the bargaining table, hammering out our roles and regulations contract. She even repeated it over and over again when regaling friends with the duties I'd be undertaking while serving as what the State Department disparagingly called "the trailing spouse" overseas ("That's nothing," a friend of mine from Vanuatu said. "My State Department form referred to me as the "alien trailing spouse'").

I had to learn to cook and learn fast. It was either that, or having fish, breadfruit and yams every night. Eventually, I prepared food that was passable and soon we had what I thought was a scrumptious weekly culinary menu: Hamburger Helper Monday, taco Tuesday, spaghetti Wednesday, pork chop Thursday, chicken and rice Friday, pizza Saturday and tuna fish on toast Sunday. This worked for a while, but it wasn't long before the food riots began. Any prison warden will tell you, when there is unrest, it's usually the food that sends them over the edge.

"I'm not eating this," Tess said, pushing the plate away from her.

"You'll eat it and you'll like it," I said, pushing the plate back while wincing that I used yet another parental cliché. In the following weeks, however, Devon and even Bette soon followed suit. It took time, more than the family would have liked, but eventually the cooking became varied and at least palatable. I even ventured into making homemade yogurt and our own bread.

Bette and I knew we had to be understanding and a lot more lenient as we adjusted to our new circumstances. The kids were going through a period of tremendous upheaval that would be especially hard for anyone, let alone anyone their age. School, of course, didn't help.

Naturally, our options were limited, even more so after we heard that public school teachers were known to show up late to class, if at all. Luckily, there were also three church affiliated schools on the island. Thank God for religion.

In their quest to save the "Godless heathens," the Protestants were the first to establish a continuous presence on Pohnpei in 1852, followed by the Catholics in 1886. As of our arrival, the majority of the island remained divided about equally between these two Christian religions. However, in recent years a heavenly host of churches had also descended on the island, including the Assembly of God, Baha'i National, Calvary Baptist, Pentecostal, Jehovah's Witness, Seventh Day Adventists, the Church of Jesus

Christ of Latter Day Saints, the Lutheran Church, the Universal Church, the Church of Christ, and the United Church of Christ which, I'm guessing, was established just to piss off the Church of Christ. Even Sun Myung Moon's Unification Church had a presence on the island.

The plethora of religions, however, only yielded three choices for schooling. The Catholic school was decent and had a few really good Jesuit teachers, but wasn't rated very high overall academically. The best, we were told, was the Calvary Christian Academy, a strict Baptist school. This was our A list school until we were told that we would have to sign a document promising there would be no alcohol in our home and – at that point I fainted and didn't hear the rest, but Bette later confirmed they added – no singing or dancing. They also adhered to corporal punishment in the school in the form of a thick stick called "The Rod of God." We politely declined, then went home and poured ourselves a drink.

That left the Seventh Day Adventist (SDA) school on the outskirts of town.

"Weren't they the ones who years ago committed suicide by drinking poisoned Kool Aid with Jim Jones in Guyana which, by the way, I'm still certain is in Africa?" I asked Bette.

"Shhhhh," she intoned as we entered the school.

I kept my mouth shut, she did the talking and the kids were accepted.

The religious affiliation of the kid's school never bothered us. Both of them attended a Jewish pre-school and a Catholic elementary school before enrolling in the Seventh Day Adventist school. I figured if we could get them into a Buddhist middle school and a Muslim high school they'd have most of their bases covered and would be sure to get into heaven one way or another.

Upon looking at the SDA curriculum, we decided to move Tess up to the 3rd grade and Devon up to the 6th grade as the courses were more in line with the 2nd and 5th grades back home. This didn't sit well with Devon's sixth grade teacher, an older Pilipino who made it clear she was not fond of

Westerners, especially pushy Americans pushing their pushy kid into her class.

"She can't come into my class," she said standing in the doorway with her arms folded. "She needs to take a test."

After Devon passed the test the teacher again blocked the doorway the next day.

"No room," she said.

"There's plenty of room," I said.

"No desk for her," she quickly added.

"I'll build the goddamn desk," I said, forcing Devon past her and into the room.

"Ok," she sighed. "We'll find a desk for her."

We were then informed the school didn't have any books for her and that she would have to share with others in her class. Apparently, this was some sort of "every child left behind" program initiative and they were starting with Devon. Determined, Bette got on the phone and immediately ordered a complete set of 6th grade books.

If the SDA school was different and difficult for us, it was, of course, even harder for the kids. The thick wire mesh windows made it stiflingly hot and let the rain in, soaking Devon and the other children seated on the outer edge of the classroom. Poor Devon also sat next to a column of giant ants that inevitably found their way into her lunch every day.

I kept telling the kids they would have plenty of stories to tell when they were older but that only went so far. They accepted the school grudgingly, and trooped along nonetheless. Fortunately, Sarah and Anya, David and Alison's kids; and Sophie and Maggie, Uta and Steve's kids also went to the school. Perhaps it was because of her dark brown hair and eyes that Devon had an easier time fitting in. Interestingly enough, she also would go on to be among her teacher's favorite students. Unfortunately for Tess, with her blonde hair and blue eyes, it would take much longer and she would have to endure more than a few bouts of bullying.

The next piece of the puzzle that needed to fall into place was getting a car. Used cars, which came from Japan, were our only option and were hard to come by because of their short life span in the salt water environment, obvious by the hundreds of moldy and rapidly rusting hulks left roadside in the exact spot where they last broke down. Our only hope was that someone who owned one in good working condition left the island, physically or spiritually.

Since gas prices reached $6.90 a gallon on the island, we were hoping to get something that had a diesel engine that could then be converted to run on coconut oil (about $2.50 per gallon). Yes, you heard right, coconut oil and no, it's not just something the professor made up on Gilligan's Island. In fact, quite a few of the island's vehicles ran on coconut oil.

We settled on a Suzuki Nomade, a compact SUV with just enough room to jam our boogie boards and snorkeling gear in the back. Having the steering wheel on the right side while driving on the right side of the road was a little freaky at first (with me engaging the windshield wipers every time I signaled a turn), and we had to adjust to a speedometer measured in kilometers. Since I wasn't about to do the metric to miles-per-hour conversion (will the rest of the world ever learn?) I could only gauge my speed as slow, slower and crawling. Nothing, and I mean NOTHING, moved fast on the island and driving was no exception.

This at first drove me crazy, but it was just another adjustment we had to accept, and one for the better. With no time commitment and really nowhere to go, what was the hurry? Rush hour simply didn't exist as there was nowhere and nothing to rush to. Even the car horns were only used for the forces of good, not evil. You beeped to say hi and you beeped to say goodbye. You beeped to let someone in, who then beeped to say thank you. And sometimes you just beeped because you were happy. Happy beeps. Back in the States, I once had to cross three lanes of traffic to make an exit ramp. Those were not happy beeps.

One of the first things we did was pile into our new car and navigate the only paved road that circled Pohnpei.

The island itself is a deeply jagged circle, some 13 roller-coaster miles across and about 130 square miles in total (about twice the size of Washington, D.C.). With a population of only about 35,000, Pohnpei contains the most uninhabited land of any place in the F.S.M. Subsistence and cash crops occupy 34 percent of the land and woods and mangrove swamps cover 64 percent of it. Businesses and offices, mostly in Kolonia, occupy the rest. The ubiquitous thatch and corrugated tin houses became more prevalent as we headed out of town and taro patches could be found everywhere. Almost every single person we passed smiled and waved, the one exception being a small boy who glared at us from behind wrap-around Ray Ban sunglasses, his T-shirt bearing a picture of 50 Cent on the front and the word "thug" emblazoned across the back.

The name of the island is taken from two local words, *pohn* (upon), and *pehi* (stone alter), and refers to a legend about how the island was created. Like most Pohnpeian legends, it contains gods, magic, men with unpronounceable names and women with incredible breasts. The men and women, lost at sea, were eventually guided by a friendly giant octopus to Pohnpei where they frolicked and populated the island.

As we drove around the island, I couldn't help but notice that the god Katinanik, who summoned the mangrove trees in the legend, did one helluva job.

"Where are the beaches?" I asked.

"There are no beaches," Bette replied. "It's all mangroves."

"No beaches?"

"No beaches."

How was that possible? How could a beautiful island in the middle of the Pacific not have even one sandy beach, not to mention a boardwalk with mega G-force rides and funnel cake stands? I was determined to find a way to get to the great blue waters beyond and discovered Nett Point, an old pier that once served as a WWII U.S. Navy fueling station. The point, the most northern tip of the Pohnpeian mainland, sat at the end of a narrow strip jutting out into the ocean near our house. The expats stayed away fearing the waters, although clear and a part of the vast blue ocean beyond, were still slightly contaminated with leptospirosis, but I noticed Pohnpeians swimming there often. A quick visit to the local Environmental Protection Agency office (total staff: 1) confirmed the waters were safe to swim in.

"Ok, kids, you go first," I said as we stood at the edge of the pier and examined the inviting water some 10 feet down.

"The EPA lady said 'relatively safe' to swim in," Devon said shaking her head.

Before they could even have the chance to tell me "no way," I whirled past them, leapt in the air and dove in. Splash! Bette and Tess jumped in and soon we were swimming and having the time of our lives. Tess went snorkeling for the first time in her life and we roared as we heard the muted "FISH, FISH" she excitedly screamed through her air tube as she pointed at the colorful reef fish darting about. Unfortunately, Devon remained on the pier and looked ridiculous just standing there with her mask over her eyes, snorkel in her mouth and fins on her feet.

"Why won't you come in?" I asked.

"Sharks, sting rays, manta rays, jellyfish," she said, holding up fingers for each terror of the sea, "barracudas, man of wars, crown of thorns, fire coral…"

"Ok, ok, we get it. Your loss," I said, floating in the warm water. "You know, you couldn't have picked a worse time to suddenly develop a fear of the ocean."

Afterwards, we sat and watched the day's final red rays streak across the sky and the sun's elusive green flash, a phenomenon which only lasts for a second at certain latitudes, before it sank into the sea. Just in front of us, tiny Lehnger Island and beyond that, nothing. The ocean stretched out before us and the stars rolled out above. I breathed a deep, contented sigh, admiring our new swimming hole, hundreds of feet deep and thousands of miles wide. We truly were on the edge of the Earth.

Once back home we made spaghetti (and no, it wasn't Wednesday) then played cards before heading upstairs to bed. After a quick tale about the ever naughty Noved and Sset, the kid's names spelled backwards, they drifted off to sleep. A great family day and it dawned on me why … no TV, no computer, no cell phones, no nothing.

Funny, less really is more.

Chapter 5

Conflict within the conventions of civilized behavior

*Surfing, alone among sports, generates laughter at its very
suggestion, and this is because it turns not only a skill into
an art, but an explicable and useless urge into a vital way
of life.*

~ Matt Warshaw

The early hue of dawn cast a bluish tint on the smoke rising up
through the trees from the morning fires across the river. Two young boys,
wearing only tattered shorts, stood in a crudely carved wooden outrigger and
slowly poled their way to the opposite shore, sending small, synchronized
ripples across the smooth, placid surface. A large white reef heron swept in
low, turned, then drifted just above the water, its eyes focusing on the
breakfast menu below. Mesmerized, I gazed through the large window
framing our kitchen sink, celebrating the solitude and the silence.

VROOOOOOMMMM! The tranquility was abruptly shattered as
first one speedboat, then another and still another ripped past, sending

tsunamis crashing against the shore. On board, several blonde, bikini-clad girls smiled and waved as they sped past. I mustered a half-hearted wave and continued to stare out of our large back windows with my mouth open.

"What the heck was that?" Devon asked, raising her sleepy head out of her bowl of cereal and confirming that it was not, in fact, a dream.

"Surfers," I said. "Lock the doors, bar the windows and for God's sake hide the beer."

The Pohnpei Surf Club had set up shop on the river just up the path from us. That afternoon I decided to walk down and introduce myself.

"What do you want?" a man said without lifting his head up from the boat engine he was working on. "Cause I really don't have time for whatever it is you're selling."

The dock was abuzz with activity as the surfers had just arrived for lunch and a brief break between sessions. While the girls ran up to change, people whirled past me, securing ropes and jumping on and off the boats with tanks of gas, camera equipment and additional surfboards.

"What if I'm selling new engines?"

"Fuck the engine," he said. "What I need is a new boat. The ones I have are pieces of shit." There was a total of four boats running from 23 to 30 feet in length moored to the small dock. They looked in good shape to me, but what the hell did I know? Finally, he looked up from the engine with a devilish smile. "You're that new guy whose wife works for the Peace Corps. I'm not allowed to talk to anyone from the Peace Corps." He paused before adding, "Well, at least not the women."

Allois Wagner Malfitani, owner of the Pohnpei Surf Club, was part Italian on his father's side, part German on his mother's side and, born and raised in San Paulo, all Brazilian which meant his priorities alternated from women to waves and back again, depending on how high the surf was breaking.

"There were these two, young female Peace Corps volunteers a few years ago that would go wild at night at the bar, lifting their shirts, doing body shots, that sort of thing," he would tell me later. "I had nothing to do with it." Behind him, the local boat hands smiled quietly and shook their heads. "Well, I mean yes, I always seemed to be there when it happened, but I certainly wasn't the instigator. The next thing you know I have this undeserved reputation and the Peace Corps director is banning all volunteers from talking to me."

Undeserved or not, Allois' reputation was that he was all libido, the id on the island. Sigmund Freud, or maybe it was Wikipedia, pointed out that libidinal drives can conflict with the conventions of civilized behavior. Allois, a case study in action, was every man's alter-ego. In fact, if I were to be perfectly honest, and I rarely am, I'd say he was the quintessential example of what every man could be, and indeed longed to be – pure instinctual psychic energy derived from biological urges. Waves and women, women and waves.

Allois wasn't about conformity. At 45, he had a soft, doughy look to him and his sleepy eyes and short brown hair shooting out in every direction corresponded with his detached, nonchalant attitude. I could never tell whether his mind-set was surfing Zen or just plain indifference, or even if I should make a distinction between the two, but rest assured, Allois had both in spades. Apathy, id, and age aside, his surfing days were still very much in front of him and, I would later learn, he could still ride the hell out of the waves. That, really, was all that mattered.

Well, that and the club he founded. The devil-may-care attitude belied the fact that he also had tremendous business acumen and a fierce determination to make the organization work as he often labored late into the night pouring over financial records, tourism information, and tidal charts. Women, waves … and the Pohnpei Surf Club.

Allois cleaned up and we headed for the large outdoor room next to the restaurant where lunch was being served to his guests.

61

"You can join us if you want," he said, "but I'm not paying for it."

Meanwhile, the loading and unloading from the boats continued and I noticed photographers toting an array of tripods and cameras, some with massive zoom lenses that looked like three-foot cannons.

"So, I'm guessing these women surfers are pretty good?" I said.

Allois stopped in his tracks. "Pretty good?" he said looking at me quizzically. "These are the best women surfers in the world. Stephanie Gilmore, the current world champion? Chelsea Hedges, a former world champion? Jessi Miley-Dyer, ranked 8th on the circuit last year?" He paused after each name, looking for something, anything that indicated I knew who he was talking about.

Nothing.

We sat down to a lunch of tuna and rice splashed with soy sauce and I listened intently as they talked about barrels and breaks and the rigors of the upcoming surfing circuit ending with the WCT (World Championship Tour), which would take them all over the world.

"France, Peru, Brazil, Australia, Hawaii …," Stephanie explained to me while ticking the countries off her fingers. "It's insane, but it's a helluva lot of fun."

I couldn't help but get caught up in the excitement. "What are the chances of me getting on a boat tomorrow?" I asked Allois after lunch.

"None," he said walking back to the boats, a large container of gas in each hand. When he reached the end of the dock he turned and shot me an exasperated look. "Be here by seven, but you're gonna work."

A first generation Brazilian after his parents came over from Europe to escape World War II, Allois spent his formative years carving up the streets of San Paulo on a skateboard.

"Back in the day, I wasn't the best, but I was good enough to travel and enter all of these competitions," he said. "I didn't make any real money, but they gave us new skateboards and T-shirts and stuff like that."

He graduated to surfing as a teenager and, like a lot of surfers, especially enjoyed the one-on-one aspect between man and wave and the overall solitude of the sport.

"I don't like people," he said.

"No shit," I replied.

"It's not that I don't like all people," he clarified. "It's just that I don't like to be with a bunch of them at one time and surfing gets you out there, away from all of that crap."

And that's what brought him to Micronesia.

"I was going through an old National Geographic and there was an article on the FSM, the birth of a nation, or something like that," he said. "What caught my attention was an aerial photo of a reef. I could see the swells. That's what surfers look for."

After touching down in Pohnpei, he quickly discovered all of the surf surrounding the island was practically his alone to explore. "There were only two expats who surfed as a hobby," he said. "Ninety-nine percent of the waves went untouched."

This was important because, as *Surfing Magazine* once put it, "crowds are the Holy Grail of surf trip buzz kills." The more surfers in the water, the fewer waves you catch, that's the reality. It's survival of the fittest, the best take off deeper, catching the wave first, and etiquette calls for everyone else to back off. Unfortunately, that's not always the case. At any given time, California, Hawaii and, particularly, the famous Gold Coast of Australia, can have what seems to be hundreds of surfers in the water, each trying to catch the same wave. This, of course, inevitably leads to fisticuffs on the beach, prompting *Tracks*, the Gold Coast magazine surfing bible, to list it as a diet supplement – "Burn Locals, Burn Fat: dropping in starts fights and fighting is an excellent workout."

And therein lay the lure of the Pohnpei surf – manageable five to eight-foot waves breaking right, in a pristine paradise with no one else around. "In other places you always have to worry about that one jackass fading you on the best right of the day," Allois said, shaking his head. "Not here. Pohnpei is one of the friendliest and most civilized places to surf."

In October 2004, he officially opened the Pohnpei Surf Club with only three guests on the register. By the time we arrived in 2007, Pohnpei had already been written up in the top surfing magazines and even visited on one memorable trip by five world champions: Andy Irons, Sonny Garcia, Mark "Occy" Occhilupo, C.J. Hopgood, and Tom Curren. Pohnpei was on the map, at least in the surfing world, but being discovered and being a destination are two different things.

"It's a love/hate relationship," said Allois, who pulled in 250 guests the previous year. "The fact that no one is here is one of my main selling points. It's hassle-free, with no tourists and you have the waves to yourself, but to fly here costs a fortune."

Continental, the only airline flying into the FSM, had a virtual lock on the islands and charged around $2,000 for a round trip ticket from the United States, never mind the 22-hours it took to reach the islands from the eastern U.S. Even the prices and the time it took to get to the FSM from Australia and other nearby locales were prohibitive as you had to fly through Guam and then island hop the rest of the way.

Pohnpei, it seemed, would forever remain a far-off island of mystery and, although a headache for Allois, that was just fine by me.

The next morning, I whistled as I made breakfast despite the smoke pouring out of the oven, which also served as our toaster.

"What are you so happy about?" Tess asked.

"He's going on a boat with a bunch of surfer girls while we have to go to school." The words dripped venom and cereal as they slid out of Devon's mouth.

Bette came downstairs to take the kids to school. "Have fun," she sang as I headed out the door. She tried to make it sound cheery, but I knew sarcasm when I heard it. I arrived at the dock promptly at seven only to find Beru and Jerry, the two local drivers, preparing the boats.

"Everyone is still sleeping, man," a voice said behind me. "And, fuck, I should be too."

Take your stereotypical California surfer dude, add Otto the bus driver from the Simpsons and you have Mitch Ferris, the Surf Club surf guide. A little over six feet tall, his rail thin frame was accentuated by a bushy blonde mustache that drooped down the sides of his mouth, and the matching stringy blonde hair pouring out from under his baseball cap all the way down his back to his waist. Even his SoCal dialect was straight out of central casting.

"The waves should be bitchin today, dude," he said. "Let's scarf up the boards and load them onto the boats before the chics get down here."

At 31, Mitch had life all figured out.

"I'm doing it backwards," he said. "I want to be retired while I'm young and then start to work when I'm, like, 65. I may have to work at a Wal-Mart handing out stickers or whatever but, fuck it, I'm not worried."

Funny, I don't remember coming across this retirement plan in any of the pamphlets handed out by H&R Block. The key to this 'Mitcheconomics,' he continued, was to avoid real work as long as possible and learn to get by with as little money as possible.

"If I made thirty grand I could live off it for, like, three years, man," he said. "Right now, I'm going to take advantage of life while I'm young. I think, like, fuck, I just want to travel more, find unique places to surf, and live in the moment. I mean, fuck, I'm not going to die with money."

I asked Mitch to try and complete a sentence without using the word fuck.

"Fuck that," he said.

His outlook, though, was carpe diem at its best and completely plausible ... for someone living on Pohnpei without a wife and kids. Still, it

65

was good to see a little youthful exuberance, albeit a tad irrational and careless, but exuberance nonetheless.

Gradually, the "chics" crept down the stairs, wiping the sleep out of their eyes and crashing at the communal breakfast table. As they slunk into the chairs, six in all, I couldn't help but notice every one of them was blonde, leading me to believe, when I included Mitch, that there was some kind of rule against dark haired surfers. Of course, the sun also might have had something to do with it as they each hailed from the world's surfing meccas, including California, Hawaii, and Bondi Beach on the Gold Coast of Australia.

"It's waaaay too early to be doing anything," the first one down said as she laid her head on the table. After a long night at the Rusty Anchor, the colorful local hang out in town, the other girls nodded their heads in agreement. They were in luck, for the time being, when Simon Williams or "Swilly," as he's known in the surfing circles, came down and announced that the wind was too high and that they would have to give it another hour or two before heading out.

"The wind kicks the spray up and it's harder to shoot," he explained to me, holding his camera up. "The boat is rocking; water gets on the lens, it's a mess."

One of the top surfing photographers in the business, Swilly was shooting stills for the surfing apparel companies sponsoring the trip and expected to sell additional shots to *Surfing* magazine in the U.S., *Surf World* in Australia, and the *Surf Girl* editions in Japan and the UK. He described this particular trip as unique, adding, "It's not often you get a high caliber of girls like this, or at least this many girl with this much talent."

At only 19 – "soon to be 20," she emphatically added – Stephanie Gilmore was the youngest of the group, but, as the reigning world champion, the one who most needed to look over her shoulder.

"Chelsea's always on my tail," Stephanie said of her fellow Tweeds Head, Gold Coast Australian neighbor, "but right now she's pregnant."

Only 24, Chelsea Hedges was still the elder of the group and yes, at three months pregnant, still surfing. Worried? "Nah, I'm teaching the baby how to surf," she said with a laugh. Having won her first major contest at only 14, Chelsea was just making sure the kid was already in line to break the family record.

Despite the talent and competition present there was a slumber party feel to the atmosphere and the girls couldn't have been more relaxed. Karina Tetroni, 21, a newcomer to the WTC, had everyone laughing by telling the story of how she actually first met Mitch while surfing in Mexico. "He was driving an old Volkswagen bus," she said. "It was baby blue with white clouds painted on it."

Finally, the real clouds outside gave way to the sun, the wind withdrew its little temper tantrum, and soon we were splashing our way across the lagoon, past the 300-foot tuna boats already processing the day's first catch, and out to the reef surrounding the island. Our own 30-foot skiff, a Yamaha Panga with a broad entry at the bow for easy access and, more importantly, fishing in the deep sea, was wide and flat with yellow benches and a blue canvas bimini to block the sun. The Panga style boat draws little water, which makes it perfect for hovering just over the reef and staying close to the surfers. Its narrow beam also allows it to slice through the water which Allois particularly liked as he knew only one speed – full throttle. The twin 150 Mercury engines roared as we flew over the water, slightly levitating off the benches with each cresting wave and bowing our heads to dodge the shower of sea spray.

While the wind whipped past, plastering my sunglasses against my face, I looked up at the bright blue sky and, just for a moment, drifted away. Let's see, I thought, it's a Tuesday morning around 8:30 a.m. I'm supposed to be in Washington, D.C., crammed into the red line train with the dark blue

suits, and on my way to work to review the department budget, but I'm ...
NOT! I had that wonderfully giddy feeling you get when you are doing
something you're really not supposed to be doing on the road, or in this case
the sea, less traveled. After inhaling a deep breath of salty air, I came back
down into the boat from the bright blue sky. Allois looked over, nodded and
shot me a smile back as if he knew exactly what I was thinking. He then
tapped me on the shoulder and pointed to a turbulent commotion of foam on
the horizon. "That's it right there," he yelled over the wind. "Palikir Pass."

Palikir Pass, or P-Pass as it's known locally, is a small channel, 75
yards long and only 20 yards wide, that cuts through the reef about a mile
offshore of the northern end of Pohnpei. Easily the best spot on the island
with the most consistent waves during the winter months, it is unusual in that
it offers surfing on both sides of the channel, with left breaks on the one side
and perfect rights coming in on the other. The way the reef is shaped and
angled, how the trade winds hit – it all comes together at Palikir. Under the
headline "Catch The Greatest Wave on Earth," the pass was highlighted in a
National Geographic Adventure magazine feature listing Pohnpei as one of
the 'Top Island Vacations.' "When the big winter swell starts breaking on
Palikir Pass ... it is one helluva wave," the article gushed, adding that "Aussie
pro surfer Dylan Longbottom has called the hollow, glassy barrel, which is
accessible only by boat, 'by far the best right in the world.'"

"It's definitely one of the better waves in the world for sure,"
Chelsea confirmed as we tethered our boat to one of the buoys in the pass.
While the sea raged on either side of us, the inside of the channel remained
surprisingly unruffled; its deep, steel blue waters emanating a calming
contrast to the aqua green waves exploding into white foam on the dazzling
turquoise reef. During high tide, as much as three feet of water would cover
the reef, providing ideal surfing and snorkeling conditions. At low tide the sea
withdrew, hovering only inches above the coral and exposing the larger rocks
to the harshness of the sun and anyone not abandoning a wave in time. Below

us, the reef wall offered an array of brightly colored fish and plant life as it plunged straight down into the dark depths of the ocean.

"It's so clear you can actually see the faces of the fish," Stephanie exclaimed.

Suddenly, the boat was abuzz with activity. As the girls readied themselves and their boards for the surf, Swilly monitored the light meter and adjusted his cameras. Jimmy, yet another Australian on board to help film video for Rip Curl, one of the top surfing accessory companies, checked then double-checked to make sure his equipment was secure. Only 17, he had already dropped out of high school a few years earlier. I asked him why.

"Cause I was shit at it," he said still rummaging through his bag.

Ok, a fair enough assessment I thought before being pushed aside by Mitch, who put his arm around Jimmy, told him school didn't mean a thing, then proceeded to tick off the benefits of his retirement plan. More sage advice from the here-and-now financial guru. When he was done, Mitch went to work preparing his board.

"I'm particular about my waxes," he said. "Sex wax is my favorite."

Of course it was.

"It beads the right way and it just feels right," he continued.

"Are we still talking about the board?" I asked.

"Yes, we are. I use something different for myself," he laughed, "although…" He contemplated the jar of surfboard wax for a moment before deciding to get serious again. Then he grabbed my shoulders and shook me.

"You gotta focus, dude. Mr. Zog's Sex Wax is one of the most popular surfboard waxes around and it's important as it helps your feet stick. You want it sticky enough so the water beads on the board. The water temperature is also important. Cold water causes it to bead differently than warm water.

"Now, the right board is everything, EVERYTHING," he continued. "I like lot of different boards, but my favorite is a six-foot, one-inch Pyzel shortboard."

"Cool," I said, nodding my head knowingly.

He grinned, recognizing I didn't know a thing about what he just said. "You use a different size board depending on the size of the wave you're going to ride, and Pyzel is the company that made this particular board."

"Oh yeah, Pyzel," I said, again nodding my head knowingly. "I prefer the six-and-seven-eighths, triple-quarter C317 Pyzel myself."

He just shook his head and mumbled, "I don't why I even try."

With the impromptu lesson over, he jumped overboard and paddled out to the surf, where several of the girls were already shooting down the walls of water. On the previous day, the girls were living billboards, modeling Billabong, Rip Curl, Quicksilver, and Vans as well as Oakley Extreme surf sunglasses, Etnies footwear and a slew of other surfing apparel. They would pull on an outfit from one company, have their photos taken while they surfed, then come back to the boat and change before heading out for yet another company advertisement.

This day, however, was for pure fun, although they still wore some of the logos and Swilly was still shooting. Jessi sat on the edge of the boat and gave me a thumbs-up. "Well, gotta work," she said before plunging over the side. Hearing her from his boat moored right next to ours, Swilly held his camera up and smiled. "It's a hell of an office to work in, isn't it?" he asked.

Beru maneuvered the photographers boat so that it sat right at the end of the break allowing Swilly to get those poster perfect close-ups. The trick was to throttle forward with just enough speed so that the momentum of the diminishing swell didn't carry the boat onto the shallows of the reef just behind them. Although he grew up handling boats at P-Pass and worked those waves thousands of times, Beru shook his head as he gunned the engines over a wave and circled back around to reposition the boat. "I always hate that part," he later told me. "Give me a small local fishing boat any day of the week."

Over on the waves, the surfing goddesses continued to walk on water, performing an impressive array of twists, turns and jumps and, of course, making it look all too easy. Karina shot to the top of a wave and spun, sending a perfect arc of spray into the sky before descending again. Jessi dive bombed into a perfect barrel then ducked down on her board content to simply float through the green, swirling tunnel. Stephanie whipped into the thick of one wave, did a few figure eights, then capped it off by shooting straight up into the air and performing a perfect dive back into the water. Chelsea dropped into a monster wall of water, then carved it back and forth playing a cat and mouse game with the churning foam crashing only a few feet behind. Somewhere deep inside her, I just knew the baby was screaming.

"So, let me get this straight," I said back at the PCR later that afternoon. "You guys get paid for doing this?"

They all laughed. "It's a living," Karina said.

"We do ok, but you should talk to the women golfers," Chelsea added. "Now that's the sport with the real money."

I sat down next to Karina and asked her to elaborate on the life she had chosen.

"Despite what it looks like, all this traveling can be a real pain in the ass sometimes," she said. "Last year I was home for at least six months, but this year I'll be lucky to get home for three months. The tournaments haven't even really started yet and I already miss my mom, dad and two older brothers terribly.

"Having said that, I'm still a total gypsy. The Earth is my home and I couldn't see myself doing anything else. I can't be indoors for any length of time and I will never, EVER do the nine-to-five thing. I just never got how my friends went from high school right into another concrete building."

Just then Stephanie came over and joined us.

"We're talking about life," I said. "So, where do you see yourself in the future?"

71

It was a vague question and she struggled for an answer. I elaborated.

"I mean, what do you see yourself doing when you're 30 or 40 years old?"

She looked out on the water and thought for a second before smiling and shrugging her shoulders. "I'm just gonna keep on surfing."

I closed my eyes and imagined banging my head against the table. The future? What a STUPID question. She was all of 19 – ok, 'soon to be 20' – with the whole world in front of her and living very much in the present, thank you very much. They all were. When I thought about it, the entire island was in a constant state of present. All you had to do was say, "hey, we're having a party tonight" and the reply would always be, "Great, I'll bring a cooler filled with beer." No checking your phone for availability dates. No "I'm booked all of June – how about August 14th or sometime next fall?"

My whole focus on work and the future – pretending for a moment that I ever really focused on anything, or actually worked in its truest sense, or ever showed any real concern for the future – was out of whack there in the land of the lost and it was apparent my head was still very much in the helter-skelter, fast-paced world back home where everything depended on the future; your retirement, the kid's college fund, the dinner party next month, that meeting next Thursday, the gifts for the holidays you need to buy NOW!

Wikipedia, or maybe it was Sigmund Freud, pointed out that it is the need to conform to society and control the libido that leads to tension and disturbance in the individual. Yes, the girls were young (and, let's not forget, surfers), but almost everyone I met on the island, young or old, seemed to be following their own agenda. Nonconformists, one and all. As a result, there was very little overall tension and disturbance in their life. Sure, the expats and the islanders had many of the same problems the rest of us had; they just

72

dealt with them, shall we say, a little more casually. On an island with few commodities, there really wasn't much you could do about it anyway.

I couldn't have been happier to be a part of this new life and watch the kids grow up in it, at least for a little while. Mitchonomics would continue to work for Mitch, at least for the time being, despite the rest of the world saying it couldn't, or shouldn't, and the Home Daddy state of mind would continue to work for me. There was a new society to conform with; one that centered on communal sharing, the present state of mind, and "island time." And as for controlling the libido, well, there was always a jar of Mr. Zog's Sex Wax.

A week later I was back out on the water and more within my age element with Allois, Mitch, and a foursome of middle-aged Aussies slathering zinc all over themselves for protection against the sun beating down on us.

"Call us Aussies again, mate, and you'll be swimming home," the two from Auckland, New Zealand cautioned.

Ok, so two of them, Teri and Martin, were Kiwis, and the other two, Chris and Lou, were Aussies. They all were on an official surf vacation and, after visiting the Wave Hunter site, discovered there were only two good 'rights' happening at that time of year. One was in Morocco and the other at Pohnpei's Palikir Pass.

"This was closer," Teri pointed out.

I looked at the pass longingly. Pohnpei, it was said, was the last place you'd want to learn to surf as the turbulent waves crashed directly onto the razor-sharp reef. It would be best if I saved face, literally, and learned somewhere else before trying it here. They plunged in with their boards while I went snorkeling safely along the reef wall.

The 80-degree water was a refreshing respite from the sun and exquisitely clear with visibility easily at 100 feet in any direction. As I investigated the coral formations, sea fans and brilliantly colored fish, I detected a dark movement about twenty feet below me. Looking down I saw two black-tip sharks five feet in length heading my way while patrolling the water for food. Sharks were a main concern and often ventured into Pohnpei's lagoon. However, of the 300 different species of shark, only 28 are known to attack swimmers. Luckily, the most dangerous – the hammerhead and the tiger sharks – patrolled the deeper, colder waters outside the reef and were rarely, if ever found inside the lagoon. That left only the less aggressive reef sharks and, while they looked menacing and awfully, well, sharky, I had already learned from previous dives that they were indeed more afraid of me than I was of them. In fact, whenever I saw a white-tip or black-tip shark nearby, I would cease all movement to draw them as close as possible since even the slightest motion would send them scurrying away.

After a while I was back on the boat when the Aussies, excuse me, Kiwis climbed in to take a lunch break. They absolutely gushed about the six-foot waves and excellent conditions and I looked out to where the other two surfers were straddling their boards with Allois and Mitch. The sea had a serene, tranquil look to it and the waves were rolling in rather calmly.

"Excellent conditions," Teri confirmed.

I looked down at the surfboards.

There are monks in Tibet who can teach you how to separate your mind from your body through transcendental meditation, creating openness to the infinite reservoir of energy that lies deep within and allowing you to arrive at the source of thought, a place where problems are absent. I believe I obtained this consciousness early on in life as my mind would frequently drift away from my body, usually while my wife was talking to me. I don't like to brag but, in fact, my mind and my body are rarely in concert. My wife points this out every time we dance. On that day, in that boat, my mind began its usual ascension.

"Would you mind if I borrowed your board?" I asked Martin.

"It's all yours, mate," he said, chomping into a sandwich.

"Whoa, whoa, WHOA," my body said to my mind. "What the hell do you think you're doing?"

"I am creating openness to the infinite reservoir of energy," my mind replied, and before my body could argue further I was in the water and paddling out to the great beyond. After a full five minutes of powerfully stroking the water, however, I turned to see the boat just 10 yards away.

"You're too far back on the board," Teri shouted. "Move up a bit and then take smooth, easy strokes."

I again started out and, although it was still awkward, began to make progress. After several minutes, however, my arms ached and it felt like someone had stuck a knife between my shoulder blades. I was quickly finding out that my reservoir of energy wasn't, in fact, infinite. How the hell do they even do this, never mind ride the waves, I thought.

My body was pissed. "Funny how painful it can be when you're working muscles you don't normally use and heading to a place you really shouldn't be," it said.

"I have arrived at the source of thought and the place where problems are absent," my mind replied ignoring my body.

Actually, I had arrived at the point of no return where the waves thundered down before the reef. Luckily, it was between sets and relatively calm. I turned to see Mitch paddling furiously over to me. "Dude, you're freaking me out," he said.

"I think I can do this," I said.

"You CAN'T do this and really, REALLY, should be learning somewhere else first."

"Too late, I'm already out here," I said. "I'm gonna do it."

Allois glided over, straddled his board and shook his head. "Fuck it," he said to Mitch. "Let him go." Turning back to me he added, "If you get all bloody you're not coming on any of my boats."

"It's your funeral, dude," Mitch added. As he paddled away he called out over his shoulder, "Just remember to keep the board tethered to you, but also keep it away from you when you go under."

Wait, what? How do you keep the board away when it's tethered to you? Suddenly, a huge swell brought me high in the air and back down again. A set was rolling in.

The first wave absolutely towered over me and I ducked under it at the last second. Six-foot waves my ass. At water level, the waves I was looking at were at least 50-feet if they were an inch. The harmless, calm water I viewed from the boat just minutes earlier had now become a living, breathing monster; a swirling tumultuous maelstrom heaving from the heavens wherein I could actually see the face of God, a vengeful, merciless god about to unleash his wrath upon me. A chilling fear enveloped me and my stomach became nauseous. I was now having issues with my mind and, frankly, began siding with my body. "What the hell have you gotten me into?" I asked my mind, which, I discovered, had suddenly left town.

The next wave rose up menacingly and began sucking me into its vortex. This was it, the moment of truth. As I paddled feverishly to catch the wave (I like that, *catch*, as in "to capture, or to seize control of") my breath became shallow – not a good thing when you know you are about to be driven to the bottom of the ocean. Fear is the mind killer, I thought. Panic and you're through. I gripped the board which became one with the wave and I felt the power of the ocean surging through it. Rising high in the air, suddenly everything became clear to me. In that enlightening instant, I knew exactly what it took to become a surfer. You had to have the courage to throw yourself in front of this thundering force of nature when every single survival instinct in your body is screaming for you to duck underneath and avoid it.

You had to have the fortitude to continue into that center of chaos despite everything a millennium of evolution, and survival, has taught us. You had to be fearless and brave but, most of all, you had to be an idiot.

The wave reached its peak and as I began hurtling down from the top of it at what now seemed to be at least 100 feet in the air, my mind sent every impulse it had at its disposal down into my body. "Jump up on the board," it screamed. "Jump!"

"Nope, not happening," my body replied, remaining rigid. "Not a chance."

The board continued to career down the steep, cavernous wave. "Just do it!" my mind yelled and at that moment it dawned on me that the nice folks over at Nike have no idea of just how reckless that slogan is. Whatever their intentions, it wasn't working. As quickly as the impulses were being sent down by my mind, my body, obeying the laws of nature I might add, was rejecting them. Instead, I laid down on the board as the wave began to crash all around and shot me out the front of it at an incredible rate of speed. I careened over the reef and, feeling exhilarated, let out a victorious roar, the victory being that I wasn't dead. I didn't surf, but at least I survived to surf another day. After paddling for what seemed like another hour, I finally reached the boat and a smiling Allois pulled me aboard. "Pussy," he said.

It took a while, but later that night my mind, my body and I were again speaking to each other after I created openness to the infinite reservoir of beer at the Surf Club, allowing all three of us to arrive at the source of thought and a place where problems were absent.

Chapter 6

Missionaries, Mercenaries & Misfits

*Few men who come to the islands leave them; they grow
grey where they alighted, the palm shades and the trade-
winds fan them till they die, perhaps cherishing to the last
the fancy of a visit home ... No part of the world exerts the
same attractive power.*

> ~ R. L. Stevenson
> *In the South Seas*

"Hey, there's that Santa Claus guy again," Devon said as we drove
through Kolonia. A penniless drifter with long, curly, graying hair and a thick
salty beard and mustache, I always thought he looked more like Jerry Garcia
of the Grateful Dead. One or the other, or perhaps both, could have been
hiding out on the island. No one would have known ... or cared.

We often saw this brawny Santa Garcia man walking through the
markets or sitting and having a cup of tea before heading toward his home a

few miles outside of town. This time, though, he seemed to be limping a bit so I beeped and pulled over to the side of the road.

"What are you doing?" Tess asked, somewhat shocked. It was time they learned that sometimes you do stop to offer a ride to a perfect stranger, at least on Pohnpei. "He's going to kill us all," Devon whispered as he opened the door.

"Oh, man, I can't thank you enough," he said, plopping down in the front seat while the girls scrunched together and pressed against the door in the back seat in order to be as far away from him as possible. "My feet are killing me."

A short time later he motioned for us to pull over by a path that led into the jungle. "Hey, you mind if we take a look?" I asked. "I'm trying to get to know as much of this island as possible."

"Not at all," he said. "Just be careful as the path can get awfully muddy."

Devon grabbed my arm as he left the car and said emphatically, "Dad, we are goners if we follow him down that path."

I pried the kid's hands off the car door handle and we followed him down the path, deep into the dark mangrove where the only thing waiting to attack us was a swarm of mosquitoes. Eventually, we were led to a small, lopsided one room corrugated tin shack nestled on wobbly stilts just above the muddy water. Inside, there was barely enough room for an old cot and two wooden shelves on which he kept a few outdated magazines. Naturally, there was no electricity or running water. "Ain't much," he said, "but it's home and it's free. The family up the hill said I could use it until someone else needs it."

He introduced himself as Garry and as the months passed we came to learn more about him each time we picked him up on his way home. "Hey, there's Garry," Devon would say. "Let's give him a ride."

It's always interesting to try and figure out how and why a person fits in where they fit in and, perhaps just as importantly, why they don't fit in. Being an outlier would serve Garry well on the island. Historically, Pohnpeians have shown a remarkable propensity to accept any and all foreigners, even if most of them have been deserters, reprobates, rascals and rogues.

One of the more famous of the castaways was James F. O'Connell, the celebrated "Tattooed Irishman," who by choice or chance resided on the island for five years around 1830. O'Connell claimed to have been shipwrecked in a vessel called the *John Bull* in 1827 and that he arrived on Pohnpei after four days at sea. He later would publish a highly imaginative account of his visit in which he claimed to have been captured by the Pohnpeians who wanted to have him for dinner – literally. To save himself, he leapt to his feet and danced a lively jig to the tune of "Garry Owens," a song about drinking, gambling and high living. The Pohnpeians, always ones to appreciate a really good show tune, let him live. O'Connell said he was then taken and forcibly tattooed by a young, beautiful Pohnpeian maiden. "I bore it like a martyr," he wrote.

Adding to his lore, O'Connell reported the beautiful maiden also happened to be the daughter of the chief, who adopted him, allowed him to marry her and then allowed O'Connell to become a chief himself. After leaving Pohnpei and undertaking several more mischievous adventures, he traveled through the United States exhibiting his tattoos and dancing in halls and circuses billed as the "Celebrated Tattooed Sailor-man."

While O'Connell portrayed the rascal, the role of rogue was played by the appropriately named Bully Hayes, who visited the island several times between 1869 and 1877. As you might have guessed, Bully had a penchant for fisticuffs and throttling those who worked for him. He also took what he could however he could. On one visit to Pohnpei, he arrived with a dozen thirty-pound cases, tightly sealed and marked "tobacco." He then traded the cases, all filled with rocks, with a local chief for a bull and three pregnant cows before quickly sailing off to engage in further trouble elsewhere.

Hayes eventually got his comeuppance aboard the schooner *Lotus* while sailing between Pohnpei and Kosrae on March 31, 1877. According to the most accepted version of the story, he took issue with his hot-tempered cook, Dutch Pete (who was actually a Norwegian). I think it's safe to say it's never a good idea to take issue with a hot-tempered cook, especially one called Dutch Pete who is actually a Norwegian. Dutch smashed Bully with a heavy metal bar as he emerged from a companionway and then rolled his 240-pound frame over the side of the boat. Another version had Dutch knock Bully overboard and then laugh as he was eaten by sharks. At any rate, the authorities never saw fit to prosecute Dutch, possibly because the demise of Bully had been circulated on several prior occasions, some by Bully himself to keep creditors and the law off his tail.

The current cast of colorful characters on the island had changed little since the beachcombers first disembarked (or jumped) from the frigates and galleons of yore. Like their castaway cousins, they didn't really mesh with the restrictive societal norms back home and sought a richer or at least more liberating life elsewhere.

"I didn't want to live, work and die in one place like my parents did back in Indiana," Garry told me one morning as he sat in the shade outside the local market watching the world go by. "I needed to get out. I didn't know where, but eventually I chose the Pacific. It always seemed to be the place to go to escape, I mean really escape."

Garry performed miscellaneous services, like helping paint the Micronesia Bible College and cleaning boats now and then. "The lord provides," he said. "What little I have goes for tea, fish … maybe a scone. I have free shelter. What else do I need?

"How old are you, Garry?" I asked.

"53," he said, then stopped himself and thought for a moment. "No, wait, 54, 55 something like that." Live out here long enough and all of your cares just drifted away along with your age.

Although by then we had become quite familiar with Pohnpei and immersed ourselves in the culture, it was hard to escape the fact that we were just visitors with a long lifeline tethered to Washington, D.C. The longer we stayed, however, the thinner that lifeline became. Would there come a time when we would sever it? More to the point, could we sever it? Most of the island expats worked without a safety net and that both frightened and fascinated me. Who were these transient wanderers? It was easy to see what attracted them – paradise beckoned, but how could they just leave everything behind and stay for good? What kind of a person flips the switch to "off," then drifts so far away they don't remember how old they are?

Alison #2 (as opposed to the country director's wife, Alison #1), was a short, elderly woman with brightly dyed red hair, who flipped the switch after arriving as a Peace Corps volunteer back in 1983. It was, in her words, "the beginning of my real life." I came across her walking down the main street in the midday heat with her full-length island skirt, red cotton blouse and woven bamboo purse clutched tightly under her arm. She was a drifter alright, although she knew exactly how old she was.

"None of your goddamn business," she said. I wasn't being so disrespectful as to ask, but I certainly was being disingenuous in asking how old she was when she joined the Peace Corps. She then gave me a devilish grin. "I was 56-years-old, and why not? My kids were grown and my husband died of a heart attack only a few years earlier. What the hell was I going to do with myself? I knew I wanted to volunteer, so I looked around and bingo, the Peace Corps was it. One of the best moves I ever made, I can tell you that."

The sun beat down on us and she apologized that she had to move on, but I had to throw one more question at her as she walked away. Was she ever going back to the United States?

"I have no idea," she said waving her hands at me and continuing on down the road. "Plans? Plans? What are those? I'm too busy living today."

Again with the here and now. Apparently, 401K retirement plans weren't big on the island.

I crossed over to a small block of stores selling local woodcarvings, produce – or what little food was left from the container ship, used clothing and other sundries. Two attractive women in their early twenties stood in the shade, leaning against the wall. They giggled as I approached and flashed a Pohnpeian hello with their dark eyes. I nodded in return and noticed the eyes of the girl closest to me locked on mine. Ascending the stairs, I gave a quick glance back. Her eyes remained focused laser-like, causing me to turn a slight shade of red.

Silly me, I could theorize and postulate all I wanted as to the reasons why so "few men who come to the islands leave them," but the answer was standing, or leaning, right in front of me. Say what you will about the palm shades, balmy trade winds and easy living, it was the women, the sirens of the South Pacific, who were the ultimate lure. With their slender, sculpted bodies, coffee brown skin, and long, silky black hair, the young women of Micronesia had a charm all their own. Bob Spegal made no bones about that.

"They're gorgeous here," he said. "I have to be honest and say the fact that they're a lot more open sexually was a factor in my decision to stay. Almost all of the women went topless in Kolonia at that time which was pretty cool."

To be fair, I also met a few American women who met and married Pohnpeian men and settled down on the island. Perhaps the fact that the men also had slender, sculpted bodies and occasionally went topless had something to do with that as well.

Bob, 58, ran the Micronesia Human Resource Development Center, an NGO specializing in health/environment related issues, and was a lifer on the island. "I'll probably die here," he said. "I'd like to be buried at sea and become part of the food chain again."

Of course, Bob had the prerequisite castaway look; wavy gray hair, with a matching beard, and a laid back, amiable attitude. He came to Pohnpei straight out of Philadelphia as a Peace Corps volunteer in 1975 and, like so many others, quickly fell under its spell.

"When I first arrived, every single person I met sat me down and offered food and coconut juice," he recalled. "On a scale of one to ten, the friendliness factor here is a 12. That's what attracted me. Well, that and the women."

After leaving the Peace Corps, he married Maria, a local girl he had met and, in addition to a one-year-old boy she already had, they had two more of their own. The relationship went well until 10 years later when he traveled to Kosrae to teach the islanders how to use computers for medical records and financial programs.

"While there I saw two local girls hitchhiking – something you almost never see – and that's how I met Sepe. Two months later I was back in Kosrae and a few months after that I got a call that she was pregnant. She had identical twin girls. I knew I had to take care of them. You need to be responsible for your actions. The funny thing was that both Maria and Sepe were pregnant at the same time." He thought for a moment, then added, "Well, I guess that isn't so funny."

It wasn't long before the coconut wireless began working and Maria heard about Sepe. However, according to Bob, although she didn't like it and was understandably upset, she put up with it and they made their marriage work. Another 11 years went by, but the cracks were ever widening. Bob struggled to keep his dual life in relative order while Maria went and got herself her own boyfriend. Not exactly your typical nuclear family unit. Then, in what has to be considered one of the more foolish and not exactly well thought out moves of the century, Bob decided to move Sepe, the twins and his six-year-old (he neglected to mention he had another kid with Sepe), over to Pohnpei to be close to him and Maria.

"Ill-advised," I added.

"That's it, that's the word," he said snapping his fingers. "Ill-advised. Anyway, that's when World War III started."

Maria arrived at the airport and threw stones at them as they drove away. A few months later Bob was at Club Cupid (I found there was never a lack of irony on the island) and she hit him in the back with a machete. "Thank God it wasn't with the sharp end," Bob recollected. Another time she hit him in the head with a huge rock. Years later, the subtle 'marital disagreements' continued when Maria's boyfriend stabbed him in the neck with a spear. Luckily it didn't go deep, but Bob did feel the need to point out that there was blood spurting everywhere.

Time heals all wounds. Eventually, Bob stopped dropping by and wounding Maria emotionally and, in turn, Maria stopped wounding Bob with rocks, machetes and spears. Over the following years, things actually became downright civil. Although they had been separated for nine years, the last I heard they were still legally married and actually became partners in running Pohnpei Waste Management.

Indeed, all was well that ended well on the island and, in the end, it was all about forgiveness. Pohnpeians reacted to transgressions as *sapwung iso* or sacred mistakes and considered absolution (along with generosity) as the noblest of virtues. Most, if not all, incidents – even murders – were resolved by the victim or the victim's family signing a "forgiveness" contract exonerating the perpetrator of all "misdeeds." Forgiveness didn't come easily, however, and was only bequeathed upon receipt of pigs, *sakau* and cash, which could total thousands of dollars. The perpetrators also had to personally ask for forgiveness from the victim or the victim's families, usually on bended knee. The local court system rarely intervened when there was a signed and heartfelt forgiveness contract in hand.

"It's a catharsis," Mat Mix explained to me at his place early one morning, "and it works both ways." Mat, 64, was yet another Peace Corps volunteer who came over in in the 1960s. Frankly, I was beginning to think of the volunteers as the dinner guests you invite over and then never leave no matter how many times you make overt references to what time, or year, it is.

"In my 40 plus years here I've never seen a repeat offender," Mat continued. "Forgiveness is almost always given. If not, it would look extremely bad and your reputation within the community is one of the only things you have around here. I was drunk one night and ran over a guy, breaking his leg, arm and jaw. The next morning I visited him in the hospital asking for forgiveness and he gave it to me. That's one of the things I like best about Pohnpei. I really didn't see much forgiveness back in the States."

True to form, Mat was also perfectly content to grow grey where he alighted. I also had the feeling that, like most of the others, forgiveness wasn't actually the real reason he came and stayed.

"Weather and women," he said through a wide smile. "The food and water just came. Plus, it's just so liberating out here. It's freedom personified. You can pretty much do as you feel. You want to build a house, you build a house. Electrical code? Fuck the electrical code.

"Within a half hour after I arrived," he added, "riding in the back of a truck on a god-forsaken, ruddy road no less, right then and there I said, 'fuck it, I'm never going back.'"

Mat was a legend on the island for several reasons, but the one that came up most often, the one that hung like pungent smoke in the air, was the rumor circulated by almost everyone that it was he who first brought marijuana to Pohnpei. He grinned when I brought it up, and then took a long pull from a bong he made out of an old plastic Gatorade bottle. It was 8 a.m. and breakfast was served. "It's a great story," he said, letting a steady stream of smoke escape from his lips, "and I really haven't done anything to dispel it, but it's not true. I'm not the Johnny Appleseed everyone thinks I am."

Life was good for Mat. Soon after arriving he married a local girl (she was 17, he was 24) and together they had eight kids. "The Pohnpeian community culture and extended family really frees daddy up to do whatever the fuck he feels like," he said. Pointing to his four-month-old granddaughter crawling in the yard, he added, "She has more people picking her up and watching over her than you could ever imagine. You got lots of arms around here."

With the help of family, Mat settled into island life and eventually started his own collection/debt receivership business. His marriage ended in divorce in 1984 after "serious sexual infidelity" on the part of his wife. "I put up with it for as long as I could and then finally I took her back to her parents and just dropped her off there," he said. "That's how you divorce here on Pohnpei."

After a few years he remarried (the second time a little more typically aligned with the expat ideal – he was 42 and she was 19) and, as he put it, lived happily ever after, playing his guitar and harmonica and tooling around town on his Chinese Kinroad 150 motorcycle. With all the sexual promiscuity that was taking place, I asked if he ever felt inclined to cheat on either of his wives. "Never, not once," he said emphatically. He took another long draw from his Gatorade bong and added, "I'm the straightest person you'll ever meet on the island."

I bid him farewell and headed out into the hot afternoon sun. It was time to pick up the kids as, unlike others, this home daddy was still far from doing "whatever the fuck he feels like." Actually, having the kids taken care of and kept busy after school was relatively easy since we were fortunate enough to have the three Australian Naval officers, two of which had kids roughly our children's age, as neighbors.

The Australian Navy compound, with its immaculate lawns and landscaped flora, was an anomaly amidst the trees, vines and dense brush of the jungle that surrounded it and kept it hidden next to the Mallarmes. Inside there was a swing set and play area for the kids, a long smooth paved driveway for skateboarding and, down by the river, a small built-in pool to cool off in chlorinated, leptospirosis-free water. Hide-and-go-seek was a staple on most afternoons. For the adults, the compound also had a huge thatch-covered *nahs* that served as a gathering place for a number of welcoming/going away barbecues or just playing poker long into the wee morning hours. The *nahs* was also THE place to watch Australian rugby matches, where we'd drink beer and listen to the same heated argument that would inevitably take place.

"Rugby Union is so much better than Rugby League."

"Ah, you're daft, mate. Rugby union is only a contact sport -- rugby league is a collision sport."

No doubt about it, the Aussies were the people to be with and at the top of the expat social order. They easily ruled the lifer list on the island and had quite a few short timers as well. That being the case, I had to learn how to decipher the Australian accent. Watching the commercials during the rugby matches helped. For instance, one kept telling us about some important horse "rice" coming up on the sports network. When I found myself saying "thudeen" (the number after twelve) months later, I knew I was spending way too much time with the Australians.

The Aussies were quick to point out that Australia wasn't just about rugby. In fact, I would soon come to learn that Australia was a complex agrarian society based on two important economic indicators – beer and barbecues. Between the two, and make no mistake about it, beer was king. You could have beer without a barbecue, but you would never, ever, have a barbecue without beer. Nobody took their beer, or drinking in general, more seriously than the Aussies. They never showed up at your house with a mere bottle of wine or, god forbid, a six-pack. They arrived wielding a huge cooler, or "eskie" as they called it, filled with beer in addition to bottles of wine and the alcohol of their choice. I was always amused to see a living room lined with blue coolers at a party.

"Hey," I said, holding an oil can-sized Foster's and offering a thumb's up to Eddie, himself a househusband of Janet, one of the officials at the Australian Embassy. "Love the Aussie beer."

He looked left and right to make sure no one saw us, stroked his handlebar mustache, then strode over and sat me down for a serious talk.

"Right, mate. The first thing you need to learn is that nobody … NOBODY … drinks Foster's in Australia and that's because no self-respecting pub would sell it. It's an export beer only and the sure way to spot a tourist is to see them drinking one."

I quickly put my Foster's under my chair.

"Contrary to what you might think," he continued, "we don't have that many beers, but what we have is good. Toohey's is one of the best, but Victoria Bitter is what most people drink and probably the best 'all-rounder.' Four X is decent but pretty much only drunk in Queensland, and then there's Carlton, which probably owns half the breweries anyway. Normally, for value, I drink Carlton and I'll drink it cold because it's more refreshing." He held up his beer and smiled as if posing for an advertisement.

And there you have it, an Australian beer primer done in 20 seconds.

Feeling I should reciprocate, I then went through my own 20-second American beer primer. Lower beer tier: Schlitz, Schaeffer, Rheingold, Pabst Blue Ribbon, Mickey's Big Mouth (if you can get it, but why would you want to); Middle beer tier: Bud, Miller, Rolling Rock, Yuengling, and Stella Artois; Upper beer tier: Sam Adams, Sierra Nevada and St. Pauli Girl. (light beer was not on my list as it fits more into a water primer; e.g. Perrier, Evian, Aquafina, Coors Light).

"Bud?" Eddie interrupted while making a face. "Who drinks that?"

While the Aussies were easily the predominant expat community on the island, they certainly weren't the only ones. Our pick up soccer matches under the lights of an old athletic field on the outskirts of Kolonia resembled a U.N. assembly. There was Yefeth Konings from the Netherlands, Tuiono Tuitaru from Fiji, Gainmore Zanamwe from Zimbabwe, Simon Ellis from England, Dilshan Senarathgoda from Sri Lanka, Dirk from Germany, Charles Musana from Uganda, Lachlan "Locky" King amongst several from Australia and, of course, Damian, Steve Finnen, myself and a few others from the United States.

Despite all of us speaking English, or something like it, our main problem was communication.

"You have to fix the pitch," Simon yelled to Michaela, a World Teach volunteer from the States who was standing on the other side of the field.

"What?" she yelled.

"Fix the pitch," he yelled back.

Michaela looked around at the field hoping a pitch would reveal itself. "Fix the what?" she asked again.

"You need to adjust the cones on the pitch," Simon said waving his arms.

"The Pitch? Isn't that the small golden thing with wings that you have to catch to win the Quidditch match at Hogwarts?" I asked.

"The pitch is the playing field," Steve interjected. He added that while playing rugby in Europe he also had to get used to preparing for the "fixture," the common name there for the match itself.

I pulled up a stool and sat down at the Rusty Anchor bar.

"Who the fock are you?" the burly man sitting next to me bellowed in an Australian accent. The ashtray in front of him, filled with mangled cigarette stubs and long unbroken strands of grey ash, sat atop a bar sticky from several Jack & Cokes, one of which he held tilted inches from his lips, poised to be finished as soon as he was through with his interrogation and got the answer he was looking for.

"I'm Jeff Martin, mate, who the fock are you?" I replied.

"Well, pleased to meet ya there Jeff," he said putting his drink down and slapping me on the back. "I'm Wayne and I run this joint. Hey Joe, give him a beer on me will ya? And by the way, that was the worst fockin' fake Aussie accent I've ever heard."

While there were a few places to wet your whistle in Kolonia – including one or two rundown *sakau* bars on the waterfront where you could muck up your whistle, the Rusty Anchor was THE place to go on a Saturday night (those of us with kids often had them assemble in one of our houses with a shared babysitter or two). If you sat at the bar long enough, and most of us did, you were bound to run into almost everyone at one point or another. It was a home away from home for locals and expats alike; a refuge for the fishermen, landlubbers, low-lifes, and the rare wandering traveler seeking to be entertained for an evening before sailing on.

"For further, um, anthropological studies," *National Geographic Adventure* magazine intoned in the same article that highlighted surfing at Palikir Pass, "stop by the Rusty Anchor, a harbor-front bar hidden in the shell of an unfinished hotel and frequented by an Altmanesque cast of expats and locals."

Even the old building itself was a castaway from a dream long since unfulfilled. Originally designed as an elegant three-story hotel, it sat majestically perched atop a bluff overlooking the picturesque harbor between Sokehs Ridge and the town of Kolonia. For reasons never fully disclosed, however, the funding dried up and construction came to an abrupt halt. The jungle soon began its unyielding encroachment and the building remained a dull grey cinderblock shell of its former potential until Wayne's wife, a local entrepreneur whose family built the hotel, patched up one of the larger back rooms and opened the Rusty Anchor. Wayne ran a local construction company and was more than happy to provide any and all building materials and support.

With no sign outside and its first-floor windows bricked up with cinder blocks, the Rusty did its best to keep customers away, posing as just another abandoned building outside of town. For the uninitiated it was hard to find during the day and at night, damn near impossible. Like a speakeasy in New York City, the best and often only way for newcomers to get there was to have an insider take them. After entering a small, unmarked side door, Bette and I were led through a darkened entryway to unfinished cement stairs that took us down into an abandoned ballroom. A thick, twisted dock rope strung along large columns guided us past a raised dusty dance floor beckoning in a ghostly manner from the left. The light and noise from a doorway at the end of the ballroom, however, quickly let us know the living were just inside the next room ... and living large at that.

A wall of sound and images hit us as soon as we entered. Wetter Than Seattle, an expat rock band, was playing Jethro Tull with their amps cranked over in a dimly lit corner. Johnny, one of the Australian naval officers, was the first to greet us; just a simple nod as he stretched across one of the pool tables for a bank shot, the smoke from his dangling cigarette curling up into his squinting eyes. His girlfriend Jade, pool cue in one hand and a cigarette and beer in the other, was running the other table with Melyann Mallarme. Donna, a tough, foul-mouthed former Aussie cop hired to help whip the Pohnpei police force into shape, blindsided us with a bear hug and dragged us over to the bar.

"You guys have been here almost 30 seconds already and you still don't have a drink in your hand," she shouted above the music while slamming her hand down on the bar to remedy the situation.

After a flurry of greetings (and salutation shots) we made our way to the few tables on the opposite side of the bar for drinks and island gossip with David and Alison, Damian and Mary, Uta (her husband, Steve, played bass in the band), and the rest of our crew. Behind us lay an unobstructed view of the harbor bathed in moonlight and, in the distance, the lights of the tuna boats being offloaded at the docks on the causeway. "Unobstructed" is a key word here because just beyond the tables the hotel simply ended; no walls, just rebar jutting outward and a 40-foot drop into the dark mangrove below. To be fair, a few potted plants were strategically placed to keep you inbounds and no one ever fell over the side, at least not to my knowledge, but then again my awareness could be called into question, and often was, whenever I was at the Rusty.

"Maybe we should play a drinking game," I said, surveying the drinks piling up in front of us.

"I have a game for ya," Nick, a huge Aussie bloke who had been buying most of the drinks, shouted while towering over our table. "It's called keep up with the Australians!" He then threw back a tall gin & tonic, I believe swallowing the lime as well, and pounded the table. "Another round's comin' in about three seconds, so these drinks better be gone," he bellowed as he ambled back to the bar.

Meanwhile, always seated on the same stool to better monitor the revelry taking place, Wayne was holding court from his throne at the corner of the bar, alternately befriending and belittling the fermenting brew of locals, expats and surfers as well as the Peace Corps, World Teach and yes, even the Jesuit, volunteers. All fell within the realm of his kingdom of comment. He was big, burly and belligerent and although I can't prove it, I am absolutely certain he was a direct descendent of Bully Hayes.

"You're full of shit, mate, and let me tell you why." Thus began many a soliloquy from Wayne and there was no interrupting him once he got started. Like all barroom philosophers, he knew a little, but not enough, about a number of topics and an awful lot about human nature. Usually, though, his facts were in order. In a wonderful snapshot of the island's informality, now and again I'd even see him sitting at the bar discussing the state of political

94

affairs with Susan Cox, the Australian ambassador to Micronesia. Ever the diplomat, she would only disclose that the discussions were "frank and candid."

"He does have, shall we say, an interesting point of view," she added.

While his wife officially ran the place, doing the bookwork, ordering the supplies and overseeing the bar in general, Wayne more or less served as manager and the bar's best customer. "I couldn't even handle the amount of Coke he drinks," Steve said, "let alone the Jack Daniels that goes with it." Mostly, though, Wayne just loved to rub elbows with the guys, flirt with the ladies and buy an occasional round on the house to make sure everyone was having a good time.

"He's not as grouchy as everyone thinks he is," Devon once told me. "I saw him at the movies for his son's birthday party and he was so nice to all of the kids, asking 'Is everyone ok? Can I get anything? Does anyone want any candy?'"

"What, do you think I'm an asshole 24 hours a day?" he asked when I told him what a nice guy my daughter thought he was. "It's only down here at the bar and that's because all of you assholes get me started."

With that I moved over as a newcomer bellied up to the bar between Wayne and I. He was in his late 50's with a weather-beaten face and calloused, leather-like hands. It wasn't difficult to guess he was a fisherman. After introducing himself, we soon learned he was the captain of the *Ocean Challenger*, a 220-foot boat offloading 1,000 tons of fish at the dock on the causeway. Like his grandfather and his dad who fished all of their lives, he already had spent more than 40 years on the seas in Mexico, Panama, Venezuela, the Caribbean, and Micronesia, "just following the cost of labor."

He turned to Wayne and told him he'd heard about Rusty's from other fishermen, but couldn't find it because there were no signs.

"You're foreigners and we don't want foreigners here," Wayne said while buying him a beer. "If you want bars with signs, go to focking Hawaii." He downed another gulp of his Jack and Coke before adding, "You found us, though. Assholes always find us."

The fisherman let out a hardy laugh and was soon sending another round of drinks our way.

On the other side of the bar, Bette was having her own cross-cultural experience. As she sat talking to Steve, an extremely drunken Pohnpeian stood close by eyeing her the way a fisherman eyes a game fish. He cast his lure.

"You're beautiful," he slurred.

"Thanks," Steve said. "I have been taking care of myself lately."

"Not you, her," he said moving a few feet closer.

Ignoring him, they continued with their conversation. For the next half hour he circled dangerously close to Bette, casting and recasting his line. Finally, he moved within inches of her and dropped the net.

"You come home with me," he said.

"I'm married," she countered.

"That's ok," he replied. "We share. This is the island way. You are on Pohnpei now."

"My husband is not a sharing kind of guy and he's standing right next to you."

He turned and upon seeing me narrowed his eyes and clenched his fists. Frankly, I was more amused than angry. As he moved toward me Steve cut in.

"Ok, this is ridiculous," Steve said rising to his full 6' 2" stature. He and Uta had been on the island 14 years and while he didn't know this man by name, the two at least recognized each other. "Come on, let me buy you a drink," Steve said, yanking him over to the bar by the arm.

Back at our table, the crew had already heard that I had been talking to some of the lifers about what it took to stay on Pohnpei. Anything and everything said or done on the island made it to everyone's ear within a three-hour period.

"Mercenaries, missionaries and misfits;" Damian said waving three fingers in the air, "the only people that make it here."

"And the trailing spouses thereof," I added. Suddenly, Aussie Nick appeared out of nowhere. "There he is," he said, thrusting a gin and tonic at me. "You got some real catching up to do, mate."

Oh good god, I thought. And just like that, another raucous Saturday night became yet another blurry Sunday morning on Pohnpei.

Chapter 7

War of the Worlds

Literature is mostly about having sex
and not much about having children;
life is the other way around.
~ David Lodge

The house was a mess.

Bette brought this to my attention. It wasn't said maliciously or to malign my housekeeping. It was more of an observation, a statement of fact. The house *was* a mess. Clothes were flung everywhere, books and games were strewn about, and a half-inch of sand, dirt, and coral covered the floor. I honestly believe that cleaning your house before the kids move out is like raking the yard before a hurricane hits but, still, I cleaned and swept every single day.

It took about five minutes to clear the cobwebs in my head as it was still early morning but eventually the primal need to defend myself reached my temporal lobe, or whatever part of the brain it is that makes you argue with your wife, and so I said, "Hey, I clean and sweep every single day."

"I know, but maybe we should get a house cleaner to come at least once a week to um, you know," she paused, "really clean."

I couldn't argue with her as our bathroom looked more like it was a part of the jungle and I could swear something actually growled at us whenever we approached it.

And so it came to be that Yone, a Pohnpeian from a few villages up the road, cleaned our house every Friday, just in time for it to be ruined by the spontaneous weekend cocktail get-togethers and the children's sleepovers, which drove us to arrange the spontaneous weekend cocktail get-togethers in the first place. Now that I think of it, Sunday morning house cleaning would have been a bit more practical, but the point was to have the house look impeccable for the guests, even if it's only for an hour and, yes, even if that guest is only seven years old. Another practicality most men don't get is that you have to pick up and straighten everything before the house cleaner arrives. "What's the point of cleaning the house before the house cleaners come," I used to say. "Isn't that what we're paying them for?" Well, I don't say it anymore and the reason is simple. You pick up the toys, games, clothes, and semi-empty juice boxes so that they spend more time sweeping, wiping, mopping and actual "cleaning" instead of picking up the toys, games, clothes, and semi-empty juice boxes.

In return for sweeping, wiping, mopping, making the beds and defoliating the bathrooms, we paid Yone U.S. $20 for an afternoon's worth of work. Yes, I know this is nothing compared to what they charge for this service back in the U.S., but it was decent pay on the island and you could be viewed as being cheap, even selfish, by the community for not employing someone locally. Thanks to Yone's half day and, I must emphasize, my six-and-a-half days of cleaning, the jungle began to recede from the house and we again had our toilet back.

The house was clean.

Of course, Bette wasn't around to appreciate it. Her job took her off island an awful lot. I wasn't complaining though. Her work was an important part of the Peace Corps' overall mission and essential in helping the Federated States of Micronesia meet its educational and social programming needs. I knew this because the official in-country Peace Corps handbook said so. It also told me that her busy schedule was to be expected. I knew just how crucial this was, so no grumbling came from me. My job was to maintain the house and take care of the kids. I mean, how could that compare to preserving the overall well-being of an entire nation? I remained completely supportive. Her incessant traveling didn't bother me a bit; never even entered my mind. As the "trailing spouse" I would just carry on cooking and cleaning, seeing the kids through college and then taking care of their grandchildren while Bette continued to jet around to god knows where, saving the world one sustenance garden at a time, but you wouldn't hear me griping about it. Nope, no complaints from me. Everything was just fine, thanks for asking.

After being home for a few days Bette was flying off again, this time to Kosrae for the induction of the new volunteers there. Did I mention how supportive I was of her work? So much so, in fact, that within only 24 hours of her arrival from her previous trip and immediately offering me several helpful suggestions on how to improve myself and increase productivity in the household, I would actually look forward to her once again fulfilling the Peace Corps' overall mission and helping the Federated States of Micronesia meet its educational and social programming needs – on the outer islands.

Devon and Tess were, of course, much more at ease when Bette was home. When she left, however, it was like the fall of Saigon with the kids hanging onto the skids of the helicopter as it wobbled up from the roof of the U.S. Embassy. Gunfire and overall chaos would erupt from the jungle as soon as her chopper left the demilitarized zone.

"It's ok, kids," I'd say trying to quell their anxieties and calm their fears in the car on the way home. "I'm going to take care of you."

"Yeah, but you're not mom," Tess would say, twirling her hair and jamming her thumb into her mouth as an immediate source of comfort.

"And you yell too much," Devon would add, twitching her head downward three times in a row, always three times in a row.

"Well, I'm working on that," I'd say, loosening my neck muscles by rotating my head three times in a row, always three times in a row. "Who wants ice cream?"

"YAY," the kids would shout and their mood would lighten considerably.

Psychiatric care for anxiety disorders wasn't exactly in abundance on the island, but ice cream always worked wonders. Actually, in many ways my life became easier with Bette gone because then it became solely my house, my family and my rules. There was a comfortable, easy flow to our schedule with no one there to tell me the same school uniform shouldn't be worn five days in a row, which of course we would never do or, strictly as a hypothetical, that waffles shouldn't be served as dinner.

Still, stress fractures had begun to form between Bette and I, the kids and I, the dogs and I, the cockroaches and I, and ... look, we can go round and round trying to find a common denominator in all of this, the point was that I was having problems, serious problems, adjusting to my new role. I don't want to over use an understatement, but even when Bette wasn't away, the Home Daddy thing was becoming just a tad problematic.

Nothing could have prepared me for the parental school of hard knocks, which offers no degree yet whose tuition costs nothing less than your soul. There are no Bell Curves, no sliding scales, no rough drafts and certainly no pre-test preparations. Every day is a final exam and, it seemed, every day I was failing this exam. The educational analogy is apt because the children's schoolwork turned out to be my undoing. Devon and Tess were excellent students, but I still had to stay on top of them with their transitions into a higher grade level than where they'd be back home. I learned that a quick review had to be done in the school parking lot before we left. Homework written down? Do we understand it? Do we have the books we need? What about worksheets?

Devon read her homework assignments to me, "Reading, pages 141 – 160; fill out reading log; review chapter four in religion; and math."

There, right there! The oversight that would lead to my eventual downfall. Did you catch it? She just skimmed over the math part. I assumed it was just a page of math problems. This assumption was wrong.

Once we were at the house we only had enough time to grab a snack and a change of clothes before we flew off for the kid's tennis lessons. The tennis courts in Kolonia looked like they were built during Magellan's stay on the island (history books often mention his deft backhand and his overpowering serve) with fissures and cracks everywhere, but the kids had fun.

We were back home again by 5:30 and I instructed, "Get your homework out and let's move!" with drill sergeant precision. I then began grating the cheese, slicing the one ragged tomato we had left and frying the fat laden mystery meat for our burrito dinner.

Meanwhile, Bette called to ask for a ride because it was pouring rain and she had had a "horrific day." The time bomb was set and the ticking began. When we got home I again got back to dinner and Bette immediately quizzed the kids on what they had for homework. As she did with me, Devon methodically went through her list, but this time she casually ended it by announcing she had a major test in Math the next morning. I dropped the Mexican seasoning on the floor. "WHAT?"

We tried to stay calm and focused but the fire was spreading further and faster, thanks to the flames shooting out of Bette's eyes at me for not having known this and keeping Devon home to study instead of going to tennis practice. We decided to separate them and had Tess do her homework upstairs in her room while Devon did hers on the dinner table. However, sensing panic, the kids rebelled. "Why DO I HAVE to do it now?" "Well, maybe I DON'T FEEL LIKE IT!"

I laid down the law. Without yelling (I think it important that fact be established), I explained that certain rules must be obeyed and that kind of behavior would not be tolerated. As with any parental lectures, we also made sure there were several interjections of "from now on..." and "I expect you to..." with the obligatory threatening conclusion of "or so help me..." Tess was then sent to do her homework with me and Bette pulled up a chair and attached herself to Devon.

By 9 p.m., a full three hours later, Tess was finally in bed, wide-awake, but in bed, while Bette and Devon were still wrestling with the math.

"THAT'S IT," Bette suddenly announced. "I can't take it anymore. Devon get your pajamas on and get into bed."

Her plan was to keep Devon home from school the next day so she could review everything and then be ready for a make-up test on Thursday. I knew this wouldn't work since Thursday was the school fair and the kids had off on Friday for Pohnpeian Independence Day.

I said I'd stay up with Devon for a little while longer to review everything, but after a while she was dividing when she should have been multiplying, adding when she should have been subtracting and sleeping with her head on the table when she should have been ... well, it just wasn't working. I took her up to bed.

When I came back down I found Bette pouring over the open books and note cards and she had that wild "fight or flee" look about her. Actually, Bette has never "fled" in her life so, naturally, she decided to fight ... me.

"She doesn't know this," she said, jamming her finger into the math book, "AT ALL!"

I braced. Here it comes, I thought to myself. Wait for it, wait ... for ... it.

"What the hell have you been doing all afternoon?"

There it was, the trump card, the arrow that all working parents sling with deadly precision at the heart of their stay-at-home partners. Nothing will start a fight faster than asking that question. Now sure, I should have rationalized the situation before answering or perhaps even offered her ice cream, but instead I decided to use the old 'answer a question with a question' trick.

"You were the one studying with her," I shot back. "What the hell have YOU been doing for the past three hours?"

Like Russia and the U.S. in the cold war days, escalation was the name of the game. We were now entering a nuclear arms race where the objective was to corner your opponent and prove the problem at hand was due to their neglect. An "I told you this would happen" was the equivalent of a first strike, followed by an "annoying habits" counter strike, which then quickly deteriorated into all-out war.

"What do you do, sleep all day?" she fired.

I went directly to the 13 mega-ton bunk buster.

"You're off flying around to exotic islands and never even home half the time, so don't even think of asking me what the hell I do all day," I said. "Apparently, you think you're some super important part of the Peace Corps' overall mission and essential in helping the Federated States of Micronesia meet its educational and social programming needs."

That last part certainly confused her, but then I had to go and make things even messier by adding "Look, it's not that big of a deal."

At that point I had committed two of the most common errors when dealing with an adversary, according to *Zen and the Art of War*: #1. Never use the Peace Corps training manual to back you up, and #2. Never, EVER, tell a woman that something, anything, isn't a big deal.

105

Bette's eyes grew wide and she bared her teeth.

"Not that big of a deal?" she asked. "NOT THAT BIG OF A DEAL?" She then took a deep breath and started. "If Devon doesn't pass this test she fails, if she fails here she's going to fail even worse back at St. Andrew's, if she fails at St. Andrew's she's going to have to go to some shitty high school where she'll probably hang out in the bathroom chain smoking all day before bowling practice and eventually dropping out to become a pole dancer at the Moulin Rouge Strip Club. Is that what you want? IS THAT WHAT YOU WANT?"

Something told me that was a rhetorical question and that it might be best if I didn't answer. But, of course, answer I did.

I'd like to think that Bette and I fight just like everyone else, but we don't. It's more like a gang fight – no, worse, a fight between relatives from New York and New Jersey with screaming and yelling and many unseemly references regarding one's mother. I recall at least one fight during our earlier parenting days that lasted for weeks and was resolved only after U.N. peacekeeping forces stepped in and NATO issued a "no fly" zone.

Eventually we calmed down and mutually agreed we needed to work more on our shared responsibilities. On my end, I agreed that I had to become more involved in dealing with the children and, especially, their homework. On Bette's end, she agreed that yes, I needed to become more involved in dealing with the children and, especially, their homework.

In addition to being a hunter I would now also become a gatherer. This meant I would have to be in the classroom everyday talking to the teacher, asking what the homework was, when the tests were, what the tests were about, reviewing snack schedules, and become the parent every teacher (and every other parent) hates.

Bette and I even had a good chuckle when, after looking at Devon's math notes, we discovered we couldn't answer a few of the problems. Prime and ordinal numbers, check, but just what the hell are cardinal numbers?

The next day, our arguing turned to joyous family hugs when after several months at sea the long-awaited container ship finally arrived with our cargo of food and about 4,000 pounds of unnecessary plastic items. I immediately broke into an Irish jig knowing that the toaster was in there somewhere. No more charred bread from the oven.

Best of all were the crates of food with boxes of canned vegetables and five- gallon containers of mayonnaise, peanut butter, maple syrup, cereal, cooking oil and salsa (the bags of chips, unfortunately, had been reduced to corn meal). Our once empty storage space now looked like a mini Costco. The girls were ecstatic as they dove into the pile of snacks. Bette and I celebrated by opening a bottle of good wine and a can of Chef Boyardee min-raviolis. Later that night as I went in to check on the girls, I noticed Tess's beloved teddy bear lying on the floor. I pulled back the covers and discovered she had fallen asleep clutching a can of Pringles.

A loud crash emanating from your kitchen in the middle of the night is never a good thing. It portends doom. It conjures up images of thieves in the night and, yes, even murder. Machete in hand, I crept down the stairs, flipped on the light and saw a trickle of warm, red liquid running across the floor from the cement pantry. Murder it was. The pungent, yet oddly sweet smell of death choked me. Our cheap shelving unit had collapsed under its new found weight and there, shattered on the floor along with all of my hopes and dreams of ever eating a decently flavored meal, lay several broken jars and bottles; a veritable gazpacho soup of apple sauce, salsa, chocolate syrup and Thai cooking sauces.

We also had another dilemma. Along with all of the goodies, the container ship also brought with it a scourge that would soon infiltrate our house and our lives. It was a plague; a curse that threatened to destroy our entire family by emitting electrodes containing light and darkness, good and evil, late night heaven and prime time hell. Our bulky, not-at-all-flat-screen TV had arrived. While the island actually did have cable services, the installers worked on island time and so the TV sat silently in the corner for another month, beckoning like the tall black monolith in *2001, A Space Odyssey.* The kids, squatting ape-like on their haunches, forearms holding them upright, would approach to within inches of it, let out a screech, then back away apprehensively.

Even after it was set up, Bette and I agreed we wouldn't tell the kids and keep it off for as long as possible, but after only a week they found it actually did work and, wielding the remote like the bone in *"2001"* they turned it on and much head shaking, shrieking and back flips ensued.

Fortunately, or unfortunately, depending upon how you want to look at it, Pohnpeian cable only offered 32 channels, most of which were devoted entirely to international programming, including the RT or Russia Today channel, the JTV or Japanese TV channel, Korean Arirang-TV, and NewsAsia, as well as religious broadcasting including JCTV or Jesus Christ Television, and the Evangelical TeleNetwork stations (one promised a special on "God's terrible wrath and hell's eternal torments" which I assumed was a show about raising children, but I watched the show for an hour and didn't see even one tip on parenting).

On the plus side, they also carried Cartoon Network for the kids, news programs (Aljazeera, BBC and CNN) for Bette, and ESPN 2, which was basically a 24-hour soccer and Australian rugby network, for me. Real Madrid vs. Lottomatica Roma anyone? The TV was also attractive to a few outside our family. Peter, Yone's husband, often would accompany her and offer support by turning the TV on and plopping down on the couch. Every now and then Bette would come home for lunch and watch reruns of *Grey's Anatomy* with Peter who was somewhat shocked to see every gorgeous physician having sex with every gorgeous physician's assistant in every gorgeous episode.

"This doesn't happen in a real hospital," Bette would have to explain every five minutes.

108

Speaking of high-quality television entertainment, host Jeff Probst and the cast and crew of *Survivor: Micronesia "Fans vs. Favorites"* had arrived on the island of Palau, marking the second time the series was filmed there. Helicopters, speedboats, and chaos descended on what the show described as the "distant, remote and unreachable Exile Island" – about a 15-minute boat ride from Koror, the capitol city of Palau.

All of this commotion made me glad we were on Pohnpei where, well, nothing was happening. Back in the helter-skelter world we used to live in I thought I'd never see "boredom" again. It became a magical, mythical place, this Boredom, a wonderful world where there was nothing to do. I used to visit it often as a child but, like Puff the Magic Dragon and all fairy tales, it slowly faded with each maturing year until I couldn't even imagine Boredom anymore and I longed to simply say "I'm bored" (of course the kids uttered it countless times since we arrived). Boredom truly is a fantastic place and I recommend stopping by as often as possible. Visit the little travel agent in your head and reacquaint yourself by perusing the Boredom brochures, which have nothing in them, then ask for a ticket to nowhere. Despite popular theory, the unexamined life truly is worth living – until someone finds you via email.

This, however, proved to be less of a nuisance than I thought it would be as the internet on the island was spotty at best and it took 20 minutes to open or send even the shortest emails. Photos? YouTube? Forget it. To save time and headaches, I simply told everyone, via email, that we didn't have email, to which they then sent emails back asking "why not."

With the scarcity of cargo and emails, CARE packages containing goodies and news from home were a godsend. I'll never forget the look on the kid's faces when, after a six-month drought of mail, a box arrived from the Stonestreets, who were friends of ours and the family of Katherine, one of Devon's best friends back home.

"What the?" Devon disappointedly exclaimed after opening the box she assumed was hers. "Wine. It's just wine."

Bette and I couldn't hear the rest of her diatribe as we were holding hands and dancing on the table. Luckily, other packages arrived with goodies for all. In case you're wondering, the quintessential CARE package, sent by our good friends Rob and Dina, contained the following items necessary to survive on a deserted island:

- Oreo Cookies
- Crunch 'n Munch popcorn
- Trident Gum and Blow Pops
- Tootsie Rolls
- Cap'n Crunch cereal
- Peanut Butter
- Wonka Nerds
- Extreme "Kickin' Cheddar" Pringles
- Beer Nuts
- Reese's Peanut Butter Cups
- A "Best of The Far Side" book

There was also a long letter describing Rob's work as pastor of his church, Dina's duties as a councilwoman in Sea Bright, what they did for Thanksgiving, yadda, yadda, yadda … before we got to the third paragraph, the letter was tossed and we all dove simultaneously for the box. A fight ensued over the Wonka Nerds, but after Bette grabbed the Oreos and I grabbed the beer nuts, we all went to our corners, happily munching away and growling if anyone else came close. For the time being, except for the munching, all was quiet on the western front.

Chapter 8

Highball of the Gods

*There is not any memory with less satisfaction than
the memory of some temptation that we resisted.*
~ James Branch Cabell

The Peace Corps' mission has three simple goals:

1. Helping the people of interested countries in meeting their need for trained men and women.

2. Helping promote a better understanding of Americans on the part of the peoples served.

3. Helping promote a better understanding of other peoples on the part of Americans.

Funny, but most of the Pohnpeians I met weren't interested in strategic marketing positioning, crafting messages to influence public perceptions, or any other public relations techniques that I could teach them, so I thought it might be best if I left it up to Bette to accomplish the first goal. The constant yelling and noise emanating from our house I believe promoted a better understanding of Americans, so the second goal was more or less taken care of. That left goal number three and when I heard the *kava*, or *sakau* as it is known locally, being pounded on a large stone one night at the Mallarmes next door, I knew it was time to partake of the sacred narcotic beverage so I could help promote a better understanding of "other peoples" on the part of Americans. Indeed, if I really wanted to know the people of Pohnpei, I needed to know *sakau*.

The Mallarmes allowed us to cut across their property, over a small stream and through a short patch of jungle to reach the "secret" back entrance to the Australian Navy compound where Melyann gave hula lessons to the kids. After dropping Devon and Tess off, a loud splash distracted me as I crossed back over the stream in the dark. Suddenly a large, soaked cat with matted fur scampered over my foot on the rock I was standing on before slipping back into the stream. This was unusual in that cats are not partial to water and don't have a long, hairless and slimy tail that ... Ughhh! That was no cat. Soaked from the knees down, I sloshed my way over to where everyone was sitting outside the Mallarme house and plopped down. It didn't take long before I became a fixture there and they always made me feel right at home. Maxson looked at me as I sat sprawled in the white plastic chair with my head tilted back looking up at the stars.

"Tough day?" he asked. "You should have some *sakau* to take your mind off it."

"Not really," I replied. "In fact it was a good day."

"Then you should have some *sakau* to celebrate," he said. Apparently, *sakau* was the solution, whatever your state of mind.

S*akau*, or if you're a bespectacled anthropologist, *piper methysticum*, is taken from the root of a pepper plant and contains a kick that has been cultivated and used for medicinal, ritual and recreational purposes for more than 3,000 years. Kavalactones, the active ingredient in sakau, is a psychoactive drug that serves as a natural tranquilizer and muscle relaxer, and has even been said to possess aphrodisiac qualities. A typical prescriptive commercial dose of kavalactones might be 80 to 150 milligrams (mg) three times a day, while a single cup of kava from Fiji, Samoa or Tonga probably contains about 250 mg alone. A cup from Pohnpei or Vanuatu, meanwhile, is said to be significantly stronger, containing up to 500 mg of kavalactones. The root's reputation had only recently taken hold overseas with its mellowing effect being marketed in Europe as an anti-anxiety drug and in America as an herbal supplement that promotes relaxation. The *South Florida Sun-Sentinel* even reported that, after a long day at work, doctors and lawyers were saddling up next to skaters and surfers at kava bars opened in Boca Raton, West Palm Beach, and Fort Lauderdale.

However, *sakau* was more than just the buzz beverage of choice on the island, it was also a highly revered way of life. Originally only those with chiefly titles (e.g. the *Nahnmwarki* and *Nahnken*) imbibed during elaborate ceremonies in which they often made ritual offerings of it to the thunder god, *Nahnsapwe*. Over the years the inebriating grog eventually became readily available to everyone and was used to celebrate weddings, funerals, the first birthday of a child, the departing and returning of fishermen and friends, or even to settle legal claims. While the Pohnpeian/English Dictionary lists 31 different *sakau* ceremonies, it was safe to say the drink had become somewhat less ceremonial by the time we arrived and was also used to celebrate the sun rising, the sun setting, completely sunny days, partly sunny days, cloudy with a chance of rain days, evenings when it was getting dark outside and, especially, throughout the night to ward off evil spirits or just reality in general. *Sakau* was even used to celebrate a feast, *uramai*, which celebrated the first use of a new *sakau* stone that would be used to celebrate future feasts serving *sakau* (I'm not sure but I think that last sentence was a *sakau* haiku).

Still shaking the wet slime off my feet, I quietly waited as the *sakau*-filled coconut shell cup made its rounds. There were about ten men and women sitting around the huge, flat stone table used to pound the *sakau*, and each one took a gulp of the muddy, sinewy liquid before passing it on. Suddenly Hilario Bermanis II, HB for short, spotted me and smiled villainously as he motored his wheelchair over. Three years earlier he lost his left arm and both of his legs to a rocket propelled grenade (RPG) while on patrol in Iraq with his unit, the 325th Airborne. The Federated States of Micronesia had been under U.S. jurisdiction since the end of WWII and, although declaring independence in 1979, many islanders still continued to serve in the U.S. military under a "Compact of Free Association." As a result, Micronesia had more Army recruits per capita than any U.S. state and, subsequently, more casualties in Iraq and Afghanistan, per capita.

"I heard the whistling noise an RPG makes and that was the last thing I remember," he later told me. "I woke up in Walter Reed Hospital in Washington, D.C. President Bush came to visit and said something like 'thank you for your service,' and Rumsfeld gave me a Secretary of Defense coin," he said, rolling his eyes.

He may have lost limbs but, apparently, he hadn't lost his thirst for life, and *sakau*. Normally extremely quiet and reserved, he still had a penchant now and then for mischief making. "Wait a minute, hold on," he said, holding up his hand and stopping the flow of the coconut shell. "We have a guest of honor here." With that the cup made its way straight to me. "Thanks so much HB, you're a real pal," I sneered staring down into the concoction. I quickly took a gulp and smiled politely while suppressing my gag reflex.

"Is that a hint of pepper I detect," I said trying to be gracious as my eyes watered and my stomach heaved. Good god, it was a cup of brown snot. The crowd laughed ... at me, not with me.

"Be gentle with him, it's his first time," HB said as the crowd continued to laugh.

The shell was refilled and again sent straight back to me. I hesitated since the last thing I wanted was more, at least not right away. As if the taste and texture weren't enough, the drink was often prepared under less than ideal hygienic conditions and with water that was, shall we say, suspect at best. Local doctors attributed maladies related to amoebas, worms, and other internal parasites to its consumption. However, I had reason to believe the Mallarmes used bottled water to help make it and, as all eyes were on me, at that point it would have been rather disrespectful to refuse. Although much of the pomp and circumstance had faded over the years, *sakau* still maintained a strong sense of tradition with considerable religious symbolism in the plant itself. I lowered my eyes, raised the shell and took another gulp.

> *"Kava here is what the cross is to the Christian;*
> *it fell from heaven and is the only means of obtaining*
> *a hearing there."*
> – Rev. Albert Sturges, 1856

The Reverend Sturges knew what he spoke of, for legend has it that *sakau* truly was the drink of the gods, with Luk, a wily god of mirth and mayhem, taking off his knee cap and using it as the first kava cup. Apparently, they got a little too rowdy and, while pounding the root, allowed some to drop down to Earth where it landed, you guessed it, in Micronesia. Another more likely story (and one told on other Pacific islands relating to kava) tells of how someone saw a rat nibbling on a root, then watched in amazement as the rat warbled off acting quite inebriated. In an interesting addendum, local legend has the powers that be, angry that the mortals misused the happy hour highball of the gods, banishing *sakau* and only allowing the more respectful people on the nearby island of Kosrae to drink it (even today, Kosrae is known to have the strongest *sakau*). Not to be outdone, the Pohnpeians, it was said, sent a woman to Kosrae, who then hid the *sakau* in her vagina and brought it back to Pohnpei.

"That's why it tastes bitter and smells that way," a woman later explained in a matter-of-fact tone.

Maybe I did get this *sakau* all wrong. I mean, if it was good enough for the gods, and if a woman would go to that length to bring it back to the island, who was I to refuse? I took another gulp.

The purpose of drinking *sakau* was to obtain a nice, warm, fuzzy feeling, and I can tell you that after an hour of drinking, and gagging, I felt – nothing. All of the talk; all of the build-up surrounding *sakau*, and then – nothing. Picking myself up and making my way back across the stream to get the kids, I felt betrayed. Hell, I'd rather spend an evening with a cheap bottle of wine and then throw up, both of which would have tasted better. "Don't worry," Maxson called out after me, "sometimes nothing happens on the first try. We'll do it again tomorrow."

Yeah, right, I thought, still retching. I crossed the stream keeping a wary eye out for that damned aquatic cat.

I have a problem learning lessons in the classroom of life. This became evident when, only a few days later, I found myself ripping the husk off of some small, date-like dry brown fruit with my teeth and chewing the betel nut, yet another natural narcotic, found within.

"This can't be good," I said through a mouthful of red liquid.

"Here, spit into this can," Regina said thrusting an empty Budweiser toward me. "Whatever you do, don't swallow."

Regina, from the island of Yap and the local Peace Corps program assistant there, was sitting on the bed in her hotel room with Hana, her local counterpart from Palau, showing me the wonderful advantages of chewing betel nut, yet another bad habit that dates back to antiquity. In the 1st century AD, Sanskrit medical writings claimed that betel nut possessed 13 qualities found in the region of heaven. That was good enough for me, as I was never

116

one to question Sanskrit medical advice anyway. It was also said to beautify the mouth, induce purification, and kindle passion. Ah, passion. I could only imagine how turned on Bette was going to be watching me lean over and let loose a gushing stream of blood red spit into a Bud can.

Because of its stimulating effects, betel nut is used in a manner similar to the western use of chewing tobacco which, I have found, possesses none of the qualities found in the region of heaven. After putting a pinch between your cheek and gum, the betelnut at first tastes like cardboard. After chewing it for a while, though, it finally begins to soften and develops into the mouth-watering flavor of wet cardboard. Lime is added to help activate the stimulant. No, not the juicy green lime you're thinking of; more like the lime you use to fertilize your lawn. This lime is coral taken from the shore which is burned in an earthen oven, then crushed into a fine white powder. The powder is wrapped in a pepper leaf to protect your mouth from getting burned due to the alkalinity of the lime. According to Hana, lime made from clamshells is best because it is stronger. "It's what you have in your mouth right now," she added. I wasn't impressed.

Like *sakau*, betel nut had a firm foothold in the Micronesian culture and it seemed to be used by everyone everywhere. It wasn't uncommon to see a 12-year-old girl, walking down the road with her school uniform on and pig tails bouncing, offer a cute smile before turning her head and spewing a torrent of red spit onto the ground.

"In Yap you have to plant a betel nut tree and watch it grow before you can enjoy the nut," Regina said. "It teaches them patience and also not to touch something they didn't work for. They usually start chewing in high school, so they plant the tree when they are 11 or 12, but nowadays I see them starting younger and younger."

As if the betel nut buzz wasn't enough, they started adding tobacco in with the lime for an extra nicotine kick. The Palauans and the Yapese had recently begun to also sprinkle vodka into the mixture.

"Yap and Palau always lead everyone into the bad habits," Hana said with a laugh.

The sickening red juice began to slide down my throat and I quickly reached for the Bud can, unable to talk for the next 15 minutes. Meanwhile, Regina and Hana not only continued chewing the betel nut, but also ate saltine crackers and drank root beer soda at the same time. I was impressed. When the room stopped spinning, I finally settled into a comfortable, mellow buzz. It was all quite interesting, but I had an inclination I wouldn't be getting into the betel nut vice; too messy.

With that experience successfully fulfilled, I waited a week before turning my attention back to the island's heady elixir. The familiar CLANG, CLANG, CLANG of rock on rock next door meant only one thing; the Mallarmes were readying the *sakau* again. I had a little time before I picked the kids up from school, so I walked over and watched the preparation step-by-step.

After dredging up the *sakau* plant, the roots were cleaned in a tub of water and then pounded with rocks on a flat basalt stone. The stone, about three feet in diameter (I had seen some as large as six feet in diameter), was raised slightly off the ground to increase the volume of sound. Shirtless men (boys and women, shirts on, would also take part), usually three at a time, pounded the *sakau* to produce a pulp. The loud melodic rock-on-rock rhythm, a ritual steeped in tradition, also served as a formal announcement that the drink would soon be ready, but I'm guessing the cell phones worked better as cars began arriving from the other side of Kolonia. After chopping down a small, willowy hibiscus tree with a machete and peeling its bark into long strips, the *sakau* pulp was then lined evenly into the strip of bark and water was added a handful at a time. The hibiscus helped increase the pulp's viscosity and, I was told, added just a hint of sweetness to it (the same way a sprinkle of sugar might add a hint of sweetness to a handful of dirt). Finally, the hibiscus strips were held up and twisted tightly to wring the pulp, rendering a thick brown fluid which was then squeezed, or rather plopped, directly into your coconut shell cup.

Soon there were a dozen people seated around the sakau stone. Being the only *men wai* there, I stood in the back and out of the way as I really didn't
want to participate, but it wasn't long before everyone was motioning for me to join them and Maxson patted an empty seat next to him near the center.

Oh who's kidding who? You and I both know the reason I was there and it wasn't to just observe the ceremony. And why shouldn't I give it another shot? If I was going to be a part of the Pohnpeian culture, I was going to have to get the *sakau* down, literally and figuratively.

As the *sakau* was twisted and squeezed then passed from person to person, I watched intently for the ceremonial procedures being observed. For example, I noticed the cup was usually passed by being held in the right hand and crossing the right forearm over the left forearm for support. The recipient also formed this arrangement with their arms. Acknowledgment that the cup was received was signaled when the recipient lifted their left forearm to touch the server's left forearm. Melyann sat next to me and explained some of the other rituals involved.

"When one drinks, one must close their eyes," she said. "This is to show respect, but also to not offend the spirits present."

"Ghosts?" I whispered. "Cool."

"Spirits," she corrected, then put her finger to her lips for me to be quiet. Although rapidly deteriorating in the developed world, respect is still of the utmost importance in Micronesia. On Pohnpei, you must show *wahu* (honor, respect, the customary ways) and speak *meing*. *Wahu* is given to high-titled persons but I saw it generally afforded to all elders on the island. The use of *meing*, a high or respected language, again used in days of old only for high-titled persons, was also afforded to everyone I came across. Both islanders and expats bowed and said "*Kasele-ehlie meing*," with the vowels elongated to show respect, whenever greeting someone.

An older gentleman sitting near us offered another reason why one must close their eyes while they drank *sakau*. "If you look into the *dahl* (cup) and see your reflection you will become blind," he said. "Sometimes you will see someone covering the top of the *dahl* to keep bad magic from going into it. This also can be done through words or herbs. It is not as common now, but it is still done."

Still clinging to the rituals of old. How silly that is, I thought as I made the sign of the cross and said three Hail Mary's. Suddenly the *sakau* was in front of me. "Ok, let's try this again," Melyann said, handing me the coconut shell. This time I did everything I was supposed to do. I crossed my forearms to receive it. I bowed my head and closed my eyes. I was respectful of the ghosts, er, spirits. I took a long pull of the slimy, brown sedative and … I didn't gag. This time it went down at least a little easier. Better yet, it stayed down and so I took yet another drink, then another and still another. First, my lips and tongue went numb and within 20 minutes the rest of my body followed. I was completely anesthetized and relaxed, but the interesting part was that I was still relatively clear headed with the ability to function, rationalize, and even hold a conversation. I could do anything, so long as I didn't move from my chair. That was difficult as my limbs refused to follow my still lucid brain. But why would I even want to move? A warm breeze lifted the leaves and the treetops swayed as they brushed against the stark blue sky. The clouds rolled past. My life rolled past. Nothing mattered.

Louis Lewin could have told me this would happen. In 1924, Lewin, a world-renowned pharmacologist and toxicologist, published *Phantastica,* a book on the use of drugs around the world. In it, he offers a wonderfully insightful description of the effects of *sakau*:

> When the mixture is not too strong, the subject attains a
> state of happy unconcern, well-being and contentment,

free of physical or psychological excitement ... The drinker never becomes angry, unpleasant, quarrelsome or noisy, as happens with alcohol ... The drinker remains master of his conscience and his reason. When consumption is excessive, however, the limbs become tired, the muscles seem no longer to respond to the orders and control of the mind, walking becomes slow and unsteady. The eyes see the objects present, but cannot or do not want to identify them accurately. The ears also perceive sounds without being able or wanting to realize what they hear. Little by little, objects become vaguer and vaguer ... [until] the drinker is overcome by somnolence.

There's something about being overcome by somnolence on a sunny weekday afternoon. It's depraved, it's decadent and something that's just not done by responsible people. Then again, responsible people don't do a lot of things, and therein lay the problem. They miss out. Not me, though. Responsibility has never been an obstacle for me. In fact, my wife thinks I'm the most irresponsible person she knows. The *sakau* had freed my mind and I relinquished the thought that by sitting there buzzed on a sunny weekday afternoon I was somehow cheating in this game of life. Cheating what? Whom? I couldn't answer that. I couldn't answer anything. Instead I simply sat in my white plastic chair amidst the green of the jungle and watched responsibility drift away with the leaves. Bette was off island and the kids were...MY GOD, THE KIDS! I was supposed to pick them up from school an hour earlier! Wait, that's right, I had previously asked Uta to pick them up from school and they were at the Finnens playing with their kids, Sophie and Maggie. Whew! What a buzz kill.

The hushed, quiet conversation continued in Pohnpeian all around me as I drifted in a dream world.

121

"I fucking hate the Dallas Cowboys," a cousin of the Mallarmes suddenly said while spitting on the ground.

What? Where the hell did that come from? I then noticed the TV, with its volume off, illuminating a N.Y. Giants/Dallas Cowboy football game through the picture window of the small structure beside us. Since we were 15 hours ahead of Eastern Standard Time in the U.S., ESPN 2 was airing Monday Night Football live at noon on Tuesday. Yet another indicator that we were in a galaxy far, far away and it was explained to me by someone in a more sober frame of mind that no, I couldn't win lots of money knowing the outcome of the game because being 15 hours ahead doesn't necessarily mean you live in the future. Others perked up at the comment as more than a few of the men in Pohnpei also followed American football.

"America's team?" the cousin scoffed. "Not anymore."

Talk about "a better understanding of Americans on the part of the peoples served" and a better understanding of other cultures, this guy was able to cover Peace Corps goals two and three with just one statement. I mean, my God, other than Dallas, is there any place in the world where, as a whole, they don't hate the Dallas Cowboys? Suddenly, it went from bright sunshine to a torrential downpour and, with great exertion, we lifted our feet away from the river that quickly formed beneath us. Mrs. Mallarme peered out from under the tarp, winced at the rain falling from the sky, then looked over at me and shrugged her shoulders. "Pohnpei," she said.

That night, I sat and smoked a cigar in our *nahs*. As I looked up at the thatch roof illuminated by candlelight and listened to the rhythm of the jungle emanating from the darkness just outside, a huge smile spread across my face, the same one I had begun wearing on a daily basis. We were no longer in the chaotic "here" back home, but officially somewhere over "there" – the happy place psychologists tell you to imagine, the island screensaver on your computer at work, the fabled "middle of nowhere" you read about. We were living the life we had always dreamed of. They say your past will always catch up with you? Not out here. Too far. All of my troubles and anxieties were still in Washington, D.C., unable to afford the airfare. This, THIS, is the way to have a mid-life crisis, I thought.

It was easily one of the best feelings I have ever felt. Seize the day? Hell, I promised to seize the next two and a half years. And, true to my word, there honestly wasn't a day that would go by without me stopping, taking in a deep breath and doing something really irresponsible.

Chapter 9

Men At Work

Everyone wants to save the earth; no one wants to help do the dishes.
~ PJ O'Rourke

Apparently there was a presidential election of some significance back in the United States. We didn't receive much news on the island, but Barack Obama's inauguration did make the Australian newscast, right after the lead story about the New Zealand All Blacks/South African Springboks rugby match.

Speaking of politics, an official straw poll posted on our refrigerator showed my household popularity had gone down several percentage points.

Devon's Family Popularity List
#1. Devon
#2. Mommy
#3. Daddy
#4. Tess

125

Throwing out the high and the low (Tess being Devon's perennial "low"), the poll showed I was the least favorite of the parental candidates. Apparently I needed to work on my messaging. Yes, I was treating my new duties as a "job," and yes, major strides were being made regarding Home Daddyship, but hey, Rome wasn't burned in a day.

I also still needed to work on my teaching skills.

It was late afternoon and we were doing our homework (I say "our" homework because I was drawn into every single sentence structure, every question about quotients, and every plea regarding the pulmonary system) when Devon looked up from her reading assignment and asked, "Dad, what's the difference between irony and coincidence?"

I had to think for a second because I never really even got what the difference was in the saying "comparing apples to oranges" since they're both fruit and they're both kind of round and...

"Dad, did you hear me?"

"Yes, of course, honey. Uh, let's see. Irony is when something happens that seems planned, but it isn't," I said rather proudly even though I wasn't entirely sure what I just said was right which was, in and of itself, ironic and made me laugh.

Devon was not laughing. "That's coincidence, dad," she deadpanned.

"No, coincidence is when something happens that wasn't supposed to happen."

"You just said that for irony," she said rolling her eyes.

"Ok, ok," I said, erasing the air in front of me with my hands to come up with a different answer. "Coincidence is when, um, uh ... say I'm in a restaurant."

"A restaurant here or a real restaurant back home?" Tess interjected. I gave her a quizzical "what?" look but she continued anyway.

"Because I hate the restaurants here," she explained, apropos of, apparently, nothing.

"Quiet Tess, I'm teaching here," I said, turning my attention back to Devon. "Ok, say I'm in a restaurant and I'm talking about you and then you show up. I would say 'hey, what a coincidence. I was just talking about you.'"

"So what's the definition?" Devon asked, obviously unimpressed with my answer.

"Coincidence is when something happens by chance." I snapped my fingers. Bingo, the answer.

"That sounds like the same answer for irony," she said.

"No, irony is when you, when you ... didn't you write down what I originally said irony was?"

She just looked at me because we both knew the answer was no.

"You want to know what irony is?" I asked. "I'll tell you what irony is. Irony is the fact that you have a dictionary sitting up in your room and yet you continue to sit here asking me what irony is. That's what irony is."

Despite the homework hardships on my end and the relentless travel on Bette's end, we still managed to have our romantic moments, sitting most evenings amongst the graying mold on the balcony overlooking the Nett River while sipping wine and eating cheese and crackers. With the humidity hovering at a constant 99 percent, however, the cheese went bad quickly and the crackers became limp in literally the time it took to open the package and pop one in your mouth, leaving us with what amounted to zesty cheese and communion wafers as appetizers.

There we'd sit and sigh as the jungle ridge across the river to the east transformed from light green to a vibrant gold reflecting the sunset, then dark green to black as the evening faded. Soon, a hazy silver glow would appear just above the ridge and within moments the moon would peer down on us from behind the treetops. Off in the distance, almost as if in a dream, we'd

127

hear "HEY, WHERE'S OUR DINNER?" A short time later the kids were eating – ahh, the magic of a poor man's pizza (tomato sauce and American cheese on toasted English muffins) – and we were back on the balcony to talk about our day. As a Home Daddy doing home work, I had little to say. Bette, on the other hand, was always full of exciting news and gossip from the Peace Corps. I'd nod my head appropriately and, tuning her out, quickly switch the radio dial in my mind to soft rock while she continued.

"So the CDO and CDA, as well as the acting DCHOPS, all agree that despite the PASA and the MOA, this is a PC initiative and USAID and PEPFAR be damned. I mean, you have the AF, IAP, EMA and half the Pacific region all working with NGOs on SBDs without so much as a SOW or a TA. I have a good mind to take a LWOP, and just rewrite the PATS myself."

I snapped my inner radio dial off. "LWOP? Did I just hear Leave Without Pay? The hell you say, girl?" Actually, I understood little to none of it but, like any loving spouse, I shrugged my shoulders, faked shocked expressions and interjected "sheesh, I can't believe it" and "boy, you're telling me" at just the right moments.

Truth be told, Bette was in the midst of a two-month long training of trainers (TOT for the acronym addicted) and orientation of some 30 new volunteers. She then would be traveling throughout the outer islands for the better part of the next two months. Add to this the fact that her office was short-staffed and it wasn't hard to see her job was running her ragged. I truly didn't envy her.

On the other hand, I was the envy of everyone back home, which I enjoyed with a certain degree of skepticism, as I felt they weren't getting the entire picture. This was confirmed in a less than lengthy letter from my two buds back in Jersey.

Hey Jeff,

Just what the hell do you do all day?

Lovingly,
Joe and Ken

Despite it being the 21st Century, friends and family, nay the entire world, still didn't see cooking and cleaning and taking care of the kids as a "real" job. With two of my (former) best friends, whose resume highlights included the formation of an unemployed "Bum's Union" which lasted well into their 30's, questioning my ambition it was clearly time to set the record straight in another of my Island Updates. I contemplated my rebuttal, but was suddenly interrupted by shrieks coming from downstairs. It was 7 a.m. The day had begun.

I descended to find Tess wildly swinging at Devon who, in turn, was grunting karate "hiiiyuhs" and keeping Tess at bay through swift, arcing kicks that swiped the air and, of course, landed nowhere. A squished brown sugar cinnamon pop tart lying on the floor was all the explanation I needed.

I quickly ended the ensuing blame game with "ENOUGH" and, pointing to the mess on the floor, added, "Pop tarts may as well be cookies and, I don't care what Kellogg says, we are NOT having cookies for breakfast." I instead poured two bowls of nutritious Lucky Charms cereal, noticeably less "magically delicious" as the kids had already eaten all of the marshmallow clovers, moons and stars, and soon they were giggling as if nothing ever happened.

This was cute until I realized the giggling was taking the place of actual cereal ingestion. "Less laughing and more eating." I separated them and remained patient ... for about 60 seconds ... before yelling "eat, eat, EAT." That's when Tess spilled her milk, which occurred with such regularity that Devon and I would do a countdown before it even happened. Of course this made Devon laugh and, while slapping the table, flip her bowl over and onto the floor. At that point I announced the kitchen was officially closed.

Still giggling, the kids, amazingly resilient and blissfully ignorant of the damage they were doing to their dad, bounced upstairs to get dressed and brush their teeth and hair. They were happy. I was shot. Create and destroy -- the universal constant.

After getting the kids breakfasted (both a verb and a noun because while it wasn't a "person or a place," it was, believe me, a "thing"), I made their lunches, dropped them off at school and Bette off at work, then stopped by the store to pick up groceries and, if the cargo ship came in, semi-rotten produce. Arriving back home, I did the dishes, cleaned the counter of bug wings, legs and heads, swept 4.7 pounds (median average based on weekday traffic only) of sand, coral, and banana leaves from the house, did 11.2 kilos of laundry (globally, I believe "kilos" is only officially used as a measurement for drugs and laundry), and brought 14 items, mostly toys, clothes and books, from downstairs back upstairs where they belonged. Once upstairs, I then brought 12 items back downstairs where they belonged. This upstairs/downstairs went on until I realized I was in some sort of irreversible cleanup continuum and managed to snap myself out of its gravitational pull.

In the afternoon, I picked Bette up for lunch so she could come home to watch a Grey's Anatomy rerun, dropped her back off, cleaned more bug wings, legs and heads, folded and put away the laundry, picked the kids up from school, helped them with their homework ("No, I don't know what an integer is. Let's look it up. Life science? What the hell is that?"), then got dinner ready, ever mindful not to use the dishes at the top of the stack in the cupboard as they were ever filled with, you guessed it, bug wings, legs and heads.

My transformation into a home daddy was taking shape. After dropping the kids off at school and Bette off at work I had been known on occasion to actually sit down and eat breakfast while reading the "latest" year-old Newsweek on the island. Apparently, the market was going gangbusters and my Lehman Brothers stock was through the roof, baby…easy street was close at hand.

The falsehoods in that last paragraph were "sit down and eat," and "read" (and, I would later find out, "Lehman Brothers" and "easy street"). On most nights I ate over the stove with an oversized serving spoon. That rule was only broken when I ate over the sink, wolfing down the cold remains of the kids 'plates before washing them. A quick last gulp of warm milk from the kids 'Sponge Bob cups ended my fine dining experience. The fact that I now can only eat while standing has made for some pretty uncomfortable situations in restaurants, I can tell you that.

As for reading, that went out the window as well. As much as I would have loved to have read that insightful Harper's article on the "Downfall of the Middle Class," I really only had time to quickly flip through the photos of People magazine and wonder why Eva Longora wore that dress to the Emmy's. Movies … forget about it, although I did see High School Musical 26 times.

Writing kept me relatively sane, however the book wasn't coming along as well I would have liked, and Bette was no longer buying the "I'm conceptualizing" tactic. She also accused me of lowering my standards when I suggested just making it a 10-page pop-up book. To make matters worse, Uta handed me a copy of *The Sex Lives of Cannibals* by J. Maarten Troost. "It's about a guy who left the rat race in Washington, D.C. to live on the nearby island of Kiribati," she said (in the vast Pacific Ocean, 5,000 miles away was considered 'nearby'). "His girlfriend worked for a nonprofit while he basically just putt around writing amusing anecdotes about his adventures."

"Yeah, so?" I asked. "What's that got to do with me? You think I just putt around all day? Completely different parallel, completely different concept."

131

"Yeah, sure, completely different," she said. "Plus, your anecdotes aren't amusing."

Crap. Who was this J. Maarten Troost anyway and why did he spell "Martin" wrong? More importantly, why was he plagiarizing my book, cleverly writing it years before I even thought of writing mine? I read it, hell everybody read it. It was a best seller. Worse, it was a thousand times better than what I was working on.

Depressed and feeling unappreciated on the home front, I went and got myself hired as a communications consultant with The Nature Conservancy, working on the Micronesia Challenge. Covering more than 1 million square miles of ocean, the Micronesia Challenge is one of the most ambitious environmental projects in the world and aims to preserve 30 percent of Micronesia's near-shore marine life and 20% of its terrestrial resources.

I didn't really seek it out; it more or less just fell into my lap from Bill Raynor, the Director of The Nature Conservancy's Pacific Division (and yet another former Peace Corps volunteer) who had become a good friend of mine on the island. Yes, I was working for a great cause and enjoyed doing the work, but it was work on top of the housework I was already working on. The fact that I utilized "work" five times in the previous sentence in a book about paradise is a clear indication that something was dreadfully wrong. What was I thinking?

I did have my outlets, though, and strumming my acoustic ovation guitar was one of them. It even allowed me fulfill in one of my lifelong fantasies. In a marketing move not seen since the Eagles recruited Joe Walsh, Van Halen enlisted Sammy Hagar, or the Captain joined Tennille, Bill Jaynes, guitarist for the island's famous rock band, actually the island's only rock band, "Wetter Than Seattle," asked me to join them.

Bill, a fourth generation Salvation Army officer, was a deluded lifelong humanitarian who served as a Salvation Army pastor in San

Francisco for several years before coming to Pohnpei and, in an attempt to make even less money, turning to journalism. He quickly became a key figure on the island writing and distributing the *Kaselehlie Press*, FSM's only newspaper. His true calling, however, was playing lead guitar and becoming the driving force behind Wetter Than Seattle. Steve Finnen, who helped Bill form the band about a decade earlier, played bass. What made it really feel like a band, however, was that they had Bill's son, a 21-year-old drummer named Nigel. You can't really call yourself a rock band unless you have someone named Nigel on board. Helen, a Canadian and one of the lawyers assisting the FSM government on the island, rounded out the band by singing the female leads and any of the high octave rock tunes, which basically meant she sang ALL of the songs.

I checked out the playlist. "Ring of Fire … Johnny Cash. That should be fun."

"Except," Steve interrupted, "we do the version by Social Distortion."

"Turn The Page," I continued. "I love Bob Seger."

"Except," Steve interrupted, "we do the version by Metallica."

"Brand New Cadillac…," I paused and looked over at Steve.

"The Clash version," he said.

"Cool," I replied, nodding my head, but I didn't mean "cool" at all. Oh good God, I thought. It was an aging heavy metal band and I was doomed to play Judas Priest and Def Leopard tunes for the rest of my stay on the island (Steve even wrote a local hit song called 'Punk is Wasted on the Young'). Luckily the band also covered the Stones, Zeppelin and several other classic rock bands and I, forever musically stuck in the 1960's and '70's, couldn't have been happier.

We played on occasional Saturday nights at the Rusty Anchor and Wayne paid us in beer. Steve and Nigel kept a steady beat, Bill (who majored in classical guitar back in college) was an excellent guitarist, and when Helen sang everyone got up and danced. Me? I was in heaven just strumming rhythm guitar and singing backup vocals.

{In an ironic musical twist, Devon flipped on MTV one day, then pointed to the screen and shouted, "Hey, it's Mitch." Sure enough, there was our surfer friend Mitch, long blonde hair poking out from under a red baseball cap, stopping his pickup truck to let Jason Mraz hop in on his "I'm Yours" video. Laid back Mitch then pretty much just hung out with an even more laid back Mr. Mraz throughout the entire laid back video. Making it to MTV without even playing an instrument, such was the life of Mitch.}

While the band fulfilled my musical itch, I needed a recreational outdoor outlet as well, something that could whisk me away at a moment's notice; something that would be easy to maintain and trouble free, requiring little to no work. I needed a boat.

Chapter 10

Das Boot Das Stinks

Never give in! Never give in! Never, never, never, never.
~ Winston Churchill

"Jeeeeffffffff," a multitude of voices called out.

I stopped sweeping our small, cramped kitchen and glanced out of our rear picture windows to see Allois and several young men and women surfers gliding across the Nett River.

"Jeeeeffffffff," they again called out from the boat while smiling and waving up at me. I smiled and waved back, trying to figure out if that was Allois being friendly or just irritating me on his way out to the wide-open sea on a gorgeous day while I swept a small, cramped kitchen. Knowing Allois the answer was, of course, both.

I continued sweeping but the smile remained on my face. Despite the inevitable mishaps, lice capades, and daily kennel show traipsing through our living room, we were leading the idyllic island life, spending our free time camping and snorkeling on the atolls, hiking the interior of Pohnpei, and playing board games or just talking during the evenings, something we rarely found the time to do back home. Still, the sight of all that beautiful blue water without any beaches and no real access to it (except through the kindness of friends with boats) was driving us crazy. That had to be remedied.

The idea that we "needed" a boat was planted by Damian when we first arrived. "Don't wait until just before you're leaving the island to get a boat like I just did," he said, pointing out that he and David, the Peace Corps country director, had just purchased a local skiff together despite the fact that he only had a few months left until his contract with the Peace Corps ran out. "I can't tell you how much we use it and how much enjoyment we get out of it."

Boating tip #1: *Be wary of boat owners spinning the virtues of boat ownership.*

A skiff is a small, allegedly seagoing, open boat with a sharp bow and a square stem. I eventually found my own 19-foot beauty, festooned in an eyesore patchwork of paint including, but not limited to, pale yellow, white, green, burnt orange and red. It was a "self-bailer," meaning it had a small compartment underneath that served to flush out all excess water which, I was told, meant the boat was unsinkable. I looked over at Devon. "Honey, do you know what foreshadowing means?"

Although it wasn't part of the negotiations discussed while I was buying it, as I understood it, the purpose of the boat was to float on top of the water. Now I'm not an engineer, and I'm not up on the whole water displacement thing, but for the life of me I couldn't understand why, less than 24 hours after I forked over $4,000 in cash, the boat was lying partially submerged in the murky Nett River alongside the Mallarme's dock they were kind enough to let me use.

Apparently, the port side of the boat (I will be using the nautical term "left side" in all future references) slipped under the dock during low

136

tide. When high tide came rolling in, the rising river pinned the left side of the boat against the bottom of the dock and, ever so slowly, began filling it with water.

Boating tip #2: *Know something about the tides.*

The kids and I jumped in and started bailing, but the newly added weight pulled the left side of the boat down and out from under the dock. Now free floating next to the dock in the disease-ridden river, the boat rocked for a moment before radically listing starboard ("right side" in all future references). Knowing the impending catastrophe about to take place, I gave the order to "abandon ship" and the kids scrambled back onto the dock, screaming as if it were an ocean liner going down – in four feet of water. I frantically began heaving water over the side using the cutout plastic Clorox container/bailer, to no avail. The boat shuddered and I watched the engine go under first, followed by the middle of the boat. As the water quickly rose to the bow and, ultimately, me standing on the very tip, somewhere off in the distance I could've sworn I heard a band playing "Nearer My God to Thee." The boat sank before we even had our maiden voyage. Self-bailer my ass.

I should have known better when I discussed buying the boat from Costan Yoma, a Pohnpeian who served for 10 years on the local police force. He smiled too much; my first clue that he couldn't be trusted. My second clue came in the form of an old Pohnpeian saying, "*Sohte me kin pangada pahn kasahn were*" (No man reveals all of the contents of his canoe.) In my case, Costan took that to mean not revealing that the boat didn't have an engine. I was later told that to remedy the situation, he simply went and "borrowed" one from his cousin, Danny O'Daniel, who was out working on a fishing vessel and not due back for several months. This meant Danny's five-stroke Honda 50 engine was fair game.

If we were anywhere else I would have immediately been suspicious that Danny O'Daniel was a made-up name or an alias of some sort. However quite a few residents tended to go with the same first and last names. The vice president of the FSM, for example, was Alik Alik, and Jack J. Jack served as the acting Postmaster General.

Names were also often related to events or everyday occurrences seen on or near the day of the birth including celestial observations (Blinking Star), children's books (Rumpel Ifamilik), and even from movies. I'll never forget the day Tess came home from school furious that Alpacino kept shooting spitballs at her in class. If the parents had trouble deciding between names, sometimes the best thing to do was just include all of them as in Rosemaryanne Kaukalougata Kamla Tagi Feitatuki Naivalurua who, wisely, just went by the name Maryanne Tagi. Meanwhile, I could only imagine the conflicts Abel Cain no doubt endured, respected the responsibilities heaped upon King Malsol Sam, and surmised that Floatup Wallaby would have a better chance of surviving at sea than his brother Mayday.

Family lineage would also play a key role in Costan's acquisition of the engine. Because clanship is inherited through the female line and Costan was a direct descendant, he outranked Danny O'Daniel, his cousin from an extended family, and thus had every right to take the engine. Apparently I was getting a look at the island's 'what's mine is yours and what's yours is mine' way of life. All well and good in the Pohnpeian culture, but while Danny boy might not have an issue with Costan, he certainly might with me, a foreign *men wai*.

Unlikely as it was, if any trouble did erupt over the engine, I would at least have Peter Shirkey as an intermediary, which, I would later find out, meant absolutely nothing. After reading James Michener's *Tales of the South Pac*ific, Peter drifted over from New Zealand some 15 years earlier to work as the chief engineer at a fish processing plant. When the plant went belly up he, like so many others before him, had already fallen in love with a beautiful young Pohnpeian and simply never left. By way of his relationship with the local woman, Costan was, in effect, his brother-in-law.

138

"Wouldn't trust 'im as far as I could throw 'im," Peter told me in his thick Kiwi accent. "But basically he's got a good heart and he's got a good boat. Can't vouch for the engine, though."

I took Devon with me to meet Costan for a test run at a dock just outside of town. The boat looked sturdy and, as Peter suggested, quite seaworthy but the engine was suspect with exposed wires duct taped together and its original steering rudder replaced with a piece of wood bolted directly into the outer casing. It started right up, though, and soon we were gliding over the channel toward Langer Island only 15 minutes away. The feeling was absolutely exhilarating as the wind whipped against our faces but I had to suppress my desire to grin from ear to ear as serious negotiating had to be done.

"You should buy it, dad," Devon yelled above the wind and the roar of the engine.

Costan smiled.

"The boat's ok," I said, "but I'm not too sure about the engine."

"Oh, the engine's good," Costan assured me. "It's about six years old but we still use it to go fishing just about every day."

"What about the hull?" I asked, putting my hand over Devon's mouth. "I'd like to check it for leaks."

"I'd buy it right now if I were you, dad," Devon said through my fingers.

"How many owners has it had?" I continued.

Devon started a chant while clapping her hands, "Buy…it, buy…it, buy…it."

"I don't know," I said. "$5,000 is way too much. I'll give you $3,000."

"$3,000?" Devon yelled. "In the car you said you'd buy it for $4,000."

Boating Tip #3: *Never take your 10-year-old daughter with you to negotiate.*

139

In an attempt to ease my mind, Costan gave me a slip of paper with his phone number on it. "Don't worry," he said shaking my hand. "You're going to have a lot of fun in this boat. Call me and we'll go out fishing in it sometime." He actually did seem like a good guy, I thought in the car on the way home. Then again, I never did check to see if that was indeed his phone number.

By the next day my concerns about the engine, especially regarding Danny O'Daniel and its ownership, had become a moot point. With it lying on the bottom of the Nett River, literally dead in the water, it was clearly mine. The kids wanted to name the boat *Island Girl* or *Island Princess*, but I finally named it the *Queen Elizabeth* for Bette.

"That's quite a compliment," she said, standing on the dock and peering down at the submerged vessel listing on the bottom of the muddy river. Actually, the name was irrelevant as henceforth Bette and I just referred to it as "that Goddamn Boat."

The road to this whole twisted affair led back to Peter Shirkey as he was one of the go-to people for boat repair or, in my case, salvaging. He had an old salty sailor quality about him and I don't think I ever saw him without a cigarette dangling out from under his bushy brownish grey mustache which drooped down the sides of his mouth and ran straight into the short, unkempt brownish grey beard that crept down his neck. About once a month he'd spring for a disposable razor and the beard would be gone. His usual ensemble was torn jeans and an old faded dress shirt with the sleeves rolled up, revealing hands and forearms perpetually covered in grease and dirt. While his signature was being able to fix anything with a hammer and duct tape, there were those who complained that was literally all he used. I, however, would remain forever in his debt.

I found him in his boat repair shop, an abandoned rusted tin warehouse overlooking the main road into town. The sign on the tin wall outside, painted in light blue and set against a fluorescent yellow background, read "Mangrove Marine" which arched above a crab holding a wrench in its one claw and a blow torch in the other.

"I fockin' hate that goddamn sign," Peter would tell me over and over again. "A crab with a blow torch? It makes my business look like a fockin' cartoon."

Daylight poured into the otherwise dark and cavernous structure from the large entryway both wide and tall enough to haul small boats inside for repair. The thin roll-down steel door remained jammed up into the top of the entryway and in its place Peter installed a rusted swinging steel link gate, which did little to keep the thieves out. Not that there was anything to steal. Other than an old boat on its side, a workbench with a few tools on it, some wooden planks and a few engine parts strewn about, the place was empty. Peter seemed overwhelmed by the large, hollow warehouse, as he sat on an overturned oil drum reading another James Michener novel. "Gotta exercise the mind," he said. "If you don't you might as well curl your toes up and buy a box." A bottle of 151 rum sat on the floor next to him. His boat repair business had him barely making ends meet, if at all, and I guessed by the book he was reading, *Hawaii*, that perhaps he was seeking to escape yet again to another tropical island paradise.

Next to him, in a stained and torn rolling office chair, sat an unshaven, emaciated man in his late 60's wearing thick round glasses and a filthy mechanic's jumpsuit unzipped all the way down to his crotch. As far as I could tell, there were no clothes to speak of underneath. He took a drag from his cigarette, already burning dangerously close to his fingers, and kicked at the freshly crushed beer cans strewn about his feet. It was only 11 a.m., but he was already well on his way to Pleasantville.

"This here is Rat," Peter said by way of introduction.

"Really?" I asked. "Rat?"

"What the fuck's it to you?" he growled while squinting up at me.

"Don't pay him any mind, he's harmless," Peter said. He then patted my shoulder and, turning to Rat, said "friend," as if addressing the Frankenstein monster. Rat again growled and slowly rocked in his chair.

"Jeff's writing a book," Peter said in an attempt to lighten the mood.

"Oh yeah," Rat slurred, "what's it about?"

"Well, it's about the characters on the island and ..."

"Well you can start by telling everyone I came here to die," he interrupted, pointing his burning fingers, still clutching the glowing cigarette ash, at me. "I haven't had anything to eat in a month. Nothing but cigarettes and beer, cigarettes and beer."

"Why?" I asked.

"Why not?" he shot back.

"Here's something you'll be interested in," Peter interjected. "Jeff's wife is with the Peace Corp."

At this, Rat's eyes lit up and I thought I could actually detect a faint smile. "I have a daughter who was in the Peace Corps," he said.

"Really? Where?"

Suddenly the spark left his eyes and they quickly darkened again. "I don't know," he snarled waving his hand dismissively in the air, "bumfuck Africa somewhere. How the hell should I know?"

I didn't want to put him on the spot and have him try to remember her name, so I just left it at that.

"Hey," I said turning to Peter, suddenly remembering why I came, "you gotta help me. My boat sunk."

He had already heard, he said. I knew nothing stayed quiet for long on the island, but Peter knowing my boat sank less than an hour after it actually went under was incredibly fast, and just a little unsettling. After laughing at my story of the boat, the tide and the dock, Peter sat back down on the oil drum with his book. Despite my jumping up and down and pointing at the river, he remained unfazed.

"Relax," he said. "The biggest mistake everyone makes is to haul the engine out of the water before they're really ready to work on it. Once it hits the air, the salt water in it will oxidize pretty damn fast and then you're screwed. We'll have to wait until it's low tide, which won't be until later this afternoon, then we'll haul it to the shore. In the meantime, you'll need to get a new battery, an oil filter, engine oil and a can of WD-40."

Later that afternoon I swam out, dragged the boat in close to the shore, and began bailing. A local islander who happened to be passing by in his boat stopped, jumped into the water, and began bailing with me. Slowly, the boat rose. After about 30 minutes of continuous bailing, we once again had it on top of the water. I looked up in time to see the islander back in his boat and waving as he disappeared up river.

"Who was that?" I later asked Peter when he arrived.

"He's Pohnpeian," he said. "That's just what they do." Then he jumped into the boat and with the precision of a surgeon, started operating on the engine. As he opened the casing, he warned me it would be extremely unlikely we'd get the engine running again.

"Yep," he said pointing to an opening with his screwdriver. "Ya got water coming out of the starter blowhole. Not good."

Damian appeared and we paced back and forth on the shore like family members in the waiting room of a hospital. The updates continued to be negative.

"The cam shaft doesn't have beads, so the water could've buggered that up as well," Peter said shaking his head.

He opened a valve and let water out with the gas. For the first time he smiled and let us know he was surprised to find less water in the engine than there should have been. Finally, an encouraging sign. He was also pleased to find the spark plugs were still miraculously, relatively dry. Then, with gas and oil layered on everything, especially his hands, he lit up another cigarette.

After connecting a hose and flushing the engine with fresh water, then spraying an entire can of WD-40 throughout the engine, we hooked up the new battery; Peter's cigarette still dangling just inches from the gas tank. Fingers crossed, we watched as he pushed the starter. Nothing. He pushed it a second time and again, nothing. Again and again he pushed, then tinkered with the wires. Suddenly, it sputtered. Peter looked at me hopefully. He pressed the starter and with a loud "VROOM" the engine roared to life.

"Well, I'll be damned. Bob's your uncle," Peter said, using an oft-used Aussie phrase meaning everything's going to be just fine. "The patient lives!"

The *Queen Elizabeth*, now rechristened the QE II, was back in business. Later that evening, Peter helped me drive plastic PCV pilings down into the mucky river bottom to prevent the boat from going under the dock again.

"That was one helluva job," I said. "How much do I owe you?"

"Ah," he said waving his hand. "Just give me $20 and a beer."

The next day I ran the engine as often as possible so the heat would evaporate any excess water still inside. The boat, however, remained at the dock since there was no way I was taking it out alone. That evening, as Bette was working late and the kids were eating with Sarah and Anya over at the Reside's house, I had Damian and Mary climb aboard with me to test the status of the engine.

We motored past the mouth of the river and into the lagoon, unusually calm after a day of wind and whitecaps. The sun was setting and I began to zigzag back and forth with the boat, carving lazy curves in the water reflecting the sky's gorgeous orange glow. All was right in the world again and at that moment, on that sea, I stood up and let out a victorious roar as the wind blew my hair back. The boat continued to purr as it skimmed across the smooth surface when, BAM, we all lurched forward and I watched in horror as the bottom of the engine kicked out of the water.

"REEF," Damian yelled.

The boat glided for a bit, then silently came to rest still only inches above the coral. "Thanks, Damian," I said quietly, still flat on my back. "I'll make note of it."

The good people at Honda knew enough to install a safety latch to free the bottom shaft upon impact so the collision doesn't rip the entire engine off the boat. I clicked the lever up to the top notch so that the engine remained out of the water. Little did I know, but utilizing this safety latch was very much in my future as the reef and I would become close, very close, personal friends. Historically, Pohnpei's lagoon has been a hazardous obstacle course for all vessels, from the tri-masted wooden sailing ships of yore to the 19-foot, pale yellow, white, red, green, and burnt orange local boats with shitty patched together engines of today. With coral heads and reefs sprinkled throughout, the depth of the lagoon could go from 300 feet to sea level in about, oh I'd say, one-millionth of a second. An axiom used around the island was "there are only two kinds of boats; those who hit a reef and those who are about to." For the rest of my stay the Queen Elizabeth would remain both the former and the latter of that phrase.

We diligently worked on the engine, which meant randomly yanking on wires and then doing roundhouse kicks to the main compartment. Oddly enough, that didn't work. The gorgeous orange glow reflecting in the water faded to purple and then to black. In the ensuing darkness, we rowed for about an hour with two planks of wood left at the bottom of the boat before reaching the dock at the Japanese Embassy. Claiming refugee status, we deboated (my guess is that if you can "deplane" you can "deboat") and called Bette to come pick us up.

Peter rewired the engine, patched up a leak or two, and soon we had the boat, re-rechristened the QE III, back in the water. Damian and I had only just started from the boat ramp of the Japanese Embassy down the channel next to the causeway when the skies opened up with rain. We peered through the wall of water that enveloped us and were just about to go through the small tunnel under the causeway bridge when the engine died. We started it. We gave it gas. It died. We started it. We gave it gas. It died.

Suddenly, from the causeway, a local man got out of his car and began shouting to us. At first we couldn't hear him over the loud roar of the rain, but as I paddled the boat closer he cupped his hands around his mouth and shouted "there's no water running through your engine. The line must be clogged. Grab a reed or something and clean it out or you'll be in big trouble." I was significantly impressed. How could someone motoring by in a driving rainstorm notice a small detail like that in a boat 100 yards away? The Pohnpeians truly were one with their boats.

We cleaned the line and with another click the engine sprung to life. It wasn't long, however, before the engine began to sputter and clank. Sputtering was ok…not good, but ok in that engines will sometimes sputter to let you know something 'minor' needs to be adjusted. The clank, however, was a dead giveaway that something was horribly amiss. I noted to Damian that we were about seven minutes away from my dock and asked if we could make it. Drawing on the sea-faring experience and wisdom he had gained over the vast three months he was actually a boat owner, he nodded confidently and said, "Easily."

Boating tip #4: *Don't trust Damian.*

If you were to think this was the time to crank it full throttle and thus, get home quicker you'd be wrong. A look of horror came over Damian's face as he stared behind me and I quickly deduced it to mean that either a) he suddenly realized the U.S. would never be able to reduce its debt to GDP ratio, or b) the engine was on fire. I turned to see smoke billowing upward, then heard a loud KACHUNK before the engine went dead. For those of you not familiar with boating mechanics, a KACHUNK is worse than a clank and much, much worse than a sputter, which, again, let's you know something minor needs to be adjusted.

In what by then had become standard procedure for the boat, Damian and I paddled to the dock at the Japanese Embassy. Denied refugee status a second time (I don't know Japanese but the verbiage coming our way from the shore didn't sound diplomatic), we then paddled in the driving rain over to a private boat ramp. We got out and made our way through the rivers of muddy water raging down the street toward my house about a mile away. Once there, Damian pulled out a bottle of rum, salve to stem the pain of losing a loved one (or unloved one, as the case was). A short while later, Peter arrived after towing the boat back to the Mallarme's dock. We didn't need a diagnosis. Our only question was whether it would be an open or a closed casket.

"Well, what can I say?" he asked, wiping his hands. "The engine melted."

It didn't simply stall or just break down, it melted. The motor cap was a thick, gooey sauce covering the gaskets and spark plugs, and the insulation a black liquid running over the *Honda* stenciling.

"Closed casket," Damian said turning to me.

I let loose a tirade meant to reach both heaven and hell at roughly the same time. Then we raised our rum in a toast to the boat and began planning for the new engine I'd buy and, more importantly, how I'd convey this wonderful news to Bette.

She finally pulled up and, utilizing that sixth sense, a sense not needed considering the almost empty bottle of rum and the grins on our faces, knew something was wrong.

"So, did you get the boat back in the water?"

I assured her we did.

"The engine started?"

I assured her it did.

"And it's now safely at our dock?"

I assured her it was. No, wait a minute, define "safely." I then regaled her with the whole story.

"How the hell does an engine melt?" she asked.

I suggested that would be a great question to type into Ask.com. Whatever answer they came up with, however, would never beat ours. Then, befitting the island way of life, Bette pulled up a chair and poured herself a glass of rum. "Fuck it," she said raising her glass.

The next day I marched right down to Yoshie's grocery store with Simon, our boat-owning friend from England. As was typical on the island, Yoshie's was a store you could go in and say, "I'll have a jar of peanut butter, a loaf of bread and, oh yeah, I'd like that Yamaha 40 Enduro engine behind the pickles." The total cost was $3,022.40, but I think they overcharged me for the peanut butter. Actually, I didn't even make the purchase; Simon did, as my credit card was embarrassingly rejected for reasons unbeknownst to me.

The reason for the credit card rejection had become frustratingly clear to us when we discovered the "middle of nowhere" wasn't a recognized geographic location and, according to most American businesses, neither was Micronesia. "We ship anywhere in the world" was often met with stunned silence whenever I mentioned where we were.

"Let's see, Madagascar, Mozambique," they'd say. "Nope, no Micronesia. We can ship it to Atlantis. Are you near there?"

Remember when I said my troubles back home could never find me? Well, neither could certain bills. Needless to say, our credit rating, once impeccable, was shot.

The new engine, however, actually proved to be a steal when the kids used the huge piece of Styrofoam that came with it as their own floatation device, thus giving us two boats, one up on blocks and the other a $3,000 Styrofoam pirate ship. That evening we took the Styrofoam pirate ship over to Nett Point where the kids paddled and played for hours. If I had known all of this from the beginning, I would have nixed the original boat, bought a new engine, thrown the new engine away, and kept the Styrofoam packaging.

The QE IV was launched with little fanfare. For its fourth maiden voyage (let's not get too particular here as it was still a maiden voyage for the family) we followed the Resides and Mary and Damian in their boat and made our way out to "Picnic Island," a 15 x 30-yard stretch of sand with scrub bushes surrounded by dazzlingly clear water. The ride, about an hour each way, was a bit nerve wracking as the boat slammed against the whitecaps, but the kids compared it to a giant log flume ride and laughed the whole time. I didn't. This seafaring business was going to take some getting used to.

Soon, however, we were taking the boat out on almost a daily basis and I must admit I cut a dashing figure as a sea captain, although the water wings were cumbersome. Our first solo excursions were to Langer Island where we had our own reef enclosed swimming hole. We'd all dive into the warm, clear water and explore the yellow, gold and green coral glowing just below us. Well, almost all of us. Once again, Devon remained on the boat looking ridiculous standing there with her mask over her eyes, snorkel in her mouth and fins on her feet.

"Sharks, sting rays, manta rays, jellyfish," she said, "barracudas, man of wars, crown of thorns, fire coral..."

Simon showed me how to clamp a long PVC pipe to the throttle so I could stand and steer the boat at the same time (which also afforded me a better view of the reefs ahead). I finally began to relax and really enjoy the ride. After several weeks I had committed a good portion of the maze of reefs on the way out past Langer Island and Palikir Pass to memory. As I flew across the water while standing in the back of the boat, PVC throttle in hand, visions of my comic book hero, the Silver Surfer, filled my head. I soared over the emerald green universe and out across the deep blue galaxy of water that lay beyond the reef with nothing but the horizon in front of me.

On several occasions, a pod of dolphins would follow within inches of the boat and spring from the water in front of us as if leading us out to sea. They loved the sound of the engine and I often obliged by carving turns around them, then gunning it through the center of the pod. Devon and Tess would shout and point excitedly whenever the Spinner dolphins jumped and twirled several feet in the air before gracefully splashing back down.

As I ventured further and further out past our known water world, however, every now and then a flash of florescent green would appear out of nowhere and I'd watch in horror as the engine kicked up out of the water. Each time though, it would start right up again and the rudder, though a bit nicked, still functioned perfectly as it propelled us back home. The new engine was a success.

150

After a few wonderful family outings and a few close encounters of the third kind – actual contact with the reef – I was lying in the hammock waiting for Maxson to let me know when the *sakau* would be ready when his nephew Ben came running over. The boat was sinking, this time from several small leaks created after hitting a reef or two, or seven. Luckily it was low tide and the water hadn't reached the engine.

Again I ran to Peter Shirkey who was standing in the late afternoon sun working on a boat just outside the Mangrove Marine garage. He pulled a coil of rope out of the back of the boat.

"Look at that," he said holding the rope close to my eyes so I could get a better look. "Ya got tar, or basically bitumen impregnated, multi-strand, nylon rope, there. The Japs invented it. Some of the best rope you can get. At $10-a-foot it better be."

I looked up at the sun as the sweat poured from my forehead. Small streams of salt water had formed and were running down my back and legs. Rat sat amongst the shadows inside the warehouse. The extra beer cans and bottle of bourbon told me that Peter was joining him on the carnival cruise line. Still, he remained, as always, a veritable encyclopedia of nautical knowledge. I tugged at my soaked shirt, but continued to politely nod as if I understood or even cared about what he was saying.

"Then, about 15 to 20 years ago the Americans, Lindgren-Pittman I believe it was, came up with a single, not braided mind you, monofilament line. The same stuff you spool off your fishing pole. It can hold 60 miles of four-meter filament." He gazed at the horizon stretched, I assumed, like a monofilament line across the sky and smiled as if admiring a Monet painting. "That line's got a breaking strain of about 1,800 pounds. Very strong. Great stuff. You have one of those snap and it's like cracking a bullwhip. I saw one guy get it while we were out at sea. Went right through all of his cold weather gear, across the back of his shoulder, then around his face. Separated his shoulder, broke his nose and teeth and cracked his lips. Ah, such is life on a boat. Another time I was out in the North Pacific…"

"Ah, Peter," I interrupted, now looking like I had gone for a swim with my shorts and shirt on. "Can we finish this story another time?"

"Of course, of course mate," he said slapping my back. "I'm boring the 'el outta ya anyway." Then he peered over his glasses at me. "Please don't tell me your boat sank again."

Chapter 11

Food Fight

To eat is a necessity, but to eat intelligently is an art.
~ La Rochefoucauld

The oppressively dense jungle surrounded me and drew tighter with each step I took. My senses heightened, and I became increasingly aware of an ethereal as well as physical presence, for this was indeed a sentient being, a single entity with vines as veins and towering trees for lungs. Its moist breath hung in the air. When it spoke, it did so in whispers, with subtle creaks and moans, and at times, with a good wind behind it, more pronounced roars and howls. It was ever cognizant; fully conscious during the day but especially awake at night and I had no doubt it was aware of my presence as well. Snap, a twig broke. Slap, a mosquito danced away. Splash, the water parted, but only for a moment. Try as I might, I couldn't help but feel an intruder; a clumsy, spastic interloper barging through its serenity. I stopped and listened, but I was not, and never would be, one with the jungle. Its beauty was deceiving, as it threateningly towered over and around me. Weeds and vines erupted from the ground and seemed to grow before my very eyes, entangling and ensnaring everything in their path. This jungle, this green beast, this living, pulsing biomass as old as the earth itself, drew me into its abyss, into its everlasting…

"Jeff! Vat de hell are you doing just standing there looking up at de trees?" It was Konrad, a German without, apparently, much of an imagination. "Ve don't haf time for fooling around. Let's go."

My Joseph Conrad *Heart of Darkness* moment would have to wait. I trudged over the roots and up a steep bank until I was back on the trail.

Konrad, 62, was a biosecurity specialist in charge of plant protection and the prevention of invasive species in Micronesia, and a fixture in the fishing/poker playing/ Australian compound/Rusty Anchor/expat community. For him, this wasn't a leisurely hike; this was a matter of life and death. Tall, with a solid build, piercing eyes and a grey goatee that disagreed with his short, fading blonde hair, he had a commanding presence and often spoke in that curt, matter-of-fact German style that made everything he said sound like a direct order. Just the day before, he had stopped by our house to enquire if I would accompany him on a trek up *Mt. Nahna Laud* to gauge the rainfall for the month.

"You vill come with me tomorrow up the mountain," was how he asked.

At 798 meters (2,617 feet), *Nahna Laud* (big mountain) was the high point of a rugged system of ridges separated by deep valleys and accessible only by little-known foot trails. Because of this, *mehn wai* had to hire local guides to direct them up the steep terrain and could count on spending the night before venturing back down. Konrad, of course, didn't need anyone to guide him up and, I was informed, we certainly weren't spending the night.

"They go so slow and make such a big deal out of it," he said, speaking of the other *mehn wai*. "We go up and down … one day!" He signaled 'one' with his forefinger and then thrust it in front of my face for emphasis.

After first stopping at the Conservation Society of Pohnpei, however, we were joined by BJ, the official recorder of rainfall. "I just had to get out of the office," he said.

A Pohnpeian, BJ had been up and down the mountain so many times the trail might as well have been an escalator to him. His record was just under four hours base to peak and back. For Konrad and I, the steep climb was more like an ascent up Mt. Everest and, after we began, I wished I'd brought along oxygen tanks. "How about we rest here and call it Base Camp 2," I said when we reached the 200-foot mark. It would be four hours before we reached the summit. The trip down, however, took three hours and I was damn proud that we made it there and back again in only the time it took to conduct a regular business day.

Of course, following BJ proved to be a bit of a problem. "Follow" isn't exactly the right word as you have to be within a certain proximity for it to be considered 'following.' We'd climb rocks, cross a stream, and hack through hanging vines with our machetes before coming upon him resting under a palm tree – probably had been there an hour already before we arrived. For the most part, though, he proved to be a patient and insightful guide, explaining the flora of the jungle and showing us some of the 'hidden' *sakau* crops.

We continued the climb, making our way through the moist air. Micronesia is home to the world's lowest elevation cloud forests and *Nahna Laud*, with an average rainfall in excess of 400 inches, is said to be one of the wettest spots on earth. Nature had been allowed to run its course on the mountain undisturbed for generations, creating a damp, misty world filled with moss-covered vegetation and spongy humus, lichens and liverworts, as well as ferns so tall and wide I expected one of those raptors from Jurassic Park to spring out at any moment.

155

Jungles, like the sea, are spiritual realms. Pohnpeians believe you can never truly own the land, only attempt to control it and even then, only the land you cultivate. Once you leave it, the spirits take over. That would explain the uneasy feeling I had as we neared the summit. As *Nahna Laud* was largely uninhabited by humans, the *sokoles* – black dwarf spirits – roamed the higher levels of the mountain. If you saw one, the legend went, you would turn black, shrivel up and die a painful death after several days. However, after learning that sakau was grown up there in massive quantities, something told me the myth had more to do with keeping people away from the crop than genuine Pohnpeian legend.

The fresh smell of the cooling air, tinged with the succulent scent of frangipani, enveloped us as we marched onward and upward. Along the way, Konrad pointed out the various plant species and "herbaceous" vegetation. Any time we got hungry or thirsty, the mountain provided. BJ cut open the top portion of a native palm and offered us a palm heart that was as soft and delicious as an artichoke. We then filled our bottles in a cold, clear stream and drank the mountain water.

The heavy vines and vegetation finally gave way to gnarled, stunted trees, which then yielded to smooth rock and finally, the summit. Gazing out over the island, I saw a vast swath of ocean stretched out in every direction with nothing, not so much as even a canoe, to dot the empty horizon. The steep ridges directly below were a watershed for life on the island and the origin of the myriad streams and rivers that peacefully glided through the untouched valley and into the coral laden sea. If the ocean was Pohnpei's fish farm, the interior was its breadbasket; the food source designed to supply the nourishment of greens, starches, fruits and vegetables to everyone on the island. At least it was supposed to be.

Breadfruit, yams, taro, coconuts, tapioca, bananas and mangoes were the most popular local foods on Pohnpei. Peanut butter and jelly sandwiches were not. The local foods on the island were easily grown and maintained and did not require extensive land clearing, machine cultivation, or commercial fertilizers. Peanut butter and jelly sandwiches were not easily grown and maintained on the island and my guess is they actually do require extensive land clearing, machine cultivation, and commercial fertilizers. All of this mattered not to an eight-year-old girl with an undefined palette.

Every day I would make a peanut butter and jelly sandwich for Tess's school lunch. Every ... single ... day. It was all she'd eat and, to her credit, most times she was completely happy with it; other times however, I'd open the Tupperware after picking her up from school and find only a bite taken. Sometimes, as a treat, I'd give the kids money to buy lunch at the school. Devon would buy chicken and rice. Tess would buy – you guessed it – peanut butter and jelly.

"Why didn't you get the pizza buns?" I asked. "You like pizza buns."

"They had yellow cheese," she said making a face. "I never eat it when it has yellow cheese."

It was just another of life's little ironies. Devon, the one who wouldn't go in the water for fear that a wild starfish might attack, ate everything; Greek, Chinese, Thai, my mom's scalloped potatoes, you name it. The food pyramid for Tess on the other hand was limited to four food groups: peanut butter, jelly, pasta, and meat, lots of meat.

"I'm practically a carnivore," she told Kristin over at the Australian Navy Compound.

Naturally, this led to our usual, and rather brief, nightly dinner conversation.

"I'm not eating it."

"Fine. Starve."

Dietary counseling was not my forte.

However, when it came to feeding the kids I made sure to meet their nutritional needs. Lunches always included a healthy dose of local fruit. You could imagine my surprise when suddenly their Phineas & Ferb lunch boxes started coming home with that same healthy dose of local fruit. I couldn't compete when a good number of the Pohnpean kids were bringing in cans of chocolate frosting and donuts for lunch – not snacks, mind you, lunch! The frosting, by the way, wasn't for the donuts; it was to eat separately with a spoon.

The Pohnpeian diet had been deteriorating for some time and, thanks to crates full of calorie dense, nutrient poor, canned and processed foods arriving regularly via the container ships, seemed to be getting worse by the boatload. Breakfast could consist solely of *Lucky Cow* sweetened condensed milk poured over donuts. In addition to the chocolate frosting, dry Kool Aid drink mix sprinkled over uncooked Raman also made for a popular lunch. For dinner, Spam and deep fried turkey tail, which was pure fat to begin with. Frankly, that would have been my diet too if I thought I could get away with it, but the fact is you can't get away with it.

In 2000, *the Atlantic* published an article on obesity, entitled "New World Syndrome," and declared, "Spam and turkey tails have turned Micronesians into Macronesians."

Certainly, the Mallarmes didn't exemplify that stereotype and a good number of the Micronesians I knew ate well and were quite fit with a hearty diet of local foods that featured, naturally, a healthy helping of fish. Still, the loss of traditional diets and increasing consumption of refined carbohydrates had led to the Pacific having some of the highest rates of diabetes in the world. One in three adults on Pohnpei had diabetes – a staggering figure, especially when you consider that diabetes was the biggest cause of amputations and loss of eyesight in the region. On the nearby island of Kosrae, more than 80 percent of adults were overweight or obese and more than half of the adults over 50 had diabetes.

Enter Dr. Lois Engleberger, Konrad's wife, and the manager of the Island Food Community of Pohnpei whose 'Go Local' campaign aimed to increase production and consumption of local foods. Dr. Engleberger was a force of nature on the island and appeared to be much younger than her 60 years. With her slim figure and silver/black hair pulled up in a bun, she looked every bit the earnest dietician she was and seemed to forever be working a dietary plan of one sort or another. Her smile and island-easy manner was magnetic and drew everyone in until it seemed there wasn't a person on Pohnpei who wasn't a part of, or at least knew of, the Go Local campaign. It was never "Dr." or even "Lois" to the islanders. Throughout Micronesia she was simply known as the Banana Lady.

The first thing she wanted to clear up, however, was a common misperception. "I'm not just the Banana Lady," she said. "I work with pandanas and taro too." Then she offered me a banana; several, in fact.

"Each banana has its own growing characteristics, its own fruit, and its own appearance, texture and taste," she explained. "Each has its own personality, just like people."

Yep, she was the Banana Lady alright.

I picked what I thought was your typical, average everyday banana, peeled the yellow skin, and took a bite.

"Ah, that's the *Daiwang*," she said. "It's mostly used to feed pigs."

I spit it out.

"Actually, it tastes just fine," she continued, "but you'll never get people to sell it because of its low status. People who grow them are considered lazy because it's easy to grow and bears fruit after only five years. You don't even have to weed it."

Lois wouldn't give up on the *Daiwang*, though. She got a few ladies at the market to start selling them and soon several more joined in. In a clever move, she got a picture of then Governor Johnny David eating it in the newspaper and its popularity began to grow.

I tried the other bananas and, to my surprise, she was right. Each had its own color, texture and taste. The *Utin Menihle*, the most common eating

159

banana on the island, was white and tasted like the bananas I'd eaten from the Safeway supermarkets back in Maryland. Not impressed. *Karat*, the state banana of Pohnpei was also, eh, ok, but the *Akadahn*, now there was a banana. White, fatter and with a beautiful aroma, it had the rich and creamy taste of a banana shake. Naturally, it was the number one preferred eating banana in Micronesia, but also was harder to grow and thus less available.

The *Utin Iap* was orange in color due to its high level of beta-carotene and probably the most important of the 50 species of banana found on the island. In fact, at one point only the *Karat* and *Utin Iap* could be given to the *Nahnmwarki* chiefs on the island. (On Yap, however, the high chiefs refused to eat the *Utin Iap*, which grew erect with its bunches going straight up in the air, because it would not bow down in respect like the other banana trees).

The *Utin Iap* was also significant for something more important than just being a chiefly fruit. More than half the children on Pohnpei suffered from vitamin A deficiency and were prone to infections and even night blindness. It became a crisis situation. The easiest solution would have been to add green leafy vegetables to the diet but, again, they were considered food for the pigs and animals. Dr. Engleberger, however, found it odd when a number of older people told her they never ate greens but also never had vitamin A deficiency. Something in their diet was protecting them.

"That's when it dawned on me," she said. "Bananas, and especially the *Utin Iap*, were loaded with beta carotene which converts to vitamin A once it gets into your body. Research is just coming out that shows bananas also protect against cancer, heart disease and – BINGO – diabetes because it has an antioxidant aspect as well.

"Bananas are so interesting, yes?" she asked.

No one had ever looked at this aspect of the banana she said, because 80 percent of the world's market of bananas is one variety (Cavendish), the kind you get at, well, the Safeway supermarket back in Maryland.

"Bananas rank fourth, behind rice, wheat and corn as the most imported food in the world," she continued. "And yet it's still neglected as a poor man's food. All of these stigmas related to it.

"We should be giving bananas the respect they deserve," The Banana Lady added, slapping her hand down on the table.

I walked out of the door of her office assured that the Micronesian diet was headed in the right direction. "Go local," she shouted after me.

Chapter 12

Gone Girl

*Parenthood is the passing of a baton, followed
by a lifelong disagreement as to who dropped it.*
~ Robert Brault

       The laid-back, peaceful, easy vibe of the island was all around me as
I stepped outside our house and into the lush jungle, bathed in a thousand
soothing shades of green. A warm breeze caressed my face as birdcalls and
the sweet fragrance of plumeria, ylang-ylang and hibiscus filled the air.
Contentment reigned and my thoughts began to drift.

       Suddenly, the front door crashed open.

       "Devon just called me a stupid butt."

       "I DID NOT. She sat on my donut and I just said get your stupid
butt off it."

       "Then she hit me," Tess interrupted.

       "LIAR!"

The peace and tranquility of the morning lasted exactly two minutes and 27 seconds. I timed it. Can paradise co-exist with kids? Of course not. A friend once told me he was going on vacation. I asked if he was taking the kids and he replied, "No, that would be a trip. This is a vacation."

I told the kids to get back inside as our Pohnpean neighbors never raised their voices, while our house was a perpetual Bruce Springsteen encore. That's when Devon, in an attempt to shut Tess out, slammed the door ... on her own finger.

Of course, she screamed.

Unaware of what just happened, I shouted at her to stop screaming (the irony of YELLING at the kids to STOP SCREAMING having long since left me), then sent her to her room. That's when I saw the trail of blood going up the stairs.

In a situation such as this it is of the utmost importance that you do not panic. As the parent/doctor you need to remain calm and exercise good judgment regarding the extent of the injury. I say parent/doctor because, despite the constant harassing phone calls from the American Medical Association ordering me to "cease and desist" and the local pharmacy ignoring my prescriptions for Valium, all parents are doctors because all children are perennial patients.

I followed the trail of blood up to her room and discovered she had torn the nail of her middle finger off ... completely. We quickly wrapped her finger and rushed her over to the dank, moldy, grey cinderblock building that had a medical sign out in front. Although it had doctors, nurses and bedpans, I just couldn't get myself to call it a hospital. "Basically, you go there to die," a Pohnpeian told me. Often, entire communities sat around and under the bed of their loved one, clanking pots and pans as they prepared food for the afflicted.

Sometimes, the food was the afflicted. "I was working the ER when a man came in carrying a huge 100-pound pig," a friend of ours who worked there told us. "He said the pig was pregnant and asked if we could do a caesarian section on it. I told him we were people doctors, not vets."

A dermatologist by trade, our friend was called to also do general practice on a regular basis (I'm guessing he prescribed Clearasil for most ailments) and, believe me, he'd seen it all.

"We had people who ate gauze to cleanse their stomachs," he said. "There were also young men inserting marbles into slits around their penis to add girth to their overall package. Don't know how the rumor started that that would actually increase pleasure with either of the participants, but we had quite a few cases that needed to be treated."

To be fair, most of the patients had the usual illnesses and complaints associated with any island and the hospital did offer relatively decent primary care. Anyone who required serious medical care was referred to the Philippines or Hawaii at the government's expense. Even the cost of primary care was often waived if the person didn't have the fee (patients also got around this by coming at night when there was no cashier around).

"Mostly we just see a lot of worms due to sakau and undercooked dog meat, that sort of thing," our friend continued. "I've seen patients vomiting worms."

Eventually Devon's doctor arrived and, I must admit, was quite professional. After sticking a needle directly into Devon's wound (which fascinated Tess but sent Bette outside holding her stomach) he assured her that her nail would be back and good as new in no time.

While at the hospital we also had Tess checked out for her constant itching at night. The diagnosis – pinworm. The medication she was given would destroy the parasite in no time, but she just had to annoy her sister while the opportunity presented itself by raising her arms like Frankenstein and slowly inching toward Devon already scrunched on the far side of the back seat of the car.

165

"Ahhhhh, keep your pinworm hands off me," Devon shouted. "DAD!!!"

"Tess," I said, "keep your pinworm hands off your sister." The inevitable back seat free-for-all melee ensued anyway.

When we arrived back home I made a beeline for the door. The house was a mess. The house was clean. It was the best of times, it was the worst of times. It was ... oh, who the hell cared anymore. All my talk about broadening society's standards for acceptable male behavior and redefining modern masculinity in the 21st Century was a crock of shit. My wife, the kids, the dogs and, yes, even Gordon Gecko were all getting on my nerves. Every time I thought I was finally getting a handle on life as Home Daddy something "in the moment" would happen sending me back several generations to square one as a grunting, growling Neanderthal dad. Every morning I'd rise chirpy and cheerful and every night I'd go to bed exhausted and utterly defeated. My life was directionless, meaningless, pointless and whatever other "less" I could think of, and it soon became painfully clear that I had no tolerance, no guidance, no game plan and, worst of all, no gin.

"Dad?"

"Yes, honey."

"Dad?"

"What do you need Tess?"

"Dad?"

"That's my name, don't wear it out," I'd say, still smiling, but that's exactly what they did. They wore it out. Like an old, tattered banner, they hoisted it up the flagpole every morning and kept it flying well into the night where it continued as a constant ringing in my ears even after they went to sleep. "Dad, dad, dad, dad, ..."

The whole Home Daddy thing was a failed experiment. It can't be done, and you know why? We're dads, not moms. It's a scientific fact, look it up. Women have been moms since before man walked upright

166

(anthropologists estimate this to be around 1964, although studies show they began slouching again in 1980). Men, on the other hand, have spent many a millennia avoiding the duties therein. We were never cut out for it. The reason lay in biological genetics.

After conducting thorough and exhaustive research (meaning I Googled the answer, then cut and pasted it here) I discovered it has to do with evolution (a change in the inherited characteristics of a population of organisms through successive generations), natural selection, and specific traits (characteristics – anatomical, biochemical or behavioral – that are the result of gene–environment interaction). Over time, say a few hundred thousand years, these traits become, more or less, common. In other words, it took a helluva long time for the Home Daddy gene to develop and it's still very much in the infancy stage.

Research also indicated that a "mutation" would have to take place in order to introduce a complete genetic change. I peruse the magazine shelves on a regular basis and I've yet to see a "better parenting through genetic mutation" article in *Family Circle*, but if it takes us becoming genetic mutants to get closer to our kids, then I think I speak for all men when I say – we'll fight it every inch of the way. Adaptation – I think not. Again, my exhaustive nano-second research came to the rescue in letting me know that "an *adaptive trait* is an aspect of the developmental pattern of the organism which enables or enhances the probability of that organism surviving and reproducing."

"Aha! Well there you go, Bette," I said tapping the computer screen. "The point is you and I are not reproducing anymore. Therefore, I have no need to adapt."

However, Bette, who was cutting out cooking articles for me to use, pointed further down the screen to where it stated that "adaptation may cause either the gain of a new feature, or the loss of an ancestral feature." I couldn't help but notice she was using the scissors to specifically point to the part

167

about losing an ancestral feature. She then smiled sweetly and closed the blades with a loud SNIP. I got up and started cooking the Asian-spiced pork stew with scallion pancakes recipe she handed me.

The note marked "Dad" slid under our bedroom door late one afternoon. I had no idea who it could be from until I saw "Devon and Tess" written in the return address. The copy got right to the point.

> "Dear Dad, we can not stay with you if you are going to get mad at me and Tess every-single DAY! It teaches us bad examples! I am going to feed myself and do my own stuff until you say sorry. Consider myself a 'runaway.' Good Bye, Devon and Tess."

I caught them at the front of the house, backpacks securely fastened. Inside were the necessities for leading a nomadic life on the road and enduring the harsh weather they would surely encounter. Devon's backpack had three hair bands, a notebook and pen, one face towel, and a key chain. Tess was a little more practical having stuffed a can of Pringles, two granola bars, two face towels, her teddy bear and blanket, and $12.47 into her backpack.

I didn't know whether to laugh or cry and, honestly, felt like doing a little of both. We all went back inside and I made them sandwiches with Nutella (basically, it's chocolate frosting despite the nutritious sounding "hazelnut spread" the label sells you, but I was going for happiness, not healthiness, here). I know just about every child does this little runaway skit at least once in their lives, but I still took it as a clear indicator that something had to give, and that something was me. What we needed was a parental paradigm shift and I immediately began to work on my Home Daddy Home Improvement Plan, Draft XXI. I would rally the troops. I would convey a positive attitude. I would perform admirably. I would fail miserably.

I was stuck in a Home Daddy quagmire and it became apparent just how badly I was losing the war. Their "shock and awe" campaign continued;

the shock mostly coming from me when I discovered Tess had once again left crayons in her pockets and I once again had to deal with tie-dyed laundry. The "awe" came when I then heard a loud thud inside the house and discovered Devon's new Rip Stick (a streamlined version of a skateboard with only one wheel in the front and one in the back, to the delight of family doctors everywhere) slammed into our book case knocking the 20-pound stone Buddha head from Cambodia off the top shelf.

"Devon! How many times have I told you not to rip inside the house?" I said, confiscating the "stick." While not the best Home Daddy, the fact that I correctly separated "rip" and "stick" as a verb and a noun at least showed I was improving as a progressive, new-age father, although Devon didn't seem impressed as she once again headed to her room.

I placed Buddha, with a fresh chip gouged into his forehead, back on the top shelf and noticed his all-knowing, serene smile was gone.

I couldn't get a break. That afternoon, after they were done playing with *Matches*, a name they gave to a cute, furry, six-week-old puppy – one of the ever-growing pack of feral dogs that now called our house "home" – he fell asleep in the only shade he could find. Unfortunately, that shade was under our Jeep. Oblivious, I made my way to the market completely unaware of the carnage I had caused, although the constant *flip, flip, flip* sound coming from the right rear tire should have given me some idea.

Upon arriving home, I was napalmed with verbal abuse from the kids and was horrified at what I had done. However, Melyann, who owned *Matches*, merely shrugged her shoulders with typical Pohnpeian indifference when I told her. "It was a dog," she said as she continued walking down the path.

Still confident I could turn all of this around, the next weekend I set up a memorable jungle excursion up Nett Ridge across the river from our house with Devon, Tess and a few of the Peace Corps volunteers. We huddled at the foot of the trail waiting for the sudden downpour to stop then, after I

169

did a quick head count to make sure we were all there, preceded up the ridge. Since I had arranged for the local guide, I hurried past everyone to catch up and entertain him with my constant, witty observations and banter for the entire trip up the arduous slope. It wouldn't be long before he knew, despite the pink Powerpuff Girls backpack I had strapped across my broad shoulders, that I was a seasoned veteran of mountain treks.

The hike started off easily enough with a gradual path but the trail quickly became more vertical than horizontal and we were soon enclosed by the humid jungle still dripping from the rain. Sweat poured off of us as our guide continued hacking away at the bush out in front. At the first clearing we turned and saw the stunning view of the Nett River meandering through the sprawling green forests below. Just as I was about to truly seize the moment for the beauty unfolding before me, a scream filled the air. Devon had been savagely attacked by a small ant and lay writhing on the ground, mortally wounded.

"For God's sake, Devon, it's an ant."

"I know, but it bit me and it REALLY hurts," she said, clamping her wrist with her other hand to stop the hemorrhaging so that she wouldn't bleed to death. I looked at the small bump on her finger.

"Why can't you be like Tess who hasn't complained once since we started?" I asked scanning the line of people below me. "Tess?" Everyone else turned to look behind them. "Where the hell is Tess?" A collection of shrugs. "Oh…my…GOD!"

At the bottom of the ridge, at the base of the trail, in a rainwater puddle, lay a tadpole. "Why, hello there little taddy," said Tess squatting down as the group began its hike, and the rest is pretty much history. The group ascended higher and higher as Tess's focus sank lower and lower into the primordial pool.

She ran to the foot of the trail then, realizing her situation, did what any eight-year-old would do and started to cry. However, and I'm proud of her, she then got herself together and asked the local family at the bottom of the hill if they had a phone. The phone message on our answering machine went something like this, "Mom (sniffle), this is Tess. I got left behind (sniffle). I'm just gonna start walking home now, ok? (sniffle)." That's when the phone went dead and, for the most part, me with it.

Meanwhile, Devon and I scrambled down the ridge and were directed to the road where we were told Tess had started walking. Two older women, who had their small flatbed truck parked on the side under a mango tree, let me know she was taken by someone in a white pickup truck. Small children being taken by a stranger in a white pickup truck sometimes can be construed as being bad. Now before you go calling Child Protection Service (Devon has them on speed dial), understand that almost everyone on the island knew the white pickup truck belonged to Rich and Mae, part of the venerable, and quite large, Adams family whose ancestors settled on Pohnpei around the time it was formed about three million years ago. They were a clan unto themselves and their compound resembled a day care center as people picked up and dropped off kids for play dates at all hours of the day or night.

Mae later told me she said to Rich as they drove down the road, "What a cute little girl....hey wait a minute, is that Tess? What the hell is she doing by herself way out here?"

As they got Tess in the pickup and calmed her down, Mae took out her cell phone and asked, "What's your dad's cell phone number?" Tess just shook her head and sobbed. "Your dad does have a cell phone, doesn't he?" Tess again shook her head and said, "A cell phone? MY DAD DOESN'T EVEN HAVE A JOB!"

I'm still not sure what my employment situation had to do with the situation.

As they were driving to their house they passed Bette, driving in the opposite direction, who smiled and waved and thought, "Hmm, odd, that looked like Tess in the truck with them." She pulled over and saw Rich and Mae swinging back around. The forces against me were beginning to align.

I have my own saying: "If you're damned if you do and damned if you don't … then do!" Sooooo, back at the trailhead, knowing that Tess was ok and that I was already a dead man, I tried to convince Devon to climb back up the ridge with me. Wise beyond her years, she wanted nothing to do with the situation. The two local women with the flatbed truck then asked, "You live by the Pohnpei Surf Club, don't you? We'll take her since we're headed that way."

"So let me get this straight," Bette would later say to me while grabbing the front of my shirt with both of her clenched hands, "you lost Tess on the side of a mountain, then you put your only other daughter in the back of a flatbed truck with two strangers and proceeded to finish your climb?"

I mentioned before that bad decisions make for great stories, but wives generally don't get that. The top of the ridge was exhilarating with spectacular views of the vibrant turquoise reef, the steel blue ocean and, inland along the Nett River, far, far down below, the thick, angry black smoke rising from our house. After the hike I stopped at a local bar for a few beers to allow Bette more time to calm down. Marriage counselors call this a "cooling off" period. I also reasoned that the more beers I had, the more time she had to cool off. It's this kind of instinct, I think, that's so crucial in keeping a family together and making it stronger.

When I finally did arrive home we all had a good laugh about it over a family game of Yahtzee. Or maybe I'm thinking of a different night.

Later, when I discovered our bedroom door was mistakenly locked, I thought it best not to bother Bette and instead commune with nature by sleeping in the *nahs* outside. Again, instinct that's crucial to keeping a family together. I also made a mental note to look up exactly how long "cooling off" periods are supposed to take.

Chapter 13

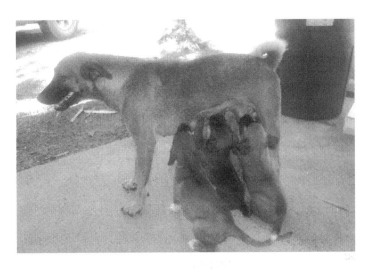

Dog Days and Nightcrawlers

Two-legged creatures we are supposed to love as we love ourselves. The four-legged, also, can come to seem pretty important. But six legs are too many from the human standpoint.

~ Joseph W. Krutch

The cockroaches appeared from behind the toaster, just four of them, a scouting party for the army no doubt gathering just under the counter. I quietly grabbed the spatula while Bette grabbed *The All New Joy of Cooking* tome and we hovered above them, ready to end their miserable little cockroach lives. Suddenly, two of them flashed heretofore unseen wings and, flying directly at us, mounted a first strike air attack.

The first cockroach buzzed past Bette's ear but the second scored a direct hit on the side of my head and then dropped immediately to the floor. "It's in my hair, get it out, get it out," I yelled slamming the side of my head with the spatula as we both retreated.

"Hey, they can't do that," Bette said, her arms awkwardly flailing the air. "They can't fly."

"They're cockroaches, Bette," I said. "They cheat. That's what they do."

We ran to the other side of the counter and watched as the second cockroach landed on the floor, then sent up flares to signal that Red Sector One was open ... or so he thought. To my surprise an enormous scaly head with bulging eyes appeared in the huge crack between the counter and the wall. It was Gordon. To his left, two smaller geckos scrambled up the wall and stopped just inches from the counter top. The two cockroaches that remained on the counter flew above them, then circled back as three more cockroaches scurried out from behind the toaster. Insect Armageddon had begun.

The cockroaches slowly advanced unaware of Gordon's presence before coming to a stop, still well out of his reach. It was as if they were responding to orders. Suddenly the earth shook, the counter trembled and out lumbered Barkley himself – eight ounces of big, black bug which easily dwarfed the other cockroaches. He twitched and felt the air with his antennae then plodded to within inches of Gordon; an in-your-face move if ever I saw one.

"This is it, this ... is ... it!" I whispered, grabbing and shaking Bette.

It was going to be the fight of the century; Gordon vs. Barkley, mano y mano, or claw y mesothorax as it was, and we were ringside.

Barkley advanced. Gordon stood unblinking. Barkley stopped and again twitched his antennae, perhaps talking smack. I could only imagine the obscenities that poured out of that filthy little antennae of his. Gordon remained unwavering, refusing to lower his dignity by responding to the barrage of insults being hurled his way. Both stood frozen for about 20 seconds. I couldn't take it any longer.

"Now, Gordon, NOW," I shouted, pounding the counter.

The pounding caused Barkley to fake right then go left, ambling only an inch in front of Gordon's nose. Nothing, not even the slightest breath

174

emanated from Gordon. Man, this guy is as cold as ice, I thought, he's good. A second later, however, Barkley continued on past Gordon and scurried down into another crack in the wall. The other cockroaches followed suit.

"What the?" My mouth fell open.

"That's it? That's the big war you've been talking about for the past year?" Bette asked.

"Gordon, do something," I yelled. "Go after him. Go get him boy. Sick 'em."

Gordon merely blinked, then slid back down between the counter and the wall. Talk about anticlimactic; what a letdown. Cockroaches and geckos, turns out you can't trust either of them. I let out a sigh, then slammed the cookbook down on a centipede squiggling along the now gecko-less counter.

Later that afternoon as we entered the Joy, a small hotel/restaurant in town we went to for our weekly fish burger fix, I overheard one of the expats talking about a nightcrawler that broke into her apartment the night before with the intention of having sex with her. And we thought we had insect problems. Later, another local woman we knew told us of how she awoke one night to find a nightcrawler standing over her bed. He fled as soon as she screamed. She added that nightcrawlers were becoming somewhat of a problem on Pohnpei. "Good God, what kind of a Kafkaesque place is this?" I whispered to Bette. We would soon find out that nightcrawlers were men, mostly adolescent boys, who lurked around and often broke into the residences of women. They rarely stayed long, fleeing as soon as the woman awakened. Although more than just a little bit bizarre (and, over the years, becoming more and more dangerous), the intrusions actually began as an innocent tradition centuries ago and had more to do with the conservative courtship culture of Micronesia than anything else.

The Western concept of openly dating rarely, if ever, took place on the islands. Holding hands or any sign of public affection, even among married men and women, was taboo. Having extended conversations (even maintaining direct eye contact) was also frowned upon and one would never risk being seen alone with a member of the opposite sex. Men and women usually sat apart at social gatherings and stuck to their own sex in almost all public activities. In the past, nightcrawling, usually done with consent, was one of the ways around this cultural conundrum. Tiptoeing the line between customs and natural primal urges has never been easy, but the Micronesians had to be particularly careful when nightcrawling, especially since the intended interest usually slept on the floor in the same room as her entire family. The boy then had the option of either rustling the thatch walls to get the girl's attention, or actually entering the hut and nudging her without awakening the father or older brothers, all of whom usually slept with machetes at their sides.

The Chuukese love stick was part of the legendary practice of courtship unique to that group of islands, and one of the cleverer ways of navigating around the communal sleeping arraignments. Traditionally, young Chuukese men would own personalized wooden love sticks on which they would carve two of the same design. A short one would be carved and usually stuck in his hair. The long one would be for the Chuukese woman. If a man liked a woman, he used his long love stick (oh, go ahead and snicker if you must) to poke into her hut and into her hair, thus waking her. She then would put her fingers around the shaft's notches and identify its owner. If the love stick's design was that of the man she liked, she would pull on the love-stick signaling for him to come in. If the woman pushed the love stick out, it meant she was not interested. This would be a crushing blow to one's ego, believe me, as Bette was forever pushing my love stick back out.

Unfortunately, the practice of nightcrawling as an innocent and consensual means began to decline over the years leading up to our arrival and had since become synonymous with straightforward breaking and entering, more for thievery or just plain voyeurism than for actual assault.

Our lunch guest, Regina, the Yapese Peace Corps program assistant, said she also once had an encounter with a nightcrawler, but added that she first wanted to make one thing perfectly clear.

"This doesn't happen on Yap," she said, "because if you are found you are beaten every which way. If someone tried, the girl's family would pound him. He's trespassing on their land, disrespecting the girl and disrespecting the family."

She then told me about the time she was visiting Pohnpei with Hana, her beetle nut buddy and fellow Peace Corps programming officer in Palau. "It was a little after 9 p.m. and we were just settling down for the night when suddenly I saw someone looking in the window. Then he started scrapping on the window and pulling on it. At first I was going to push him out of the window, but instead I grabbed a kitchen knife. Then he ran off."

My guess is that he knew the kitchen knife wasn't a love stick and he wasn't waiting around to feel it and determine to whom it belonged.

That night, as I turned up our dirt road, Mali, Jamaica, Yoshi and the other dogs surrounded the car and led the usual barking procession back to the house. Nightcrawlers didn't stand a chance down our way as the mangy, malevolent pack flew into a howling frenzy at anyone, or any "thing," that approached, either real or imagined. "To serve & protect" was their motto and, to our dismay, they let us know of this protection all night, every night.

The "serve" component, however, didn't really register at first. Fed just enough to keep them from going too far astray, the dogs on the island foraged for their own food and were generally regarded, or rather disregarded by the locals as, well, animals. Small in stature with pointed ears, short fur and thin, hardened bodies, they often bore the gouges and open wounds of war from the constant battles over turf, food, and mating dominance – it wasn't at all uncommon to see a male and a female facing in opposite directions, yet still stuck in a reproductive pose that I called the "I can't quit you" position.

It was the eyes of the local dogs, however, that unnerved me the most as they presented the cold, predatory soul of a coyote or perhaps a dingo.

Poor Tess found this out while playing up the road with a chicken and her four chicks. Suddenly, Mali, Jamaica and Yoshi appeared out of nowhere and pounced on the chicks, sending blood and feathers flying everywhere. Tess ran back to our house in a state of shock.

"The…the…the dogs killed the chicks," she sobbed. We ran back and were able to save one of them, Devon and Tess making a bed of hay and giving it water, but hours later it too died.

When they attacked again a week later, this time the chicks living on the other side of us, Tess seemed relatively unfazed (psycho killer alert) and merely went about trying to chase the dogs away with a stick. "They had feathers sticking out of their mouths," she said.

Speaking of which, pet dentists say dogs need their teeth brushed three times a week and should get a professional cleaning (which can cost up to $600) every year to reduce bad breath, according to an article in *Washingtonian Magazine*. Doggie braces and protective crowns ranged from $1,000 to $3,000 each. Americans spend about $75 billion a year on their pets – yes, you read that right. A dog owner can typically expect to pour out well over $10,000 into the care, feeding and entertainment of their pet over the course of its lifetime. Fortunately, few people on Pohnpei received *Washingtonian,* which was just as well. You could imagine how embarrassed they would have been, knowing their dogs had gingivitis because of poor dental habits … and baby chick feathers.

Mali, Jamaica, Yoshi and Clairie (yet another name given to one of the dogs by the kids) were quite happy with the lure of the wild. Around us, though, they were extremely friendly and, thanks to Devon and Tess, frequent guests at our house. The kids would play with them for hours at a time and it did our hearts good to see Tess rolling on the ground as they happily gnawed

178

and slobbered all over her. Eventually they would become one big, happy, entangled ball of confusion and you could actually see the fleas, lice and ticks jumping back and forth between the dog fur and Tess's hair. When they were through, the dogs were cleaner than Tess. We continually had to give her post-dog baths until we just gave up and submitted to the fact that she had become a permanent part of the jungle.

The companionship of the dogs was especially important for Tess and they helped immensely with her transition to the island. Other than Sarah who lived a few miles away (the two of them were inseparable whenever they were together) she still didn't have any other friends, either local or expat, that were her age. She was always invited over to Maggie's or the Australian Navy compound to play with Devon and her friends but it just wasn't the same and, to be honest, Devon was reaching the age where she didn't want her little sister hanging around all of the time.

Being the only *men-wai* in her class at school didn't help either as she was bullied by three particularly mean girls, an axis of evil, in her class. It was stereotypical in that there was the local bully; her two larger henchmen or henchgirls as it were, and the rest of the class pointing and laughing. The local bully called Tess "stupid" or "idiot" on a regular basis. Whenever they played jump rope, Tess was forever the holder, making it all "rope" and no "jump." I told Tess to play with the others and ignore the bully and her henchgirls, adding that if they approached her, she should just put her hand up and say "whatever," then walk away (she seemed to do this to me easily enough at home).

After hearing of the incidents, I stepped in and told her teacher who then had a discussion with the girls. Apparently they sorted it all out and it ended with a group hug.

Apparently not.

Tess came home and said that while out at recess, the local bully had stepped on the back of her flip-flop causing her to fall down, much to the

179

amusement of everyone in the schoolyard. That was it. It was time to introduce the local bully to the Bronx; time to teach Tess how to conceal brass knuckles in her lunchbox and make a shiv out of a bar of soap; time to show Tess that she didn't have to have her coconut milk money taken from her every day. I'd had it with the group hugs. It was clobberin' time.

"Don't worry dad," Tess told me. "Teacher said that bullies never win."

"Actually, honey," I replied, "bullies eventually become managers and CEOs and end up taking your comp time and personal days away. Better to deal with them now."

We had another discussion with the teacher who, determined to put an end to it, called the bully and the henchgirls in and threatened them with homework for the rest of the year if the bullying didn't end. Eyes wide, they agreed it would. The teacher then asked Tess if she knew what she should do if it ever did happen again.

"My dad said that whatever they do to me, I should do back to them, only harder," she said with her arms folded across her chest.

Uh-oh! Turning to Tess, I said in a weak attempt to clarify, or outright lie, "No, no, honey, I said that you should ignore them and tell the teacher here what the problem is." Wink, wink, WINK! The winks were pointless.

"Whatever," she said holding her hand up to me. Then they all ran outside to play.

Although there were a few incidents throughout the remainder of the year, the mean girls mostly stayed away from Tess. She was a tough kid and able to shake most of it off, and her laughter continued to light up the room more often than not. Still, it wasn't hard to notice that her overall mood was rapidly changing from bright and cheery to sullen and withdrawn.

The cracks in our idyllic island life were starting to widen. It was especially important that I prevented this since there was no way in hell I was going back to that office cubicle prison in D.C. No, wait, that's not what I meant to say. What I meant to say was that it was especially vital that I prevent this as the health and happiness of my wife and children were of the utmost importance. Actually, this was true. You're only as happy as your unhappiest child and, at the time, Tess's situation was affecting the entire family. Also, there was no way in hell I was going back to that office cubicle prison in D.C.

Bette quickly made an appointment for me to take the kids to see a counselor in Saipan to help us assess and remedy the impact the change in our lifestyle was having on them (counselor, of course, being a code word for [whisper] "psychologist"). Even though we were the very model of a modern 21st Century family, lord help us if we ever actually admitted our kids had to see a [whisper] "psychologist." Counselor it was, but the fact that they called it "psycho-educational" testing didn't help matters any.

Saipan is in the Northern Mariana island chain about a hundred miles north of Guam and a million miles from anywhere else (local marketing mascot gimmick: the Saipanda). Rimmed with beautiful beaches, the island at first appeared to have little to offer as we passed row after row of food marts, liquor stores and pawn shops until we came to the DFS Galleria, a wildly out-of-place shopping mall offering Louis Vuitton, Cartier, Gucci, Fendi, Givenchi, Burberry, and several other high-end stores. Before I could even finish my "who the hell on this island would shop here" question, several double-decker buses pulled up teeming with Asian tourists looking to buy anything and everything that had the Saipanda logo on it. Yeah, and we were the ones undergoing psycho-educational testing.

The testing went better than we expected as Devon and Tess were found to be intellectually bright with superior overall intelligence. Both were emotionally healthy but also demonstrated moderate anxiety at being away from the States. Particularly, they noted Tess's social difficulties with her peers in Pohnpei. To help remedy this, she was to practice firm, calm

181

responses to the teasing and name calling, like "Your name calling is making me angry, so please stop," and "I watch your little sister walk to school…it'd be a shame if something should happen to her" (Ok, I may have added that last one). They also specifically noted her separation anxieties regarding us, her parents. That we knew. Neither Bette nor I could so much as step in the bathroom without Tess anxiously asking where we were going.

We headed back loaded with substantial evaluations and recommendations, but not before the kids and I had the time of our lives hitting every waterslide on the island.

While the advice from the counselors was extremely helpful, the real turnaround came when friends called to tell us they had a puppy that needed a home. The kids did back flips when they saw the emaciated and flea-ridden, yet absolutely adorable little golden ball of fur.

Of course, we let the kids name the dog. This could have been a mistake. Our neighbor back home let his daughters name their new dog … Precious. He shook his head when he told me. "When that dog gets loose there is absolutely no way I'm going around the neighborhood yelling, "Precious. Where are you Precious?" he said. I reminded the kids that "Doggie" and "Clairie" were already taken and that they had to be more original. Buddy it was. So much for the originality, but I had to admit, it suited him just fine. He looked like a Buddy.

Although we knew it was only a psychological Band Aid, the transformation was immediate for both kids, but especially for Tess. She ran from her classroom at the end of every school day and absolutely beamed when she saw Buddy jumping up and down in the car. She awoke to feed him in the morning and she took him to bed with her every night. Both kids cleaned and groomed him and we quickly had to teach them that giving Buddy a bath twice a day wasn't exactly the best thing for him.

The months passed and it wasn't long before Buddy was not only large enough to run with the big dogs in the neighborhood, but leading them frothing and barking through our house every time I opened the front door.

"Out, OUT," I'd yell. "Goddamn dogs."

Damian finally accepted a Peace Corps position in Mauritania and, after tears, beers and several farewell parties (one offering pig tongue; a little chewy and gamey but not as bad as I thought), he, Mary and the dogs were on to another adventure. We watched their plane take off then, deeply saddened, drove back, went into their house and made off with a water hose, three sofa cushions, two glue sticks and a pack of staples. Island life dictates you pilfer whatever you can.

With Mali and Jamaica gone, that meant Buddy was the new alpha male and he had acquired all of the nicks, cuts and gouges to prove it. It wasn't long before that adorable little puppy with the soft brown eyes was gone and a coyote with a scarred face and hardened, soulless eyes had taken over. Try as we might, we could never keep him indoors for long. Although he still remained very much Devon and Tess's dog and couldn't wait for them to come home from school and play with him, Buddy had grown into what he was born to be: a scrappy, tough Pohnpeian dog and part of the wild, scavenging pack that howled every night. The natural order in the universe would prevail and the dogs of Pohnpei would simply go on living the way they had for centuries, crooked teeth and all. Unfortunately, they'd also go on dying, very few from old age.

This is where the "to serve" part comes in. Yes, dogs were eaten on Pohnpei, and quite frequently I might add. Besides keeping away nightcrawlers and other intruders, an equally important function of the dogs on the island was to be served as the main course of a feast. Historically, dogs have always been considered a delicacy on the island and a main source of protein, along with pigs, chicken and fish. Baked in an outdoor oven called an *uhmw* in the same manner as pigs, they remained a most prized offering to chiefs but were also eaten during special occasions by all Pohnpeians.

Needless to say, dogs went missing on a daily basis. While the Mallarmes and others in the neighborhood respected Buddy (and Mali and Jamaica while they were around) as being off limits, we all still kept a watchful eye on them since they were well fed and clean and, thus, easy targets. A World Teach volunteer told me he once saw two men stop their car, whack a dog over the head, then throw it into the trunk and disappear into the evening. It was as easy, and natural, as that. The rules of acceptability weren't right or wrong out in this part of the world, just different.

Coincidentally, the Mallarmes were busy next door preparing for Ben's 9th birthday and a cousin leaving for high school in Chuuk. That meant another gathering and, of course, another excuse for *sakau*. It was still late morning when I went over and met Peteriko, a friend of the family. Together we sat down and cleaned the pepper roots in a large tub filled with brown water. Suddenly he laughed out loud and I looked quizzically at him. "Never mind," he said, continuing to scrub the roots. "It's just that I've never seen a white man cleaning sakau before."

"Well, if I'm going to drink it … and I am," I said as he laughed again, "then I might as well help prepare it."

When I asked what he did for a living, he shrugged his shoulders and replied matter-of-factly that he didn't do anything. Silence followed. I then asked if his wife worked and he said that, no, she didn't work either. I quickly asked if he had kids. "Two," he replied, "One living with me and one living with my wife." My guess was that, as was the case in many parts of the island, he ate what he fished and the family/community took care of the rest. The conversation went quite until we finish our scrubbing.

As we cut the strips of hibiscus, I asked how that part of the process helped the sakau.

"It makes it slimy," he said.

"And this is good, how?"

"Slimy is better than gritty."

Later that night after several shells of sakau, I sauntered over to the table by the smoldering *uhmw*. The sweet, smoky smell of barbeque filled the air and I noticed not just one or two, but four pigs roasted for the occasion. As they lay on the table with the roasting sticks shoved through them, their moist meat glistening in the fire light, I noticed the set of teeth didn't seem right on the smaller one on the end. A closer look revealed that was because it was, indeed, a dog. I recoiled slightly.

"Hopefully, no one I know," I said.

After assuring me it wasn't, Maxson cut a piece off the hindquarters and gave it to me. Well, I thought, this would be yet another oddity to add to my culinary taste test list along with fried grasshoppers, dung beetles, grubs, bull testicles, and Reese's Peanut Butter Cups cereal. I looked over at Buddy. The irony was lost on him as he circled the perimeter of the feast with the rest of the pack hoping to get a few scraps. I blew on the sizzling, juicy piece of meat and passed it from hand to hand to cool it off before popping it in my mouth, sure that it would taste both gamey and tough. I was pleasantly surprised. Despite the moral ethics involved, and what the ASPCA would have you believe, it was actually quite good; some gristle, but with an overall taste of beef and decent beef at that. I had a second and third piece of the dog to make sure. Yes, it definitely had a beef quality to it.

"Younger is better, about a year old," Melinda said. She then added with a smile, "About the age of your dog."

The crowd laughed; a little too loud as far as I was concerned and with what I detected as just a slightly sinister tone. I smacked Buddy on the nose and pointed to our house. "Buddy, go home."

Chapter 14

Reefer Madness

I need the sea because it teaches me!
~ Pablo Neruda

"Well, I'm off to work," Simon said. "See you at the office." And with that he flipped over the side of the boat. Frankly, after watching the pro surfers say and do that, I was getting tired of these people flipping over the sides of boats in their floral Hawaiian swim trunks and getting paid for it.

"Get a real job," I shouted after him, but it was too late. He had already disappeared beneath the water's rippling surface. I would have really let him have it too if only I had a real job*. Instead, I shoved the respirator into my mouth, flipped over the side, and followed him in.

The "office" Simon spoke of was 20 feet below, where several tables, each two feet wide and eight feet long, were nestled on the sandy

---

* [Constitutes real paying job; housekeeping, parenting and volunteering as T-Ball coach not included in accordance with U.S. Census Bureau guidelines]

bottom. Hundreds of small corals, about an inch to two inches in length, lay in trays across the tabletops. Our job, with a few of his other employees, was to gently brush the residue off each of them and transfer the larger corals to the tables at the perimeter. The hard part, for me at least, was maintaining equilibrium with my scuba gear and holding steady while floating horizontal to the table. I would brush, brush, brush but then notice the table rising above me. Not enough air in my vest. Then I'd brush, brush, brush some more and notice the table falling away from me; too much air. Finally, I got the hang of it (literally). With everyone working their tables and rushing about, it looked like your average everyday office, except maybe for the co-workers wearing fins, masks and breathing apparatus and the water cooler being a bit bigger. Also, just like in any other office, we had to work fast. It was a gorgeous day with a beautiful blue sky and the sun shining brightly – and that was the problem.

"These are probably the worst conditions we could get," Simon said.

Coral is extremely sensitive and reacts negatively to even the slightest movement or water changes. El Niño conditions had caused the tides to be almost a foot lower, and the water temperature several degrees higher, than normal. Cooler water from the bottom had to be pumped into the coral filled ice chests on the boat along with a certain amount of oxygen to offset the higher water temperature. Simon explained that while fresh water holds about 10 parts of oxygen per milliliter, tropical seawater only has about six parts of oxygen per milliliter (the more salt and the higher the temperature, the less oxygen). He added that anyone handling the coral would also have to wash their hands as the oils and dirt would further agitate the live animals.

Live animals?

"You have to be careful around them, especially the wild coral," he said. "Nasty temperament."

I actually believed him for a second regarding the "wild" coral. With his piercing eyes set beneath thick, dark eyebrows, a neatly trimmed salt &

pepper beard, and his soothingly sophisticated Alistair Cooke British accent, Simon maintained an air of reassuring scientific respectability. Besides, the only coral that I ever saw back home was at the bottom of a fish tank in the dentist's office. If you watch them closely, and I have while drooling and waiting for the dental gas to wear off, they can look pretty scary.

Corals are made up of many small animals called polyps, according to "Living Treasures of the Pacific," a poster I found in Simon's above water office (I gather most of my research from posters, which was probably why my Master's thesis wasn't accepted). These polyps have a mouth surrounded by tentacles and can eat, defend themselves and kill plankton for food. In the process they also secrete calcium carbonate that becomes the basis for an external skeleton on which they sit. These calcified deposits can grow to enormous sizes over long periods of time and help to form the nearly 100,000 square miles of coral reefs that cover the world's shallow marine areas.

Besides serving as barriers protecting the shoreline, reefs provide an essential habitat for thousands of underwater sea creatures. However, research has shown they are rapidly deteriorating or disappearing altogether due to climate change – about one-quarter of coral reefs around the world have already been lost and another 24 percent are gravely threatened. It's simple, no coral reef means no sea life; no sea life means no Red Lobster restaurants.

So much for my thinking coral was just a bunch of underwater rocks. From then on, every time I threw my boat anchor onto the coral I could swear I heard them screaming. Ha, ha … no, I'm just kidding. We were environmentally conscious, eco-friendly boaters and always moored the QE V to a buoy – except for when we didn't. Hey, when your engine conks out and you're drifting with your kids over the reef and out into the Pacific, the coral can scream all it wants, that anchor is going in.

By late morning the larger corals were brushed and hoisted up into the coolers above. Phase one completed. "That was fun," I exclaimed after we

boarded the boat. Then I used the same line I threw out to the surfers …
"Honestly, you guys get paid for this?"

"I don't know where the money comes from but all my checks seem to clear," said Shaun, a good friend of ours who worked with Simon after his tour as the IT guy with Peace Corps was up.

Simon inspected the three species of hard coral we had hauled up – two species of *Acropora*, and one species of *Euphyllia*. Simon could get away with saying words like *Acropora* and *Eyphyllia* because he served as affiliate faculty and Pacific coordinator at the University of Hawaii's Hilo Pacific Aquaculture and Coastal Resources Center, affiliate faculty at the College of the Marshall Islands, director of Mid-Pacific Marine Consultants, director of the Marine and Environmental Research Institute of Pohnpei (MERIP), and as the Micronesia representative for Seacology, an organization that issues grants to communities involved in conservation. The need for all of those titles escaped me, but it certainly helped to answer Shaun's question regarding where at least some of the funds came from. There was, however, one title that certainly seemed to suit Simon best.

"I'm a gentleman pearl farmer," he liked to say in a self-effacing reference to the pearls he also cultivated as a side hobby.

Shaun thought long and hard about the previous jobs and titles he once held. "I once drove an ice cream truck," he finally said. "That job sucked."

It was still dark out the next morning when Simon and Shaun picked me up. We were getting a jump on the morning so that we could have the corals neatly packed and sent on the day's only plane out of Pohnpei. Dawn broke as we reached MERIP. In the early morning light the grounds had more the look and feel of a Columbian drug cartel than an institute as the jungle buzzed with helpers readying air guns and plastic wrap in preparation for the shipment. The product: pure homegrown coral with a street value up to 25 times its original price. The purchaser: strung out dentists who would pay that price. Dentists need coral; oh, how they crave the coral for their aquariums.

On that day we were preparing to ship 2,300 pieces. Simon would sell the coral, at $3.50 apiece, to a purchaser in the Marshall Islands who would then sell them, at about $12 apiece to a huge aquarium company in Florida. That company would have to pay clearance fees to the U.S. Fish & Wildlife Department, and thus would up the price to $25 - $30 per coral for pet stores throughout the country, who would then offer them to consumers at $50 - $75 apiece.

"It's called the value chain," Simon said.

Polyp tip: larger companies like PETCO work directly with large distributors and thus keep the price at $25 - $30 per coral. Most companies, including PETCO, also now only buy coral that is farmed and not stolen from the wild. Simon, who only works on managed farms outside of marine protected areas, added that more and more consumers are becoming environmentally savvy and asking for farmed coral – score points for the dentists.

Simon was particularly excited about this shipment as it included two new corals he had been working on; one that radiated a vibrant green color and the other a dark blue.

"Where do the brown ones go?" Shaun asked.

"There is no 'brown' in the marine ornamental trade," Simon corrected. "We tell them they're gold."

We worked throughout the morning wrapping the soft coral in moistened paper towels and placing them into crates, 15 per bag. When they were finally all packed, we rushed to the airport, filled out the proper paperwork, and let out a satisfied sigh as the plane flew out over the crystalline blue waters of the Pacific.

Back at MERIP later that evening, we stood at the water's edge and watched the rusty orange sun disappear into the water. "Beautiful," I said.

191

"Movie directors like to call this the magic hour as it's one of the best times to film."

"It is beautiful," Simon said. His gaze, however, was not on the sunset, but deep into the water below.

"We call it the crepuscular hour," he said. "It's the hour right after dawn and dusk when all of the crustaceans and sea life like to feed."

"You're weird, Simon," I said.

"I know," he replied, "and thank God for that."

As life giving and sustaining as it was, the reef also had a malicious, dark side to it. Ancient mariners often told tales of its treachery and lord knows I certainly could attest to its temperament as well. However, thanks to the environmentalists, it wasn't politically correct to speak ill of it anymore.

"I'm on to you," I said to the yellow and dull green coral flashing by as we skimmed over the vast array of life just beneath the smooth, glassy surface of the water. Diverse, fragile ecosystem my ass. The reef was indeed a living entity and didn't just defend itself, it outright provoked me. Just ask my boat, the QE V. Never mind Shark Week, they ought to have Reef Week or better yet, When Reefs Attack.

I don't know; maybe I was taking it too personally, but how could I not? There was a natural correlation between the two – the reef and my boat had become one, too often literally. Scientists call this process symbiosis, but I saw nothing mutually beneficial with the arrangement.

Fortunately, as we sped into the Ahnd Atoll lagoon, we were not on my boat, we were on Johnny David's boat and, since he was a Pohnpeian, the reef had no quarrel with him. Instead of throwing his anchor, he moored the vessel to a buoy and the reef breathed a sigh of relief. We readied the snorkeling gear with our friends accompanying us on the trip and dropped into the water. Down below, the coral watched, and waited.

Located a short eight miles southwest of Pohnpei, Ahnd Atoll was THE ideal island setting you dream about and arguably one of the most breathtakingly beautiful places on Earth. The vibrant, luxuriant atoll pulsated with brilliant color. The sky was bluer, the jungles greener, and the pristine white sandy beaches lined with swaying coconut palms slipped into emerald waters that absolutely shimmered. Best of all, the atoll remained undeveloped and very nearly untouched by humans. Because of this, the reefs were absolutely teeming with marine life scurrying about in water so clear you had to remind yourself to breathe through your snorkel. Orange and white clownfish weaved around fluorescently flamed angelfish, while a zebra lionfish, its pink gills forming an odd mane over its forehead, swam through a school of blue-green chromis.

The 80-degree water temperature was an ideal breeding ground for the more than 500 species of coral found in Pohnpei, the most common of which were the stag horn coral and the brain coral which, with its bulbous pink ridges and veins perfectly fit the name bestowed upon it.

Perhaps due to all of this natural beauty, Devon finally overcame her fears and jumped in, snorkel gear and all. We were happy for her … for about two seconds, as an abnormally strong current swiftly swept her and Tess toward a patch of mustard colored coral only two feet below the water's surface at the edge of the reef. This would be the bad coral; the red-light district of the reef, the neighborhood where no self-respecting polyp would dare venture late at night. Although known as fire coral, they technically were more closely related to jellyfish and other stinging anemones, and contain tiny tentacles that protrude from the surface and scrap the skin causing an immediate and intense burning sensation.

Several summers of expensive swim lessons apparently taught Devon to panic and scream and thrash about in the water as if she were going over the edge of Victoria Falls. This then caused Tess to panic and scream and thrash about in the water as they edged closer to the reef. Being the ever-vigilant parent, I had my head down in the back of the boat trying to put my fins on and was yelling at the kids to stop making all that racket. No help there. Luckily, Bette was able to reach Tess and our good friend Joanna reached Devon just as they were swept onto the reef. In true hero fashion they turned their bodies to protect the kids while they were raked over the fire coral. Yowww! Johnny dove in and rescued the kids, allowing Bette and Jo to swim back to the boat. As they boarded, I finally secured my snorkel, mask and fins in time to stand up and ask, "So what's all this then?"

Bette and Jo were in an extreme amount of pain as an ugly red rash spread across the backs of their thighs. The recommended treatment included a topical acetic acid (vinegar), ibuprofen and copious amounts of alcohol. That last prescription was suggested by Jo herself and although she wasn't a doctor, she was a lawyer and we figured that was close enough.

Devon stared at Jo's wounds in a state of shock. It would be another year before she would even consider entering the water again. Final score: Polyps – 4, Humans – 0.

We headed further down the lagoon and set up camp in a jungle clearing just off the sandy banks of one of the islets. The entire atoll was owned by the Nanpei family of Pohnpei, and visitors were allowed to stay as long as they liked for a fee of about $60 per person which included the boat ride to and from the atoll. No clue as to why it was named Ahnd other than it was done so by a Russian captain, Fedor Lütke, while on a scientific journey around the world in 1828. The atoll is also popularly but erroneously spelled *Ant*, perhaps because the 13 small islets contain just 0.72 square miles of land and are dwarfed by an enormous lagoon almost 29 square miles in diameter.

Somewhere around the fourth gin and tonic the pain subsided and both Bette and Jo were happy again. Maggie, Devon and Tess explored the tiny islet while Jo's husband, Ben, and I got the fire going. As usual, Uta, Steve, Simon and Tanya, a World Teach volunteer, were arguing over

Scrabble, a game where cheating is not only tolerated, but rewarded with points.

"It's not a word," Uta protested.

"Look it up," Tanya, our young, well-traveled and general know-it-all friend demanded.

Sure enough, the Scrabble bible described "za" as being acceptable slang for "pizza." Since Tanya was using the letter 'z' and it was on a "septuple word score," she ended up with something like 842 ½ points for the word. She later pulled out "ta" as in "ta ta" goodbye. Again, an official Scrabble word. A wonderful vocabulary builder, that game.

While they argued on into the evening, Johnny, our driver, and I ventured into the jungle in search of the giant coconut crab – the largest land-living arthropod in the world, with a body length of up to 16 inches, a weight of up to 9 pounds, and a leg span of more than 3 feet. Also known as the robber crab or the palm thief, the coconut crab has been known to climb tall palm trees to cut the coconuts down. If the coconut doesn't break on a rock below, the crab will grab it with its claw and carry it back up a tree to drop it again. They often descend from the trees by falling, and can survive a fall of at least 15 feet unhurt.

The crab will then use its powerful claws to rip off strips, always starting from the side with the three small circles found on the outside of the coconut. Once the pores are visible, the coconut crab will bang its pincers on one of them until they break. Afterwards, it will turn around and use the smaller pincers on its other legs to pull out the white flesh of the coconut. Sometimes it can take several days before the coconut is opened.

It wasn't long before we came upon trails in the sand around the base of a coconut palm and saw shredded coconut husks lying about. One was

Hotel Nowhere, Ahnd Atoll

close by. Johnny pointed to a dead branch on a tree about ten feet away. "That's exactly where I'd be if I were him," he said, taking the wooden handle of his machete and tapping it along the branch – hollow, hollow … clunk! He hacked with his machete until the outer portion of the dead branch fell away just past the "clunk" and then stuck his hand in. We heard movement.

"Are you crazy?" I asked incredulously.

"Oh, he's in there alright," he said pulling his hand out. He grabbed a short, stout stick and thrust his arm back inside. SNATCH, the crab grabbed the stick and, as they're wont to do, wouldn't let go. Johnny yanked and yanked and, wedging his machete inside the branch for leverage, finally pulled out a beautiful aqua blue coconut crab with a claw span of about two feet.

I wondered how I went from admiring his beauty to helping Johnny cook him on an open fire, but the ugly truth was that it wasn't as hard as it should have been. Sure, there were reservations and plenty of guilt, but I have to tell you I've never tasted meat more savory and succulent in my life. Johnny also showed us how to use the juices in its abdomen as a dipping

196

sauce, which gave the meat an even richer coconut flavor. God, could I be any more indifferent to life? Crab killer, destroyer of reefs. Oh, I was going to hell alright; no doubt about that.

That night a full yellow moon rose out of the ocean and revealed an odd, crescent sandbar about two yards wide, arcing from our islet out into the lagoon and over to the islet about 75 yards across the channel from us – a direct pathway to Pahnuhn Ahnd, better known as Ghost Island. Where had the surreal bridge come from and why was it only visible by the light of the full moon? The answer was easy. The Pohnpeian spirit world was densely populated with *eni,* the island's all-embracing word for spirits, gods, ghosts, and demons and it was common knowledge that Ahnd Atoll was one of the sacred places where the *eni aramas* (spirits of the dead) would gather to dance and make general merriment. Johnny said he knew people who swore they heard tortured moans and saw mysterious lights on that particular islet and that no Pohnpeian would ever spend the night there.

The moonlight cast an iridescent glow on the small silver waves lapping onto the strange sandbar as we slowly made our way over. When we stood on Pahnuhn Ahnd's ghostly shores, however, the only moans and mysterious lights we heard and saw came from the kids who, flashlights and sticks in hand, decided to "attack" the islet. The tortured ghosts beat a hasty retreat and soon after, so did we to make our own merriment back at the camp.

Several months later Bette and I decided to celebrate our wedding anniversary in style and had Johnny David drop us off on Ahnd where we had the entire atoll to ourselves for the weekend. After adjusting a few bent tent poles, starting and restarting the fire and, in the process, surviving several attempts to vote me off the island, I finally got the camp where I thought it should be and we settled in; nothing but a raging bond fire, lobster, several bottles of champagne, and the two of us on a deserted island.

Now that's how you celebrate an anniversary.

197

The weekend flew by and soon Johnny arrived, ready to whisk us back. Before we left the lagoon, however, we had him stop the boat so we could dive into the emerald waters and view the spectacular, and dangerous I might add, coral one last time. Ten minutes into our swim, however, Johnny motioned for me to come to the boat. "I have to show you something," he yelled. "Come in quick; you've got to see this." I swam over and hoisted myself aboard. He then went to the back of the boat and waved Bette in. "Come on Bette," he said calmly. "Atta girl." As he reached down for her hand, he smiled at me and nodded out toward the water. There, about 15 yards behind Bette was a six-foot black tipped shark, its dorsal fin above water and heading straight for her.

"He was circling the two of you," Johnny said. "When I saw the circles becoming tighter and his body turning inward, I knew it was a sign of aggressive behavior and not just curiosity."

Bette and I just stood there with our mouths open, unable to speak. We watched the shark glide past the boat and dive back down into the depths again. It was indeed a majestic and beautiful creature to behold, but secretly I was hoping it would scrape against some fire coral on the way down.

Chapter 15

At Home Abroad

Life begins at the end of your comfort zone.
~ Neale Donald Walsch

Flies are a bad sign. They are primary indicators of filth and contamination. There is nothing redemptive about them. They do not sing, transfer pollen, or weave silk. They do not display vibrant colors or transform into butterflies. They are monochrome and infectious. They swarm all over your food even, as I learned firsthand on the outer islands, when that food is already in your mouth. Flies are evil omens from hell. If you see flies in a movie you are more than likely watching *The Amityville Horror* or *The Exorcist*. They are harbingers of death, which, again, is a bad sign.

That is why, as I strolled down the path in front of our house on a clear blue sunny day, the deafening drone coming from the jungle just beyond had me stop dead in my tracks. I pushed my way in a few feet but the swarm and the smell had me beating a hasty retreat. Something had died, that was for sure. Judging by the thousands of flies, I guessed it was either a human body or a large … dog.

"Have you seen Yoshi?" the kids asked when I reached our house.

"Uh, no," I replied. The nausea in my stomach began to grow. "Why?"

"We haven't seen him for a few days," Devon said then, having already put two and two together, added, "and you know what that means."

"He was eaten," Tess said as a matter of fact. "His carcass was probably just dumped somewhere."

With Mali and Jamaica gone after Damian and Mary left, Yoshi was the last of the original howling dog pack. The doggie dynasty had officially come to an inglorious end. The kids, while still hoping for the best for Yoshi, already knew to expect the worst and merely continued playing jump rope. They were getting the full "cycle of life" education on the island, complete with actual demonstrations.

"Come here, you gotta see this," Devon called out from our kitchen. "Two geckos are fighting."

Tess and I came running over. Sure enough, one gecko had another gecko by the neck. However, things took a rather interesting turn when he then twisted around, mounted her from behind and began pumping his hips.

"Oh gross," Devon said turning away. "They're mating."

Killing something by crushing its neck apparently was cool but having sex was, well, just gross.

"Is that how babies are made?" Tess asked.

"Yes, well, no, um, sort of," I stammered, adding, "There's a lot more involved." Of course, there really isn't, but it was a little too soon to go through that whole "the birds and the geckos" talk. Luckily, Devon, who was already outside, called for Tess to join her and she quickly scampered up the stairs and out the door.

Later that week, another unfortunate and untimely death had us bowing our heads. The violence from the reptile/bug gang wars had escalated and, alas, the big bug was no more. Yes, Barkley bit it. I found him upside down in a bowl of tomato soup left out overnight, an obvious sign that it was the work of the Gordon Gecko family who sent him to sleep with the tomatoes. It wasn't long before the cockroaches retaliated. The next morning two geckos were found squished in the hinges of the kid's bedroom door, although that may have had more to do with the constantly slamming of the doors than the work of the cockroaches.

A tremendous transition in our little insect world was taking place. When Gordon went into hiding after the hit on Barkley, the army ants quickly took over kitchen cabinets 2, 3 and 4 with alarming precision, the spiders ran rampant on the ceiling, and the termites rained sawdust down onto the counter on a daily basis. Also, some curly, furry, purple centipede looking thingy had arrived on the scene. If thousands of years of self-preservation and survival instincts have taught us anything it is that you never ever mess with a curly, furry, purple centipede looking thingy. It appeared the reign of the geckos and the cockroaches had come to an end along with the Mali/Jamaica/Yoshi Dynasty.

Our dog Buddy's reign almost came to a premature end as well. Devon and I were folding clothes upstairs when we heard a deep unnatural growl and the snapping of teeth followed by an unearthly scream. We flew down the stairs to find Tess with blood streaming down her face. Apparently, she had been playfully wrestling with Buddy and rolled onto his hind leg, already sore from a previous scrape with the wild pack outside. Buddy reacted by biting her, but not just a nip or your typical bite. He literally placed his mouth over her entire face; a bottom tooth penetrating below the right side of Tess 'mouth and a top fang piercing her skin only a quarter of an inch past her left eye. She continued to scream.

Animal behaviorists would point out that Buddy was merely reacting to a "stressor" and that biting is a natural and normal means of canine communication and defense. You can manage this by implementing a comprehensive behavior modification program and remember, they'd add, never discipline a dog with physical force.

I made a mental note to begin implementing that comprehensive behavior modification program right after sending the tennis racket across the room, hitting Buddy square in the head and sending him yelping out the back door.

A trip to the hospital and a few stitches later, Tess was back and pretending to be mad at Buddy. "I thought you loved me," she scolded. That evening the two were right where they usually were, on the floor in front of the TV sleeping on top of each other.

While we all had our moments of strain on Pohnpei, for some reason the island continued to take a particularly hard swipe at Tess. This, however, drew the family even closer together as we circled our wagons to protect her from bites, bugs and bullies. Devon now included her in all play dates and kept a watchful eye while on the school playground, her friends Sarah and Anya rallied around her, Bette and I took her with us everywhere we went and, despite the bite, she and Buddy continued to be inseparable. Every evening we played card and board games, and every night we'd all crawl into bed to read books and make up the continuing adventures of Noved and Sset. Finally, with the lights off, I'd play my guitar until both her and Devon drifted off to sleep.

Tess was nothing if not resilient and it wasn't long before her infectious laugh filled the room again, just in time for the holidays.

On Christmas Eve, Bette and I sat on the balcony enjoying a bottle of wine with a warm breeze blowing across the Nett River and a spectacularly huge, yellow full moon rising over the bluff directly in front of us. Downstairs, the kids were putting the finishing touches on the lopped off top of a pine-like tree that grew near their school. Not exactly a Christmas tree, but close enough. Despite their best efforts hanging homemade cutout paper ornaments on the spindly branches, it still looked like a Charlie Brown tree. Good grief. Even the Mallarme compound was festively decorated with blinking red and green lights to celebrate the season.

All the world seemed to truly be at peace. That peace, however, ended as soon as I entered the kitchen.

A full moon usually meant lobsters were available as the bright moonlight made it easier for the local fishermen to snatch them from the reef. With lobster selling at only $1.25 per pound, all I needed each month was $10 and a stick of butter to make me the happiest man alive. Unfortunately, as it was Christmas Eve, an earlier trip to the market revealed the *men wai* had already wiped out every available lobster. However, the Pohnpeians were quick to point out the mangrove crab was the real delicacy on the island. These weren't your rinky-dink Blue Point crabs. They were huge with the larger females measuring a good nine inches across and seven inches in length, chock full of mouth-watering succulent meat. With that in mind I bought a few and prepared myself for battle.

The first thing you need to understand is that this isn't like doing away with some small, simpering shellfish. Due to their size, mangrove crabs are more like large animals, monsters from the deep, and they don't take kindly to someone coming at them with a knife. You can't just kill them by dipping them into a pot of boiling water. No, you have to look them in their beady little eyes and stab them to death before cleaning and cooking them as you please.

David Reside, a professional crab eater himself, made the preparation sound easy and "humane" when he had earlier instructed me to insert the knife about two inches behind the crab's eyes and just push it through. A fun-filled holiday activity for the whole family. I positioned the knife just so, and BAM, brought it down right between the eyes. Nothing, not even a little crab scream. I turned and twisted the knife, however it didn't even show the first signs of dying.

This was murderer, pure and simple, and on Christmas Eve no less. I wrestled with the crab, stabbing it relentlessly while a children's choir sang comforting carols on our radio in the background. "Silent night…" Down came the knife. "Holy night…" Stab, stab, stab. "All is calm…" Die already, DIE! Just then, in a desperate act of self-preservation, the crab snapped the rubber band ties and, I swear this is true, actually grabbed the knife with both its claws in an attempt to pull it out. The sight made me nauseas but I knew I had to put it out of its misery. Like some lunatic from a bad Halloween movie, I yanked the knife from its claws and slammed it down into the crab, two, six, ten times, sending a mysterious yellow liquid spraying everywhere. Finally, it slowly dropped its claws. "Sleep in heavenly peace you son of a bitch," I roared victoriously while still holding the knife high in the air, the sweat and crab juice pouring down my face. That's when I suddenly noticed Bette and the kids in the kitchen with their mouths open, slowly backing away from me.

With three more crabs to take care of, I decided to play it safe and enlist the Mallarmes for help. Mrs. Mallarme called out in Pohnpeian and Melinda set her sakau aside to assist. Back in our kitchen, she simply flipped the next crab over and thrust the knife into its underbelly at the spot where the inner tip of the tail met the body of the shell. With the crab still kicking, she ripped the shell open and started pulling the legs off. All three crabs were decimated within seconds. Fast, efficient and emotionless.

"They're best when they're boiled or steamed with coconut milk," she advised before leaving.

The Christmas Eve appetizer was served, although I vowed the following year I'd just get a jar of dates.

Other than the screaming crabs, Christmas remained relatively quiet. With limited resources the kids really only had a few presents to open and, surprise, they were just fine with that. To a great extent, the island life was having a positive effect on them regarding expectations, what truly was important, and just what they could and couldn't live without. Bette and I let out a contented sigh knowing our kids were finally shedding the bonds of the material world back home.

"Hey, wait a minute," Devon suddenly piped up. "I asked for a Nintendo."

New Year's is a rather raucous affair throughout Micronesia with everyone banging drums, pots, pans and anything else that would make noise. The idea is to chase the evil spirits of the previous year away, and that they did – all night, every night, sometimes for a week or longer. For fireworks they put gunpowder in bamboo shoots and set them off with a deafening roar depending on the width and length of the bamboo.

That year, however, we decided to skip the celebrations and instead camp out and relax for the weekend with Steve and Uta, their kids Sophie and Maggie, and a few other couples on Black Coral, a tiny patch of an island about seven miles off the shores of Pohnpei. Another small island lay only 50 yards away. The sparkling blue water separating the two was broken by a narrow turquoise channel where the coral from both islands fell sharply into a sandy bottom 15 yards below. As the channel was the shortest distance between two points, one could snorkel on the surface and take in the vibrantly colored fish, stingrays and small reef sharks gliding through the bypass.

Meanwhile, poor Tess, dog bites covered in salve, could only wade up to her chest so that the bacteria and tiny coral bits in the water wouldn't splash into her wounds. She folded her arms, pouted and said, "I wish Buddy would have bitten me on a Monday instead of a Friday."

Our time there was spent chatting, playing Scrabble and bocce ball, or just stretching out in a hammock and reading a favorite book. It was the ultimate island getaway from our island getaway, with nothing to do but close your eyes and listen to the wind and the waves.

The family was back in harmony and life was good in Micronesia; an endless vacation, except when I was cooking or cleaning or taking care of the kids. Then it was work. I guess you could call it a working vacation. While sweeping I'd gaze out the big picture window and see someone slowly drifting by in a wooden outrigger canoe, fishing with a hand line. They'd wave to me and I'd wave back. And, of course, there was always Allois motoring his surfers back and forth to Palikir Pass, yelling out, "Jeeeeeffff," every time he passed by. One day he pulled me aside.

"When are you going to paint that shit-can boat of yours?" he asked only half-jokingly. "It's an eyesore and I have to pass it with my customers every day. I tell ya I'm losing business because of it."

He was right. The paint was peeling and, after spending more time under the water rather than above, it started to actually look like the bottom of the river. I enlisted Walik, one of Allois's boat hands, and we painted it a classy white with a dark blue trim. "Perfect," Peter, my boat mechanic friend, said upon inspection. "Now you'll blend right in with the ocean and they'll never spot you when you get lost out at sea." On his advice we then painted the hatch covers a fluorescent orange. In this case it definitely was better to feel good than to look good.

After being patched and painted, the QE VI was launched with even less fanfare than the QE V, and once again our hopes rose with the tide of optimism. The boat was our ticket to the real SeaWorld and we took it everywhere … inside the lagoon. That gave us more than enough room as the lagoon could stretch a few miles out to the barrier reef and, of course, 23 miles around the island. However, once you passed the outer reef you were in no man's land, or ocean as it were. Thar be dragons out there. If your engine quit inside the lagoon you had a good chance of survival. Squalls would whip up out of nowhere leaving me with zero visibility, but as long as we were on the inside I could slowly troll along until I found a reef, weigh anchor and wait it out. If a storm hit or your engine quit outside the lagoon, you had two options – ride the waves and crash onto the reef where both you and your boat would likely be destroyed, or drift out to sea.

That said, I still found myself venturing far out into the forbidden zone now and again to follow a pod of dolphins or a school of flying fish skimming across the water. What's life without an occasional risk? However, I rarely took the kids out past the reef.

Inside the lagoon was definitely the place to be with the family. Besides, it was absolutely teeming with sea life. One of our favorite spots was Manta Road just past Langer Island, so named for the huge manta rays which arrived on almost a daily basis at the "cleaning station" – a spot where you could actually see the tiny fish eating parasitic insects and leftover food clinging from the animal's gills and skin. Although they can grow up to 25 feet in length with a wingspan of 15 feet, the manta rays were harmless (sting rays sting, mantas don't). They'd approach, gliding up from the depths to within only a few feet of us as we snorkeled, then gracefully arc back downward only to circle back up again moments later. A wonderfully majestic acrobatic show.

Another preferred outing was to take the boat along a narrow waterway, only 10 feet wide, that began just outside the Rusty Anchor and led through a dark, dank mangrove. The kids just loved this place as the trees grew right out of the water and the twisted branches and ivy overhead seemed to form one long, eerie tunnel causing us to duck under wayward limbs in certain places.

On one trip through the cavernous swamp, I let Bette take over the controls. "Just turn the throttle a tiny bit and feel yourself slowly glide along," I said. With that she turned it full throttle and I flipped right over the back of the boat, landing in the murky waist-deep water. "Release the throttle," I yelled, pulling seaweed off my face. "Release the throttle." The boat continued on and disappeared around a bend. She can say what she likes about it being her first time, but I just knew she did that on purpose.

207

The mangrove was one of our favorite trips and reminded me of being down the Bayou. Around every bend I always expected to see a barefoot Cajun playing a banjo over on the bank. Once through the mangrove it was a straight shot to Palikir Pass where we would spend the afternoon snorkeling (sans Devon thanks to the fire coral).

On the way home we'd always weave around the commercial fishing boats and pretend to attack the huge gray tuna ships. Certainly, they were up to no good. Yet day after day these monoliths sat silently, stoically in the water as if they had nothing at all to do with the fish around Pohnpei and throughout the Western Pacific disappearing by the megaton.

Our free time also afforded us the opportunity to become a real part of the community, taking part in local Pohnpeian feasts or just hanging out with the Mallarmes. I attended lunches, traded recipes and even played Mahjong with the other moms. Sure, the gossip flew and it got pretty petty at times, however it was important to overcome most of the social slights; you had to on a small island. It seemed there were always get-togethers on the weekdays and parties on the weekends.

Of course, we had also come to appreciate all things Australian. On Anzac Day, the national day of remembrance to honor members of the Australian and New Zealand Army Corps (ANZAC) who fought at Gallipoli in Turkey during World War I, we'd attend the traditional "gunfire breakfast" (coffee with rum) which occurred shortly after the early dawn ceremony and recalled the breakfast taken by many soldiers before facing battle. The gunfire breakfast would then spill over to a gunfire brunch (less coffee, more rum) and a gunfire lunch (just rum), but it was truly an honor to be a part of that occasion. We'd also commemorate Labour Day, Boxing Day and Foundation Day; honor the Queen's Birthday; and observe Canberra Day as well as Australia Day. Some of our favorite occasions, though, were the impromptu get-togethers at the Australian Ambassador's residence; posh affairs requiring a polo shirt and clean shorts.

208

The ebb and flow of the island continued and, sadly, the Reside's Peace Corps tour came to an end. While we would surely miss them (and their wonderful parties), our biggest concern was how Tess would adjust sans Sarah and Anya, her constant companions. Fortunately, by this time the kids had made a number of new friends, both local and expat, and if they weren't playing over at the Australian Navy compound with Skyla and Zara, two new friends, they were at the Finnen's or over at the Adams 'compound.

We were now officially a part of the island, but more importantly the island was a part of us. We were home. Island life had become routine – not normal mind you (it would forever remain anything but) – and the family unit was tighter than ever. I was yelling less and cooking and cleaning more efficiently. Or maybe I was yelling more efficiently and cooking and cleaning less. No matter, for the time being, peace and harmony reigned.

Chapter 16

Moby Marlin

The gods do not deduct from man's allotted span the hours spent fishing.
~ Babylonian Proverb

Dawn approached the Australian Navy compound. The morning light nudged the black sky awake and a warm breeze blew as the sleepy Nett River drifted silently out to sea. Birdcalls slowly filled the air and were soon joined by those of humans.

"Ok, we ain't here to fock spiders," Johnny said with his thick Australian accent as he bound across the dock. "Let's get fishin'."

I looked over at Steve, his navy mate, and silently mouthed the question, "fock spiders?" He looked just as perplexed as me but merely shrugged his shoulders and continued untying the boat.

It was 6 a.m. and while Steve chugged an orange juice, Chris "Johnny" O'Keefe was already dragging on his third cigarette of the day. Their sturdy builds, crew cut hair and boyish faces belied the fact that both of them had already spent a good portion of their lives in the navy and the services of her majesty, the queen.

"We're not subjects of England and haven't been for some time," Steve said. "Jesus, get it straight will ya."

The True Blue, a 28-foot speedboat with twin 135 Mercury engines, was normally used for seeking out poachers and other evildoers while patrolling the waters off Pohnpei. It was Sunday, however, and that meant fishing. More specifically, it meant yet another attempt at hooking the big fish, the ultimate trophy – the mighty marlin. For the past two years Johnny had heroically tried, and failed, to reel one in. Correction: he reeled several in but, for one reason or another, failed to actually haul them over and into the boat. Funny thing – fishermen love to hear a good fish story, but most actually require the fish to be hoisted and photographed on the dock before considering it "caught." In that regard they're a skeptical lot, adhering only to 'seeing is believing' theorem. Time after time, Johnny returned to tell the tale of how either the marlin unhooked itself, his line snapped, or they lost it as it thrashed about alongside the boat.

When there is nothing but ocean, it just stands to reason there is also nothing but fish. In fact, there were more than 1,200 kinds of fish tooling around in the Pohnpeian waters. The main fish were bonito, yellow fin and skip jack tuna, mahi mahi, barracuda, sea bass, sharks, snapper, stone fish, gobies, parrotfish, archer fish, flounder, surgeon fish, and trigger fish. Sailfish and dolphin were also abundant. None of these would do, however, as Johnny, a skilled fisherman, had already caught most of them. No, it had to be marlin. The fish had become his white whale and, like Captain Ahab, he wouldn't sleep until it was wrested from the depths of the ocean.

We skimmed past the small lighthouse perched precariously on the outer reef, through the pass and out to sea. I looked back and saw the steel grey and white tuna ships, some well over 200 feet in length and flying the flags of Japan, China and Papua New Guinea, as they sat waiting to process the days catch. To my surprise, the six ships I had seen the day before had suddenly doubled to a dozen anchored inside the reef. "I've seen as many as 30 sitting there," Johnny said, shaking his head.

Beru, the skilled captain who also piloted Allois' boats, gunned the engines. At birth, like all Pohnpeians, Beru was given a hook and a hand line instead of a pacifier. Having grown up on the water, he had developed an uncanny sense and an eagle eye for spotting fish. "There they are," he said pointing to the horizon. "Mahi birds and terns. A whole bunch of them." I looked; nothing but sky and water. He leaned over and placed his outstretched arm next to my face so I could follow his line of sight. I strained and squinted and sure enough saw ... nothing but sky and water. "There they are," Johnny reiterated with the help of binoculars.

We soon found ourselves smack in the middle of an aerial feeding frenzy. A dark cloud of birds screamed and swirled around us, then swooped down into the foaming white water churning with fish. After a brief moment, they would rocket back out, desperately trying to swallow the fish before being attacked by other less fortunate and, let's face it, incredibly lazy birds which refused to get wet. We manned our poles as the flurry of activity continued.

"Skip Jack," Johnny shouted. "There must be something big down there that's forcing them to the surface." While Steve and I stayed with our smaller lines and lures, he instead grabbed his 230-pound line and special Marlin lure. "Oh, he's down there alright," he said, jamming his rod into one of the boat's gunnels.

Without warning, the birds shot low across the dark blue water to a point about 300 yards to our left. We turned and with a thrust of the engines, forged ahead in pursuit. I straddled the side of the boat like a bronco rider and held on to my fishing pole for dear life, shaking my head after each torrent of warm sea spray splashed over us as we slammed into the oncoming waves.

Suddenly Steve's reel clicked and his line whirred feverishly out into the water with a loud "fizzzzzzz." He jumped on the reel and started winding the fish in. Minutes later the fish was close enough that we could see its bright blue, green and yellow colors flashing in the water just behind the boat. It was a good-sized mahi mahi. Johnny hoisted the fish onto the boat and yelled for me to grab the club.

"What?"

"The club! The club!"

I lifted the lid of one of the chests, found a small wooden club and slipped my hand through the leather strap dangling at the end of it.

"Don't just focking stand there, hit it just behind the eye," he yelled as the fish thrashed about.

Hit it? I always thought you just caught the fish and threw it into an ice chest. I didn't know there was a baby harp seal clubbing aspect to it. What the hell?

"Hit it, hit it."

I raised the club high and brought it down hard about two inches behind the eye. Nothing. It continued to thrash violently. I brought the club down three more times. Bam, bam, BAM!

"What are you doing?" Steve called out. "He didn't say break his back. Hit him right above the eye."

Oh, so now it's above the eye, not behind the eye, I thought. I straightened up and started to tell them there was a huge difference between those two points and that I wished they'd been more specific, because then I would have….

"HIT 'EM, just hit the focking thing," Johnny screamed as the fish began to flip violently. I looked at the fish. It had become personal. I smacked him and he went still.

"Well, yeah, he's still," Steve said with a wink. "You'd be still too if someone just broke your back instead of putting you out of your misery by hitting ABOVE the eye."

I watched the brilliant yellow, green and blue colors of the fish fade away. The colors, Johnny explained, become especially vibrant when the fish is struggling on the line just before being hoisted into the boat. "The fading is really the life force going out of him," he added. He then opened the ice chest, tossed it in, and slammed the lid shut.

Dave Barry once observed, "Fishing is boring, unless you catch an actual fish, and then it is disgusting." I had been fishing only a few times before in my life, but it was usually tiny perch which you flipped right out of the creek and into the cooler. No fuss, no muss. But this, this clubbing huge animals dragged out of the deep sea, was something else altogether. Still, I had conflicting emotions as the adrenalin coursed through my veins. It was a rush, no doubt about it; a tad repellent perhaps, but a rush nonetheless.

Apparently, there was a lot I needed to learn about fishing out there on Pohnpei. While at the Rusty Anchor the previous night I received sound advice from Konrad, himself an avid (some might say rabid) fisherman.

"No bananas, money or unmarried women on the boat," he said with his authoritative German guttural tone. "And definitely no sex the night before."

I looked incredulously over at Johnny to make sure Konrad wasn't pulling my leg. "He's serious," he said, and everyone around the bar nodded solemnly.

These weren't mere recommendations founded on silly superstitions mind you; these were hard, cold facts based on lessons learned at sea. Questioning these facts is out of the question. You don't ask why. When you're out there in the middle of the ocean doing battle with a fish, you just better be damn sure you didn't have sex or bananas the night before is all I can tell you.

215

In addition to the conventions Konrad mentioned, the Pohnpeians have several more steadfast rules that must be adhered to before and during all fishing excursions, just a few of which include:

- ✓ Never allow women to sit in or on your canoe before going fishing.

- ✓ Pointing a finger at a flock of birds following a school of fish should never be done because the fish will disappear.

- ✓ If you look back while trolling, you will not catch a fish.

- ✓ If a fisherman dreams about blood, many fish will be caught.

- ✓ If you make noise while fishing, ghosts of the dead will join you and scare away all of the fish.

- ✓ If a fisherman is aboard his boat and prepared to depart he must never return to get something he has forgotten. (A Pohnpeian at the bar said that when he was little he once forgot his lunch on the shore. "We were only about 20 yards away but my dad never even looked back. 'You go hungry,' he told me.").

- ✓ It is bad luck to yawn while fishing

Ok, no women, no pointing, don't look forward, don't look back, and no food, ghosts or, God forbid, yawning. I got it. We weren't there to "fock spiders," we were there to fish, dammit! Besides, the Pohnpeians were skilled fishermen and knew of what they spoke. When you're dependent upon the sea for survival, you better be good. In the not too distant "old days" they used the shells of mollusks and turtles as fish hooks and wove the fibers from coconut husks into sennit for fishing lines. Local fisherman also fashioned hooks from mother-of-pearl, the composite on the inner shell of a mollusk and the material of which pearls are composed, because of its glitter. Eventually these were replaced with metal hooks, but to this day many still use hand lines instead of fishing poles to great effect. I rarely saw a boat return that wasn't filled with fish. One Pohnpeian, Bronson Solomon, caught a monster 445-pound grouper using only a hand line during an epic hour-long struggle. The fish had to be towed back to shore. My guess was that Bronson didn't have sex the entire previous month to catch something that size.

Again, you don't question the fishing wisdom of Pohnpeians. With this in mind, I jumped back up on the side of the boat where my pole stood fast in its gunnel.

The birds soared over to another spot several hundred yards away and again we were off and careening toward the frenzied water. As soon as we arrived, my line sprang to life and whirred out at an incredible rate. I started to reel him in and pulled the pole back so the tip went high in the air. This helped tire the fish out. I gritted my teeth and pulled the pole back again. This fish had met his match.

"What are you doing?" Johnny said with his hands in the air.

"I'm pulling the pole up and tiring the fish out," I replied.

He smiled and shook his head. "Just leave the pole in the hole and reel boy, reel like you mean it."

He reached over and switched the reel into what I assumed was second gear, which brought the fish in quicker but also made it harder to pull. I reeled, and reeled, and reeled some more. My arms ached. Both Johnny and Steve were laughing and enjoying every agonizing second I spent pulling him in.

"Reel. Reel him in or you're gonna lose 'em."

My muscles tensed and I pulled harder. Steve took his camera out and started taking close-ups about two feet from my face. "Come on, give me that porn face," he said clicking away. "That's it, close your eyes, grit your teeth. That's it, now arch your back." I wanted to kill him.

I continued reeling, at one point using both hands to pull on the knob. Johnny coaxed me on. "It's a yellow-fin and I think this is a big one," he said, peering out into the water. The line dropped straight down as the fish came closer to the boat.

"I've got color," Johnny said. "Jesus, he's HUGE."

I looked over and saw the flash of yellow, which, despite my burning arms, made me reel even faster. Thirty feet, twenty feet, fifteen.

"He's immense. Look at 'em." Johnny grabbed the line and readied the hook. Suddenly, the fish darted left, bringing the line directly under the propeller of the motor. SNAP! My reeling became wonderfully easy, and that wasn't good.

Johnny merely shrugged. It was a huge part of fishing and it happened more often than not. "Too bad," he said and then, turning to Steve, added, "You should have seen 'em." He held his hands as far apart as he could. "More than three feet and my guess is close to 100 pounds," he said. "Would've been the biggest yellow-fin this boat ever caught."

I groaned. My first fish and all I had was a clichéd "the one that got away" story.

The birds were gone and soon we were heading off in the bright blue sunshine to Pakin Atoll, where Bette had visited the school and, more importantly, where the fish were plentiful. On the way, Beru pointed out to the horizon and said, "Ships." We all looked. I squinted and once again didn't see a thing, not even a speck. "Where," we all said in unison. He again pointed to the horizon. "Three of them, there," he said, moving his finger a few feet to the left, "there," his arm moved a little more to the left, "and there."

Steve shook his head and murmured, "He's amazing."

We came within only a few hundred yards of the atoll, which looked to be completely covered by the green jungle; nothing, not even an outrigger or a single person to be found. I knew, however, that small village with the Peace Corp volunteer was in there somewhere. The sun beat down. It was hot, damn hot and I wondered what the volunteer did all day, day after day, and how he could stand it. Ask any Peace Corps worker about life as a volunteer and the two words that come up time and again are patience and flexibility.

218

Beru slowed the boat to a crawl and the air became unsettlingly still. The sky, a cloudless light blue dome stretched from one end of the Earth to the other, seemed to sizzle in the sun, or maybe that was just me sizzling.

"How hot is it?" I asked, dipping a towel into the water and draping it over my head so that I looked like a wet sheik.

"It's gotta be about 39 degrees Celsius," Steve said looking up at the sun.

"That's like, really, really hot in Fahrenheit degrees, right?" I asked. "How about if we just say it's really, really hot?"

Steve shook his head and mumbled, "Bloody Americans." He then began the lesson. "$F° = (C° \times 9/5) + 32$," he said. I'm not making that up; that's how he talked, including arching his fingers to form the parenthesis.

"English please."

He rolled his eyes and began again. "Ok, to convert Celsius to Fahrenheit you multiply the Celsius temperature by 9, divide by 5, then add 32."

I peered out from under my turban and just stared at him the same way I used to stare at my elementary school teachers before they finally cracked. An interminable silence followed.

"102," he finally said. "39 Celsius is 102 in bloody American degrees."

Sheesh, so touchy.

As we rounded the tip of the atoll we spotted one of the ships Beru had seen earlier. It was several miles away from us, and a relatively small dot on the horizon at that, but it was clearly visible.

"They're not moving," Johnny said, squinting with his hands cupped over his eyes. "They're fishing. I'll bet my ass on it. Beru, let's try to swing as close as we can. We'll see if we can take pictures and maybe get a number."

Beru pushed the throttle and we headed toward the ship. According to FSM maritime law, ships are not allowed to fish or exchange cargo within 12 nautical miles of the island.

I looked over at Steve.

"A nautical mile is based on the circumference of the Earth," he said, "and is one minute of arc of latitude along any meridian, or about a minute of arc of longitude along ... never mind." He waved his hands at me. "It's about 1,800 meters or a little over a mile."

"Hey, that's right," I said looking at the ship in the distance. "You guys are Navy. Shouldn't we be looking for drug smugglers or something?"

Steve just smiled. "It's Sunday," he said. "We work Monday through Friday." He then pointed to the ship in the distance and added, "they work weekends."

I laughed and he continued his explanation. "No, I'm serious. We have one of the best tracking technologies in the world. It tells us exactly where every ship is. We contact the ships and get reports, but we don't have the staff to man it over the weekend." He again pointed to the ship on the horizon. "And they know it."

There had been recent reports that they also had been smuggling people, mostly Pilipino prostitutes and laborers, into Pohnpei. The Australian Navy on Pohnpei did what it could, frequently going above and beyond the call of duty. Earlier that month they had collaborated with the FSM Marine Surveillance Office and hauled in a vessel fishing well within the 12-mile limit. A listing of the stock confiscated from the fishing boat included:

Barracuda: 112 pieces
Shark stomach: 56 pieces
Wahoo: 47 pieces
Oil fish: 11 pieces
Shark: 1,766 pieces
Mahi mahi: 75 pieces
Yellow fin: 18 pieces
Big eye tuna: 363 pieces
Sword fish: 20 pieces

The value of the fish was estimated to be worth about $250,000. The month before that they confiscated 50 tons of shark from a trawler. The fins, a delicacy throughout Asia, had already been chopped off. Both confiscations, however, were a mere drop in the bucket. Illegal commercial fishing was a mainstay in Micronesia and, unfortunately, would continue unabated.

About 15 minutes after we lit out for the fishing vessel, our chase became, well, not really a chase at all. They had spotted us and the ship moved rapidly off the horizon.

While trolling back around Pakin Atoll Steve caught a good 25-pound yellow fin tuna which Beru quickly carved into melt-in-your-mouth sashimi (raw tuna) for our lunch (wasabi and soy sauce were part of the fishing gear out there). From the ocean to your paper plate in minutes – it doesn't get any fresher than that.

After lunch, a good hour had gone by with nothing, not even a nibble on our lines. Finally, Beru spotted yet another dark cloud of birds circling the water and our relaxing respite was replaced with a bustle of activity. We spun around and approached. It didn't take long before we heard one of the reels snap to attention. This time it was Johnny's line a-whirrin'. "Skipjack," he said, his cigarette still dangling from his mouth. "Not that big." He continued slowly reeling it in when suddenly, BAM, something hit his line hard. In the distance a monstrous fish burst out of the water and into the air.

"MARLIN," Beru shouted. It seemed to twist and turn in slow motion before falling down with a huge splash. My jaw dropped and all I could elicit was a silent "WOW." The small Skipjack tuna go for the bait, I was told, and the Marlin go for the Skipjack.

Johnny quickly flicked his cigarette overboard and began reeling with all of his might. We watched as the line shifted far to the right, then back over to the left. Beru turned the boat accordingly and assisted Johnny by alternately easing the engines forward, neutralizing them, or going in reverse depending on the movements of the fish. Johnny opened his reel and let his

221

line spin feverishly out into the water. He then clicked it and began reeling it back in when suddenly the marlin vaulted into the air yet again. Its sleek cobalt blue-black top and silver-white underside flashed amongst the sparkling rivulets of water and its long, pointed bill pierced the sky before it plunged back into the ocean. Like mahi mahi and other fish, marlin can rapidly change color, which become especially vibrant when they are hunting – or being hunted.

The battle raged on for another 15 minutes. The marlin was huge and, understandably, unwilling. Johnny, however, was just as determined. It was a grudge match, and not just between him and the fish.

Over the course of seven trips during the previous month, Allois had hooked seven marlins, losing four of them. The three he did catch were progressively bigger – 100 lbs, 158 lbs, and 258 lbs. I was always the first to know he caught something worthwhile. "JEFF, HEY JEFF," he'd call out, prouder than a peacock as his boat glided past our house. "Get your camera." Apparently, I'd become his personal photographer.

The 258-pounder was big enough to land him an $800 prize for the biggest fish caught during that particular Pohnpei Fishing Club outing and he immediately regaled me with the story behind it.

"We were fishing out by And Island when it jumped," he said still pumped with adrenaline. "Took one hour to reel it in. I hit him using a small Penn five-O (50) reel. The line spooled out fast and I knew I had about 30 seconds left on it, so I grabbed a twelve-O (120) reel, clipped the snap-swivel to the reel the fish was already hooked to, and then threw that whole rod and reel into the water. I figured it was only about a $200-$300 reel; not much of a loss." He shrugged his shoulders. "Anyway, it was worth it," he added, smiling at the dead fish. "Come on, take a picture, no, take several pictures of me with it."

I'm sure the photo of Allois in the *Kaselehlie Press* was still prominently displayed in Johnny's mind as he worked the giant fish. He relentlessly continued to tire it out – reel, hold steady, reel, hold steady, release; reel, hold steady, reel, hold steady, release – and slowly began winning the war as the fish drew closer and closer to the boat. "Reel him, Johnny, reel him," we coaxed. We grabbed the hooks and began clearing an area for it when the line suddenly snapped and went limp in the water. Gone, just like that.

"Son of a…." Steve didn't even finish the sentence. We stood there in stunned silence for a few moments.

Johnny just smiled. "Fock it," he said. There really wasn't anything more to add.

The rest of the afternoon was relatively quiet, but Johnny and I still managed to land five Barracudas between us. Despite their razor teeth and fierce expressions, they reeled in easier than the tuna and didn't put up much of a fight. Steve did the clubbing which was a lot less traumatic for the fish and, I might add, me.

As the sun readied itself for its daily plunge into the ocean, we headed back, quite content with our haul, and our day. Still, I had to ask Johnny how disappointed he was. He stretched his arms out wide and let the wind whip directly into his face. "This," he roared over the sound of the engines, "this is my office. How the hell could anyone be disappointed in anything when this is where you work?" He looked around for a moment and took a long sniff of the salty air before adding, "Life is good, isn't it?"

Yes, indeed, life was good. And somewhere out there, deep below us, life was good for a certain marlin as well. Johnny's elusive great white whale remained, still beckoning from the dark depths of the steel blue sea. Despite his "office" and positive outlook, you could tell that one thought still weighed heavy on Johnny's mind. He gazed back out over the water to the distant point where the fish had been.

"It'll come," he said. "It'll come."

223

Chapter 17

Happy Pizza

The formula for complete happiness is
to be very busy with the unimportant.
~ A. Edward Newton

"I'm worried about Peter," Rat said, "I think he's dead."

That troubled me as Rat wasn't exactly one to be concerned about anything, or anyone. His cigarette glowed as he sat unshaven and alone in the dark, cavernous garage, unintentionally wobbling at odd angles in his stained and torn rolling office chair. It was 9 a.m. and already the beer cans were beginning to pile up around him.

"He drinks too much," he said.

"*He* drinks too much?" I asked.

"What? Is there a fucking echo in here?" he growled. In fact, there was, but I made it a point not to play games with Rat.

"It's been three days and he hasn't showed up," he continued in his smoky, gravelly voice. "Let's hope it's just another bender."

I pictured Rat coming into the garage and just sitting there, the flies buzzing around him as he smoked and drank with his filthy mechanic jumpsuit unzipped down to his crotch. At 5 p.m. he'd suddenly realize Peter wasn't coming in, so he'd get up and leave. He had put in a day and he had done this each day for the past three days. The thought of asking around or tracking Peter down never even occurred to him.

"I'll go check his house," I said.

"Well, if you see him and he's alive," Rat said, pausing to take another chug of beer, "tell him I'm here."

Peter's house was a roomy and tidy corrugated tin structure, which lay in Kolonia proper about a half mile from the main road. When no one answered my knocking or loud hellos and "*kaselehlias*," I pushed the door open, went inside, and began looking for a body. I found one on the front room couch, motionless, but the empty bottles of 151 rum on the coffee table next to it told me all I needed to know. He had indeed been on a bender, a somewhat intellectual one I gathered from the *NY Times* crossword puzzle books piled up next to the bottles of rum, but a bender nonetheless. I nudged, then shoved him until he awoke and sat up.

"How many times have I told you?" I asked. "Alcohol and crossword puzzles don't mix."

He groaned and made his way over to the cabinet where the instant coffee was. "What day is it?" he asked, lighting up a cigarette. After watching him down three cups of coffee and being assured he was at least somewhat coherent, I mentioned I needed help with the boat again and that I'd be stopping by the garage after he got it together. His wife was sitting in their neighbor's *nahs* with another Pohnpeian as I made my way back to the car.

226

"He's alive," I said.

She smiled and waved. "I was better off with him the other way," she said.

The next day I found Peter in his garage bent over what looked like a large metal container.

"It's a galley refrigeration unit with a water-cooled condenser," he said straightening up and wiping his hands. "Built in Spain for a Polish fishing boat. It's only six-years-old but it was built for North Atlantic conditions where the sea temperatures are a lot colder."

Oh no, I thought, here we go again. Peter was always just dying to explain the intricacies of the work he did to someone, anyone, especially when the company he kept wasn't exactly the most capable of listeners.

"Who the fuck cares?" Rat bellowed from the shadows. "Just fix the damn thing."

Peter dismissed Rat with a wave of his hand and continued.

"Because there is a larger temperature difference between the sea water and the refrigerant, you don't need to pass as much seawater through the condenser to do the job. But way down here near the South Pacific the water is at a much, much higher temperature."

I nodded.

"Ya see," he elaborated, "in these waters there's a closer temperature between the sea water and the condenser. A closer temperature difference means you need to pass more seawater at a faster rate in order to remove the heat."

He gazed upon my blank expression, then took a cigarette out, lit it, and stepped closer as if that was going to increase my interest.

"You just have to get a pocket calculator and work out your heat loads," he continued. "You work out the heat that has to be removed, then add your heater compressor, which is the work done to bump up the pressure on the gas, which condenses the gas back down to a liquid at an ambient air temperature, which then goes back through the evaporator and expands. With any expansion of gas you get a temperature drop and that allows you to absorb the heat from whatever it is you're trying to cool down.

"It not rocket science," he added, shrugging shoulders, "just basic thermodynamics."

His detractors, and there were a lot of them, could say what they wanted about him (for some, getting him to arrive on time, if at all, was problematic), but the guy knew his stuff.

"I'll keep that in mind the next time I put a galley refrigeration unit with a water-cooled condenser on my boat," I said. "Which reminds me; I need help with my boat."

"Can't get to it until next week," he said rolling up his sleeves and sticking his head back into the refrigeration unit. He had a lot of catching up to do … thanks to his bender.

It was just as well since we had already planned a trip that week to visit a specialist over in Thailand as Devon needed to get her nighttime back brace replaced.

While in Maryland a few years earlier, we noticed she had a noticeable curve in her upper spine. After having X-rays at the world-renowned Children's Hospital in Washington, DC, the doctor there explained that she had scoliosis. Because I don't believe that doctors are unquestionable "gods" however, I challenged her, asking what bad breath had to do with her back. Apparently, she took this challenge personally and I was asked to wait outside while she continued talking to Bette and Devon.

The scoliosis didn't require surgery (yet) but the prescription was that every night she had to wear an awkward back brace that contorted her body and twisted her left shoulder slightly forward and far higher than her right. We assured her it would only be for a while and that it would help her in the long run, and much to her credit she took it all in stride.

At first, Devon and I were supposed to go to Thailand alone. Later, after our tickets had been purchased, we decided to make a family vacation out of it and visit Angkor Wat in Cambodia as well. Thanks to some real wheeling and dealing from Bette and the incredible value of airline miles – with 600,000 miles you get an upgrade, but only on a morning flight out of Denver (weekdays, weekends and holidays not applicable) – Bette and Tess got their tickets as well.

Our divide and conquer plan was simple in that international airline flight arrangement kind of way. Bette, Tess, Devon and I flew from Pohnpei to Chuuk to Guam. Devon and I then flew to Tokyo, where we met up with Bette and Tess who arrived on a different flight later that day. From there, Devon and I flew directly to Bangkok, while Bette and Tess flew to Manila, spent the night, then flew into Bangkok the following day which, by the way, ended up being the same day because their plane landed ahead of schedule. Confused? Me too. The divide I got, the conquer part I didn't.

My plan of attack regarding the ridiculous eight-hour layover in Tokyo was to hit the nearest bar, drink Sapporo beer for five of the eight hours, find a barren gate, then pass out and drool on the gum encrusted, green and brown Continental carpet until nudged by a kindly, snappily uniformed airport security officer. Devon was quick to find fault with that, however, so we drudged on over and purchased a quaint, quiet, 10 X 10 ft. airport dayroom at about $50 for a six-hour stay.

Best airport sleeping decision I (ok, Devon) ever made. The room was a sensory deprivation tank, a veritable black hole impenetrable by outside light or noise unless, of course, breached by children. Devon immediately began flicking the various reading lights on and off while making laser noises, then used the removable, multi-massage shower nozzle as a pulsating super-soaker death ray. It wasn't long before Bette and Tess met up with us and the decimation of the deprivation tank was complete. With Tess jumping from bed to bed, my fortress of solitude had become a moon bounce.

Of course, all that jumping makes one thirsty, and Tess kept coming out of the bathroom smacking her lips and wiping the excess water from her mouth with a satisfied "Ahhhhh." As she went back in for yet another thirst-quenching draught from what she kept calling "the fountain," it suddenly dawned on me. I bolted to the bathroom.

"Ah, Tess, that's not a fountain," I said as calmly as I could.

"It's not?"

"No, it's a bidet."

"A what?"

"A bidet, Tess, a bidet!"

"What's that for?" she asked.

"It for … it cleans your … never mind, just please stop drinking from it. It's nasty toilet water, is what it is."

A few hours later, Devon and I were off to Bangkok, leaving Bette and Tess to fend for themselves that night at the dank and depressing, yet wonderfully convenient airport motel in Manila. They jumped into the single bed early and snuggled down only to discover the bed made a loud crinkly noise every time they moved. Bette pulled the thin, worn sheet back and discovered the mattress was entirely encased in a polyethylene plastic. "Yuck, who sleeps here?" Tess asked. Bette thought it best not to inform her the regulars didn't exactly "sleep" there.

While Tess soon fell asleep, Bette tossed and turned and struggled against the plastic comfort of the bed. She told herself she was not overreacting to her fears of safety, but also wondered if the chair she jammed up at an angle against the door handle was as snug as it could have been. Hours later, still sleepless and racked with anxiety, she got out of bed and, with the forethought and rationale only a mother could appreciate, wrote a farewell note to Tess, complete with several "" I love you" lines and emergency phone numbers in case Bette suddenly died during the night from a massive cerebral hemorrhage or plastic mattress asphyxiation.

She should have kept the note as proof of her motherly devotion. The next morning, Manila airport officials gave Bette back her passport but held on to Tess's. They looked at Tess's blonde hair and blue eyes, then suspiciously over at Bette's silver/black hair and dark brown eyes.

"You say you are mother and daughter?" the official asked.

"Yes, I say that," Bette replied, the anger swelling.

He smiled then quickly went for the jugular. "Then how come she has a different last name than you? Her last name is Martin, yours is Neason."

Bette remained calm. "Listen, I understand child trafficking is something you have to watch for and I do appreciate your checking, but this is my child and we're now late for our flight. To answer your question, I never changed my name after I got married."

"Why not?" he asked, positioning himself between Bette and Tess.

At this point you could hear the air being sucked out of the airport and, if I were there, I would have whispered to the officer, "I wouldn't push this if I were you" and then I would have run away very fast.

"Why not?" Bette asked back through gritted teeth. "Because it's none of your business why not."

"You should have a birth certificate," he said, clearly getting agitated himself.

Bette put her hands on her hips and moved to within inches of him. "Well, I don't have a birth certificate. I gave you both our passports, which is all I do have. This is my child. MY CHILD! I want an American Embassy official right now. Get on the phone and call the American Embassy NOW!"

It was good they were being vigilant. It was just bad they were being vigilant with Bette and Tess as the departure time approached.

The official called several airport managers over and they conferred. A good 20 minutes passed. Finally, one of them looked at her ticket and said, "Wait a minute. She's in transit and hasn't stayed in Manila for any length of time." He turned to Bette. "You can go."

They ran to the gate and just made the plane.

Meanwhile, Devon and I arrived at Thailand's brand new Suvarnabuhim Airport and were whisked away to the Srinakharindra Ville Hotel, across from the Samitivej Srinakarin Hospital.

Speaking of pronunciation, I had a hard time following the pretty serious national development taking place in Thailand with implications of anarchy and a military coup.

Apparently, while we were out looking for Tom Ka Gai soup, about 100,000 People's Alliance for Democracy (PAD) protesters surrounded the government house asking for the resignation of Prime Minister Samak Sundaravej, whom PAD leader Chamlong Srimuang accused of being a proxy for former prime minister Thaksin Shinawatra, who was ousted in a 2006 military coup.

Making the situation hotter, and the pronunciation harder, Samak then held a tense, hour-long meeting with Army Chief General Anupong Paochinda, police chief Patcharawat Wongsuwan and Lt-General Prayuth Chan-ocha at the Army Sports Club on Vibhavadi-Rangsit Road. Meanwhile, inside the People Power Party, Thaksin was reported to have signaled to Yongyuth Tiyapairat and deputy leaders Newin Chidchob, and Khunying Sudarat Keyuraphan that they should monitor the situation closely.

The Tom Ka Gai soup, by the way, was delicious.

Thai has always been by far my favorite food (and, I might add, just a tad tastier than the Pohnpeian staples of taro, breadfruit and yam). Flavor is the name of the game there with a taste you can actually see as the rich oils and spices swirl in your very first spoonful of soup. The exotic aroma alone was worth the trip. My personal favorite was the Yen Ta Four Noodle Soup: glass noodles with fish balls, squid, white jelly mushrooms, minced pork, morning glory and bean sprouts. Cost – about $1.50 at the corner street stand.

Thailand, it is said, is the land of 1,000 smiles. Or maybe that was Cambodia. Either way, in both countries we were always greeted with smiling faces and friendly waves. With her blond hair and blue eyes, Tess attracted a crowd everywhere we went and Devon, ever inquisitive, approached and asked questions to anyone within range, regardless of whether they spoke English or not. You can imagine her surprise after speaking to a beautiful female *katoey* (transvestite), for the first time.

After a brief stay in Bangkok we flew to Phnom Penh, a crowded city of sewage and tin shacks along fetid rivers juxtaposed against wonderfully exotic markets and luxurious hotels with beautiful fountains. It was a city yearning to establish a new identity amidst the undying ghost of the Khmer Rouge, which still hung heavy in the air.

In a curious quest for the morbid, we stayed in a hostel right across the street from S-21, the elementary school turned into a notorious death camp when the Khmer Rouge took over in 1975. It had become the Genocide Museum and looked exactly the way it did during the reign of terror with concrete walls pockmarked with bullet holes and rusty barbed wire surrounding the classrooms turned torture chambers. Bette and I took turns watching the kids while the other went separately to see the school and, just outside of town, the killings fields where two million people were massacred; the skulls, bones and vivid descriptions of torture on full display. Overwhelmed with nausea, each of us came back and quietly held Devon and Tess close for the rest of the afternoon. I must admit, it was also more than just a little unsettling knowing there was an estimated four to six million unexploded landmines still strewn about the countryside.

While fast becoming a vibrant city once again, Phnom Penh still managed to maintain a wonderful old world charm with a touch of the bizarre to keep you on your toes. For example, while we were eating breakfast at a sidewalk café, a huge elephant came bounding down the middle of the main road during morning rush hour, the cars and mopeds zipping past him only inches from collision. Suddenly, the elephant took a sharp left turn, without a blinker I might add, and quickly disappeared down a side street.

233

Although the Six Flags Great Adventure amusement park has a number of scream-filled, life-threatening rides back in the U.S., I might suggest adding a recreation of the six-hour Mekong Express bus trip from Phnom Penh to Siem Reap. As anywhere in the world, the rules are pretty basic in that the larger vehicles rule the road. Careening in a driving rainstorm, we alternated between the left and right lanes through the oncoming gaggle of mopeds and *tuk-tuks*, the motorized carts used to ferry passengers to and fro.

At first, the kids began wrestling with the "my side, your side" routine, then went through the "I'm hungry-hot-thirsty-bored-tired-itchy" phase, but eventually settled down playing "count the monks" on the side of the road and taking turns looking for lice in each other's hair. I must admit, they had become professional travelers in every way and, for the most part, kept themselves amused throughout the trip.

In Siem Reap, the temples of Angkor Wat were every bit the majestic, magnificent wonders I expected them to be. We took three days to investigate the separate ruins but wished we had more like three weeks to explore. Bette had been there before and was anxious to show us the various carvings and catacombs as we meandered about the ancient sandstone structures built between AD 802 and 1432.

On the way back into town for lunch I noticed a sign that offered "happy" pizza.

"It's made with marijuana," Bette whispered.

"Get outta here," I whispered back.

She pulled out the Lonely Planet guide and pointed to the paragraph on happy pizza.

"STOP," I shout to our *tuk-tuk* driver.

Inside, Bette and the kids ordered the regular pizza and I went for the happy.

"In fact, make it extra happy," I said to the waiter with a wink. Bette interjected and told the waiter not to listen. He agreed, but winked back at me before entering the kitchen.

Bette was dead set against it, but I assured her that nothing was going to happen, calmly explaining that while in my youth I tried countless special brownies and practically never got off on them. "It's like Jell-O shooters," I said. "A nice gimmick, but they don't really do anything."

The pizza came and it was surprisingly delicious. I devoured it. Later, after a little shopping in the local markets, we headed over to pick up the van that would take us back to the ruins. More than a half hour had passed and other than maybe a very slight buzz, I was completely fine. Nothing; a nice gimmick just as I suspected. It was worth it, though, if only to tell the folks back home.

The van sped along and I watched the ancient red rosewood trees, once sacred amongst the Hindus, sweep past my window. It was quite an interesting site until I turned and noticed Bette still standing outside the van with the door open, ushering the kids inside. Tinny, surreal Thai music – a melodic sitar accompanied by high-pitched female singers – emanated from the radio as the driver twisted in his seat, stared at me with a wide Cheshire cat grin and asked over and over again, "You good? You good?" I quickly turned my head back and forth; trees moving on the right, Bette standing still on the left, surreal Thai music, driver with the Cheshire grin, "You good? You good?"; trees moving on the right, Bette standing still on the left, surreal Thai music, driver with the Cheshire grin, "You good?" You good?" No, apparently I was not good.

Soon the van was bumping along the road. I looked up. The sky above was a vibrant blue and the white billowing clouds were cascading down onto the trees which, to my amusement, were still moving with the van. Oh...my...God, I thought, I'm stoned. And not just a quick hit at a party stoned – I was psychedelic weed, bongs-away-freshman-year-at-college stoned. Good lord, it had been at least 30 years.

My face was numb and I just prayed I wasn't drooling. Paranoia set in. Why does the driver keep looking at me with that Cheshire grin? What if I couldn't walk when the van stopped? Was I talking to myself or, God forbid, out loud? And why did I have this sudden urge to listen to Alice Cooper's Billion Dollar Babies -- the album not the CD? No, this definitely wasn't you're your normal wake-and-bake stoned; this was something far more powerful. Maybe they put opium instead of marijuana in the pizza. I could just see them laughing and high-fiving back in the happy kitchen.

Just then a relaxed feeling came over me as I remembered that I used to be a pro at this back in college. Accept the situation, I thought. Take charge, nix the paranoia and just accept and enjoy it; be one with the buzz.

I turned to see Bette staring at me, her face only inches away from mine. Nix the paranoia. Nix the paranoia.

"Anything yet," she whispered.

"Nah, nothin."

"Good," she said, folding her arms across her chest. "You shouldn't have had it in the first place."

Of course, our last stop would have to be *Ta Prohm*. Constructed in the early 12th Century, the temple is only partially cleared of the jungle growth and is famous for the 100-foot Banyan trees growing on top of its ruins, their vast roots, more than two feet in diameter, snaking over, around and through the dark walls and doorways. Bette and the kids ooohed and aaaaahed, but in my state, it was a slithering arboreal nightmare.

I took amazing photos documenting the unnatural battle between tree and stone, which upon development weeks later turned out to include 87 out-of-focus close-ups of the same tree root. I also had the munchies big time. Surely amongst all of those ancient wats there had to be a Wat Burger or a Waffle Wat or someplace to eat. Alas, nothing.

After what seemed like days hiking around the enchanted forest, we eventually made it back to our hotel. I was about to dive into bed to sleep it off when Bette announced she was sick and asked if I would take the kids out for dinner. Wait a minute, I thought. She's sick? What about me? She ran to the bathroom and threw up. Yup, she was sick alright. She didn't know my state and I wasn't about to tell her.

After splashing water on my face, which, contrary to popular belief, does nothing for the interior of your head, I remained just as high as I was six hours earlier. Again, proof that what they gave me was much stronger than marijuana. I then took the kids out to dinner – about 60 feet "out" to the hotel restaurant. The strangeness of the afternoon ebbed into the evening and I noticed we were the only people in the place. After ordering, I looked over at the kids who were uncharacteristically quite. In the stillness of the room, Devon then casually mentioned, "You know, every single thing in this place can kill you." I just stared at her. She went on to explain how the ceiling fan could chop your head off, the glasses could slice you, the chairs could break, the plates could severe an artery and so on. Strange kid, that one. I couldn't help but think, "Wait a minute, who's stoned here, me or you?

237

The rest of the trip, thank god, was uneventful.

After we landed back in Pohnpei I notice a Muslim couple in traditional dress gathering their kids to deplane. Instead of heading out, however, the youngest boy went to the back of the plane. The father shouted in Arabic for him to come back. He didn't. The older boy then tried to take the huge suitcase out of the overhead compartment, yanking and yanking until it landed on the floor and opened. The father clenched his fists, rolled his eyes upward and muttered something I couldn't comprehend except for the word "Allah."

At that point, right on cue, Devon and Tess started fighting over who would head out the door first. The man looked at me and give me a wink before turning and heading out the door; an international moment of understanding.

While going through customs and filling out my arrival form I came across the section that asked for my occupation. "Senior management executive, clerical/sales, trade/technical....ah, here we go."

I checked "homemaker" then hustled everyone into the car knowing back home there was dinner to be made, dishes to clean and 4.7 pounds (median average based on weekday traffic only) of sand, coral, and banana leaves to be swept.

Chapter 18

Attitudinal Adjustment

I can't control the wind but I can adjust the sail.
~ Ricky Skaggs

"Finally," Tess exclaimed as she passed me while I was deciding whether to do three normal loads of wash, or just one huge, crammed in load, "someone is doing the laundry around here!"

She then continued down the stairs, flopped onto the couch, turned on the TV and stared at the same Jimmy Neutron episode she's seen a hundred times, the one where he's battling a huge alien mother jellyfish floating over his house looking for her baby, which of course, Carl and Sheen were hiding.

Her comment immediately elicited three very distinct responses from me: #1. Ignore the remark altogether; #2. use it as a "teachable moment" whereby I'd have her help me with the laundry and show her how working together helps us grow as a family, or #3. stuff her into the already overloaded washing machine.

I chose response #1; while not exactly the correct answer, it at least showed I was heading in the right direction regarding fatherhood. Just the night before I was using a backhoe to dredge the wads of hair that clogged our shower drain on a daily basis – rich, thick hair I'd like to add, with enough L'Oréal honey-guava-green tea conditioner to choke a horse – when it hit me like a moldy, wet towel that had been lying on the bathroom floor for five days because to pick something up would constitute someone actually doing something to help clean our house and … I lost my train of thought. You see, that's what happens. If you get three coherent thoughts a day you're lucky. Where was I? Oh yeah … that's when it hit me – the secret to parenthood. Quit! Give up!

It dawned on me as I watched the water slowly go down the drain (symbolism alert!). To obtain true parental oneness, you must relinquish your worldly possessions; abandon your selfish hopes and dreams, and give yourself up entirely.* You must die so that others may live. You are merely the booster rocket that falls away as scrap metal after propelling the rocket into outer space (those of you with kids will understand the similarity between "kids," and "rocket" as well as "outer space"). Once you get that it is no longer about you, your next step is to tear down the decaying bricks of ineffective behavior and build anew. It all became so much easier when I finally realized I couldn't just assume respect, I had to earn it and to earn it I had to WORK! I had to look at it not as an extracurricular activity but as what it truly was, a full-time job. That's it. That's the key to being a Home Daddy.

Like any job, it takes time, dedication, determination, and the ability to quickly delete the game of solitaire from your computer screen when the boss shows up unexpectedly. You have to wake up every morning and commit yourself to the task at hand. It took me a while, but that was

---

* Offer not valid on weekends during football season

understandable. If, as Erma Bombeck pointed out, motherhood is the second oldest profession, then the avoidance of fatherhood is easily a close third. In *American Parent: My Strange and Surprising Adventures in Modern Babyland*, Sam Apple called fatherhood "the longest-running identity crisis of all time."

The typical father spends about seven hours per week in "primary child care," which doesn't sound like a lot until you realize it's more than twice as much as it was in 1965. Seven hours! Not that I need to remind you, but there are exactly 168 hours in a week, two of which the baby will actually spend sleeping.

Part of the problem, it seems, is marriage itself. According to a *USA TODAY* article by Sharon Jayson, an international study found that married men worldwide reported doing less housework than unmarried cohabiting men. In short, the institution of marriage seems to have an effect on couples that traditionalizes their behavior. "The very word 'marriage' is so deeply associated with the idea that it involves men having to do less housework," Stephanie Coontz, a professor of history and family studies at Evergreen State College in Olympia, Wash., and author of the book *Marriage: A History*, said in the article. "Even the most untraditional couples will fall into it after marriage, unless they are very conscious of it. They judge themselves against this centuries-old standard of what a wife does, which they had to do when they were just living together."

In a graph that accompanied the *USA TODAY* piece, a *Journal of Family Issues* study illustrated the average percentage of housework that men in eight countries (out of 28 surveyed) reported performing. Australia had the high with 39.1 percent, the United States was close behind with 37.3 percent, and Israel was at the bottom with 29.7 percent of the housework being performed by men. [I question the Australian percentage as my guess is that most men included barbequing as housework].

Let's face it, I could use all of the charts, statistics and cute quotes I want but, like most men, it really boiled down to me not wanting to do that particular "job." I still have my 3rd grade report card, the one with all C's and D's. Under 'teacher comments,' Mrs. Lawrence wrote in alarmingly red ink, "Appears not to try!" The story of my life and, unfortunately, it looked like the same remarks would be printed, in alarmingly red ink, in my parental report card as well.

I was determined not to make that so. This time, I would turn things around and "appear to try." No, better than that, I would get it done! I later met with Bette who quickly agreed to all of my new employment demands although, in hindsight, I really should have put the three personal days, two weeks vacation, and health benefits down in writing.

Once I got it through my head that it was indeed a job – it took exactly one year, two months and five days – I got busy. I woke up early to get the kids fed and off to school as usual, but after they were gone, instead of going back to sleep I found myself making the beds, cleaning the bathrooms, and doing the laundry. I stayed on Devon and Tess to get their homework and chores done. Eventually, they got to be quite good at doing the dishes (I was about to absolve Tess from dish duty after she broke the tenth dish in ten days but, to my credit, I felt the lesson was more important than the dishes and kept her at the sink). I also marched them out and showed them an amazing machine they never knew existed. You put your dirty clothes in here, measure this much detergent, set it on "regular wash," and viola, your clothes are clean. Bingo, a miracle of the modern world; not the machine – the fact that a nine-year-old and an eleven-year-old could, and did, perform this function with ease. Let me tell you something, if they can knock an F-14 fighter jet out of the sky on a computer game, they can handle a washer AND a dryer.

I got busy – and possessive. The kitchen was mine. I rearranged the spice rack so that the ones I used the most, like the sugar 'n cinnamon mixture and the liquid smoke, for example, were in front of the boring cumin,

242

oregano, rosemary and basil which nobody uses when cooking. I positioned the glasses so that the cheap plastic Sponge Bob cups were easier to reach and my pilsner beer glass, the only one remaining out of a set of eight, was in the deep recesses, far away from little prying hands. I put the huge spaghetti pot up front and the double boiler, again, an item nobody uses, in the back. I even had that mom look down. Whenever Bette tried to rearrange something all I had to do was shoot her that look and she'd put her hands up while quietly backing away from the kitchen. Mine!

Ok, so the kitchen wasn't entirely mine

Like the creation of the Earth, the miraculous transformation took exactly six days, and on the seventh day ... I had a gin & tonic. Order was restored, or at least some semblance thereof. With less yelling, a raucous coliseum became a house, the house became a home and, inside, the family was happy.

The transformation was later confirmed when Bette returned bearing gifts from Palau, an island with a greater supply of goods and services (as Rat put it, "They got a lot more shit over there"). The kids scrambled for the clothes, hair bands, Archie comic books and candy like it was Christmas morning. And for me….Pam non-stick butter spray. I couldn't have been happier.

I think it's important to note that I was able to do this without reading yet another bestselling book on parenting ("Although it's 3 a.m., talk calmly with your drug induced teenager and, without getting angry, quietly ask them how they feel about totaling your car while drinking whiskey with their pregnant girlfriend whose nipple ring got caught on the steering wheel. Remember, they have feelings too and need to be heard"), or getting caught up in the media induced frenzy regarding a new classification of moms (re: Soccer Moms, Tiger Moms, Hockey Moms, Helicopter Moms, The Real Moms of Beverly Hills).

No, it wasn't a book, or a parental fad, or even Oprah that turned things around for me. In the end, like water pounding away at a rock, it was just life grinding me down until I was somewhat polished. I finally got tired of yelling and no longer had the energy to fight anymore. Do not confuse this with defeat, however; quite the opposite. Instead of getting angry, Bette and I calmly took away privileges – TV, games, sleepovers – for weeks at a time and no, behaving for just a day does not win back your privileges. We finally slept through the nights and woke up fresh every day. I loved the smell of silence in the morning. It smelled like … victory!

I had my own way of raising my kids and, if you must know, I was receiving compliments from high-ranking officials. Kevin, the new Peace Corps country director had arrived and, in an effort to observe the nefarious bars around Kolonia so that he could recommend that volunteers not go there, appeared at The Rusty Anchor late one afternoon to find Devon and Tess doing their homework at the bar. Our band, Wetter Than Seattle, was busy setting up for that night's performance and, with no one else around, Joe the bartender babysat, although I'd later find out most of the trigonometry answers he gave them were wrong.

"And Bette approves of this?" Kevin asked, pointing with both hands toward the kids.

"Well, she'll approve of them getting their homework done," I said. "She doesn't have to know where they got it done." I then bought him a beer, as a friend, not as a bribe or anything like that.

"I am impressed," he said.

Another time he arrived, this time to make doubly sure it was a place that volunteers shouldn't frequent, and found the kids shooting pool – a game I might add that greatly increases one's understanding of geometry and angles – while I had a cleansing afternoon ale.

"I have to know," he inquired, "how DO you get away with this?"

The sincerest accolade came during Superbowl Monday (yes, Monday, as we were 16 hours ahead). The phone at the Rusty Anchor rang and, after a brief conversation, Joe the bartender handed it over to me. Devon was not feeling well. After picking her up from school I rushed her back to Rusty's as we all know nothing settles the stomach like warm ginger ale and screaming at the Steelers/Cardinals game (to be honest, she suddenly seemed better as soon as we left school … hmmmm). Once back on my barstool I noticed the country director looking at me with his mouth wide open.

"Not only did she know you'd be here on a Monday afternoon, but she knew the phone number and talked to Joe like he was an old friend," he said. "Wow, now I am really impressed."

A word of caution: don't try this at home. Home Daddies are trained professionals experienced in the nuances and intricacies of raising their children in a bar room setting without burdening mom with the full details or, for that matter, any information whatsoever. I like to think it's all part of "embracing mistakes as wonderful learning experiences to raise respectful, responsible, and caring children." I read that on the back cover of *Parenting with Logic & Love*, a book promoted "As seen nationally on Public Television." I didn't actually read the book, just the back cover. I find you can get a lot of useful information just by reading the covers of books on parenting; that is until the security guard at the book store makes a big deal of it and asks you to move along. For example, the cover of this book told me that according to its authors, Dr. Foster Cline, a trend-setting child and adult psychiatrist, and Jim Fay, one of America's top educational consultants, "parents who try to ensure their children's success often raise unsuccessful kids." Now I'm not bragging or anything but, believe me, I've done very little to ensure my kid's success.

Speaking of ensuring success, things couldn't have been better over at the Seventh Day Adventist school. Tess had just received an A+ on her math test and, better than that, Lydia, one of the class bullies that had been bothering her, got an F. Tess told me she managed to whisper "nice job, Lydia," before the teacher collected the papers again. Atta girl, Tess.

Devon relayed that she had had a wonderful day as well, the highlight being when Amanda Hawkins, one of her best friends, opened her desk and found a big, fat gecko staring back at her. Of course, she screamed, which made everyone else scream. The teacher calmed everyone down, then tried to whack the gecko with her ruler and, after missing it several times, managed to fling it onto Devon's desk whereby Devon screamed, making everyone else scream. The teacher flung it again, this time onto the floor where Rickson, the boy sitting in front of Devon, killed the big, fat gecko by crushing it with a rock. I ask you, how can your day be anything but great after that?

The day got even better as on the way home from school we also had Maggie and Skyla in the car along with Buddy, who showed everyone just how happy he was.

"Ewwww," shouted Tess. "Buddy's worm is getting big and red."

"Ewwww," the girls all screamed.

I calmly explained that's what dogs do when they get excited. The girls calmed down, but only for a second before Skyla screamed, "Ewww, he's licking his excited thing!"

"EWWWW," the girls all squealed as they squished themselves against the far side of the car.

"Oh, it's going down," Devon said to the relief of everyone except Buddy. "No, wait, it's back again."

This went on for the rest of the ride home. It was down, it was up. "EWWWW!" It was down, it was up. "EWWWW!"

School was working. The sex education wasn't.

"Now that you're 11, what is puberty?" Tess innocently asked Devon on her birthday.

"I'm not telling YOU," Devon said folding her arms across her chest, hiding the fact that she didn't know either. The teachable moments continued and, as part of my "new & improved" Home Daddy duties, I was addressing them ... sort of. Alone in the car with me while coming back from school one afternoon, Tess said she heard a secret from her classmate but added that she couldn't tell anyone.

"Good," I said.

"I mean no one, not even you," she added, hoping I would pry her for clues. After a few seconds of silence, she blurted out, "Ok, I'll just tell you. Ok, ok, sooooo, Destiny said that Allynda said that she heard her mother 'doing it.' Then she said that Allynda has hair down there and so that means she's doing it too."

247

Okaaaay, just a little more inaccurate information than a nine-year-old needed to hear. I have to admit, I was more than a little startled. Apparently the gecko mating ballet they had witnessed at our house months earlier, while visually entertaining, didn't provide enough information regarding sexual reproduction (then again, geckos don't have hair down there so maybe they weren't "doing it"). Knowing that Tess had no idea what "doing it" was, I simply said, "That's the stupidest thing I ever heard."

"I know," she answered.

"The next time she mentions it, just ignore it and walk away," I added.

"I'm going to," Tess said defiantly.

This time, however, I used the moment to briefly, and hopefully accurately, explain the process of puberty. The "doing it" conversation would come a little bit further down the road of life. The topic quickly changed to Devon's birthday party sleepover and I pulled my baseball cap a little lower over my eyes. Still, I had to admit the best part of being a Home Daddy was that I got to not only witness, but actually be a real part of their growing up which, apparently, was happening even quicker than I had anticipated.

"I'm now a pre-teen," Devon announced after her birthday.

"Really?" I asked turning to Bette. "Eleven-years-old is a preteen?"

Of course, being a pre-preteen, Devon had all of the answers.

"When you're dead, do you have a future?" I overheard Tess asking her one day.

"Of course you do," Devon said emphatically. "But only if you've been good; then you go to heaven and have a big future because you live forever … unless you're reincarnated."

Tess thought for a moment before asking, "Was Jesus reincarnated?"

It was getting way too deep for me, but in my defense, if there is such a thing as reincarnation, this is definitely my first time around.

Religion had always been Devon's strong point. After a battle I had with her a few weeks earlier, she stormed off to her room and quickly returned, slamming an open bible down on the table in front of me. "It says right here that you won't get into heaven by being ruthless, cruel, callous or," she stabbed at the page for emphasis, "ANGRY!

"You see, dad," she continued, now a soldier of God armed with revelational information. "YOU...ARE NOT ... GETTING INTO...HEAVEN!"

I didn't question what passage she was reading. I didn't even glance down at the page as I was afraid I actually would see my name written down there. She was that good.

"I'm practically a Mormon," Devon stated rather emphatically during another discussion.

"You're not a Mormon," I said rather emphatically myself.

"Well, I went to the temple almost every Sunday with the Elwells when we were home."

This was true. The Elwells, our neighbors back in the States, were Mormon and Devon was inseparable from her two best friends in the whole world, Sheila and Anna Elwell. In fact, before we ripped her away from her perfect life, Devon let us know at least once a week that, compared to our family, the Elwells were perfect in every way.

"Yep, that's us," Bill Elwell would say rolling his eyes. "Perfect in every way."

"They never yell over there and you ALWAYS do," Devon would point out. "And they always have family nights with movies."

"I just rented *Horton Hears a Who* for this Friday night," I said, somewhat hurt.

"Can't," she replied. "I'm sleeping over at the Elwell's."

Back on the island, Devon had plenty of religious role models to choose from. Megan, a young Jesuit from Denver, was certainly a savior to us, graciously devoting her time after teaching at the Catholic school to work with Devon as a math tutor. She also worked long hours at the church helping with administrative duties and, of course, early mass on Sundays – a feat that was particularly impressive as she often spent her Saturday nights at Rusty's drinking with the World Teach volunteers (and the rest of us expats) well into the ungodly wee Sunday morning hours. Ah, Megan, the perfect island combination – part missionary, part mercenary.

The transformation from bespectacled, hair-in-a-bun, school teacher to T-shirt and jeans rocker was solidified when she literally let her hair down and joined the band as our lead singer. She had a great voice, which meant Bill and I no longer had to screech "been a long time since I rock 'n rolled" in our falsetto voices. It was a role Megan was born to play and she played it to the hilt, grabbing the mike and belting out everything from Pink to Pat Benatar and, thank God, AC/DC. The crowd loved it and the band was back in black.

In addition to playing with the band, I decided to also go solo, playing country and mellow rock during off Saturday nights with just a mike and my acoustic guitar. It's important to have a band to cover up your mistakes, but I learned that in a pinch alcohol can do just as well. The more the crowd drank, the better I sounded; that is if the crowd was listening at all. Often, I was just the guy over in the corner playing background music. There were times, though, when people, sometimes surprising people, listened.

One night, Ron, a cantankerous construction worker who had been on the island for years, sat at the bar right in front of me and pulled his stool out so that he was no more than a few feet away. An American expat, he had a reputation for being a heavy drinker (on an island of drinkers, that was saying a lot) and not exactly the most agreeable person. He never smiled or even acknowledged me whenever I saw him around town and said hello. In fact, like Rat, whom he sometimes hung out with, I could swear he actually growled whenever I was around him. Still, he sat there nodding to the music.

When I was done with my first set he shot off his bar stool to shake my hand. "You played *King of the Road*," he said with his eyes beaming. "That's my most favorite song of all time." He put his arm around me and guided me to the bar. "Let me buy you a beer." I thanked him and mentioned that Wayne let me drink for free while I played, but that didn't deter him. "Two Buds," he ordered and Joe complied. Suddenly we were best friends talking about Roger Miller and other old time "greats." I guess music really does calm the savage beast.

Music can do a lot of things. For example, it can foster peace, love and understanding. I have found, however, that it isn't always the best medium for fostering a meaningful understanding of sex and our bodies, especially for the "pre-preteen" crowd. During a function, at the Our Lady of Mercy church no less, Devon, Tess and Maggie naturally gravitated toward Megan and began peppering her with frivolous questions. Well, maybe not all of them were frivolous.

"I think that's something you should ask your dad," Megan laughed red-faced as I approached, "and look, here he comes now."

I knew it wasn't going to be good.

"Devon here wants to know what 'You and Your Hand,' the song by Pink, is about."

I winced; the one topic that wouldn't go away. Does it ever? Thanks to Pink, I now had to delve into much deeper, darker, territory, even deeper and darker than the hairless geckos and Buddy's happy worm. "We'll answer that in the car," I said, hoping the ensuing chaos of herding the kids inside would confuse them. As we drove away I tried to skirt the issue, but Devon was nothing if not persistent.

"How about those Yankees?" I asked.

"Dad...?" Devon began.

"Boy, I'll tell you," I continued, "global warming is really affecting the reefs. Who wants ice cream?"

251

Silence.

"Oh alright," I finally said. "It means touching yourself down there."

"I knew it!" Devon shouted, high-fiving with Maggie. Tess remained silent and just continued looking out the window. And there you have it. Sex education made easy … at least until Lady Gaga came out a year later.

Chapter 19

For Whom The Bell Atolls

How hopelessly we signal; how dark the sky; how big the waves. We are all lost at sea, washed between hope and despair, hailing something that may never come to rescue us.

~ Julian Barnes

It was early evening and we were slowly drifting along with the current in the far reaches of the Pacific Ocean. This, however, was not a hazy, laid back, Jimmy Buffet wasted away again kind of drifting and even the five locals on board with me, although indeed seaworthy men, were, shall we say, somewhat concerned. With the engine sputtering and no land in sight, the seriousness of our situation had become frighteningly apparent. Raging storms frequently slashed through the seas of Micronesia at night and, without power to steer into the waves, it was likely we would capsize and drown in the dark, black, yet pleasantly warm water.

Panic began to rise with each rolling swell, sending my lunch of fish and rice, the only food available all day, sloshing back up into my throat which reduced the flow of air already depleted by my shallow breathing. I was drowning without having even entered the water.

Only 48 hours earlier, I was in this same small boat on this same storm-tossed sea and swore I would not get on again under the same circumstances. Having been dropped off on a speck of sand in the middle of the ocean, however, leaves one with few transportation options. So, in the early morning hours, against my better instincts, we set sail, already leaving a wake of mind-bending mishaps behind us, not the least of which included a ridiculously overloaded boat that turned a short, day trip over to the Sapwauhfik Atoll into a harrowing 15-hour nightmare through a roiling midnight squall.

Eleven hours into our four-hour trip back home, Captain John informed us of yet another mishap that might be of concern.

"I think we're out of gas," he said tapping the gas gauge. We were about 30 miles off the island of Pohnpei. "About" is as close a guess as we were going to get, as the boat's global positioning system wasn't working.

"Oh, it's working," he said. "The display won't light up and we just can't see it."

Captain John was young, in his late 20's maybe, and while not really a captain, he was one of only two on board who knew how to operate the brand-new Seventh Day Adventist (SDA) boat and that was old enough and captain enough for me. Mr. Benjamin, the Pohnpeian principal of the SDA school where my kids attended, was the other and at that moment he was fishing. No pole, just the preferred hand line with a hook on the end of it. As soon as Captain John made his ethanol announcement, Mr. Benjamin let out an exasperated groan and I was hoping he would then focus on the situation at hand and offer an experienced local remedy for squeezing out more gas.

"Ahhh, almost had that one." He cast his line back out. Eliciting any sort of real concern from a Pohnpeian about anything, including life or death, was simply too much to ask.

The fact that we were on an SDA boat offered little comfort. Perhaps because many Seventh Day Adventists believe the world will end sooner rather than later, both Captain John and Mr. Benjamin seemed to find our predicament merely inconvenient and remained stoically, disturbingly calm.

The amount of gas was somewhat of a guessing game because the maker of the boat, a 32-foot Penga-Marine, either didn't calibrate the gauge correctly or more than likely decided to compensate for this situation and "E" didn't necessarily mean "empty."

"The last time it was on empty we still had about 60 gallons of gas."

"That's good," I said.

"It would be except we passed 'E' a few hours ago."

"That's bad," I said.

I was tempted to ask just how many times he had been on empty, but it was a question best not answered considering all that had gone wrong, and continued to go wrong, on the trip. We were well out of reach for a cell phone signal and although we occasionally heard a static voice now and then on the ship-to-shore radio, Captain John's calls through the distress channel went unheeded. "I think we can hear them but they can't hear us," he said hanging up the receiver.

The powerful twin 150 Evinrude engines sat idle, out of the water and looking rather emasculated. The trade winds that Mark Twain told me to catch, died down and an eerie silence enveloped the boat as we quietly rolled up and down the swells. Besides an extremely elderly Pohnpeian man who had either been dead or sleeping in the bow the entire day, there were only two other passengers on board, both islanders. They quickly got to work and fastened a blue tarp from the front of the boat to the console, which served as a sail – kind of. It billowed with the dying breeze but, as far as I could tell, took us nowhere.

John slouched next to me on a cooler in the rear of the boat, then folded his arms, tilted his head back and put his baseball cap over his face as if going to sleep.

"So … we're just going to drift?" I asked.

"Yep."

I slumped back and put my cap over my face, but I certainly was not going to sleep.

After an hour of silence, Mr. Benjamin coolly remarked that land had appeared and we all poked our heads up. Pohnpei was now a barely visible thin jagged line on the horizon. My spirits rose. With a little luck we'd hit the island at some point. The winds had picked up again, blowing in from the southwest with Pohnpei lying northwest. Wait a minute, that didn't sound right. Hope quickly turned to despair as I deduced the wind and current were taking us to the right of Pohnpei, far to the right.

"We're drifting the wrong way, aren't we?"

"Yep," John replied through the baseball cap still covering his face.

"If we drift through the night, we're probably going to miss Pohnpei," I added, stating the obvious. My mind was like the boat's GPS; it worked, but the display wouldn't light up and you just couldn't see it.

We continued to drift; the swells picking us up and gently placing us back down again just a few feet along. The sky, set ablaze in burnt orange and gold only moments earlier, faded to black and the ocean before us disappeared beyond the small arc of light cast by the boat. The horizon was important to the Pohnpeian ancestors for a number of navigational reasons, but also because they believed it was visual proof of heaven since that was where the earth touched the sky. Heaven and earth were one; that is until the Pohnpeian god *Tau Katau*, in a fit of jealous rage, separated them from each other so that he could possess heaven for himself. That meant not only were we going in the wrong direction, but thanks to a rather selfish *Tau Katau,* we wouldn't physically sail straight into heaven which had been my plan B all along.

Again, silence filled the boat. I tilted my head back and closed my eyes appearing cool and collected, but inside I repeated a mantra over and over again, "calm blue ocean, calm blue ocean, calm blue ocean."

The middle of nowhere carries with it certain risks and, unfortunately, our situation was not without precedent. Each and every year, without fail, sailing a small boat in a large ocean has led to big problems out there. Three years earlier, a local political candidate took a boat with his wife and children to campaign on the outer islands of Chuuk. The boat was lost at sea. Two years earlier, another boat with four passengers also disappeared in the Chuuk lagoon and was never found. the year before, two youths from Yap went missing, and only a few months before our journey one of the village mayors went fishing off the island of Kosrae and never returned.

Rescues! I needed to think about the rescues that took place. I had recently read about yet another group who were set adrift, this time four residents of the Mortlock Islands who spent 33 days at sea before being picked up in the Marshall Islands some 1,045 miles away. "We always encouraged each other not to be thinking negatively," Denter Rickysam, one of the survivors, said.

All well and good for Rickysam but, let me tell you, if we didn't reach land in 33 days, hell, by midnight, I was going to be negative, damn negative, extremely negative.

I had Nikki to blame for this. Born in the wilds of Utah, her short blonde hair perpetually tucked underneath a well-worn John Deere baseball cap, she was perfectly Peace Corps with a laidback attitude and patience galore. "Come to Sapwuahfik," she said. "The most beautiful atoll in all of

Micronesia," she said. "It's an easy, relaxing sail," she said. "Three, four hours tops." Twelve hours into the trip I began to hate, not dislike mind you, but hate Nikki.

About a year earlier she had arrived at headquarters in Pohnpei from her site on Ngatik (nat-chik) island in the Sapwuahfik Atoll carrying only a bottle of Clorox. "Try some," she said, thrusting the plastic container at me. Peace Corps volunteers are known for ingesting the most disgusting things they can find in an effort to out-volunteer each other (e.g. larvae sandwiches washed down with bat's milk). I raised my hand to stop her. "Relax, it's only *Tuba*," she added.

Fortunately, I had heard of *Tuba*, a local coconut wine made by cutting the uppermost palm leaf and angling it so that the sap drips into a container tied to the end of the palm. If drunk immediately, the almost colorless, milky substance has a sweet taste to it. Islanders, however, have also been known to let it ferment for several days, weeks even, until it becomes a lethal, foul smelling, hard alcohol. I took a long pull from the detergent container. "Fruity with a coconut consistency and just a hint of bleach," I said. It actually was sweeter and more palatable than I thought it would be; not as good as MD 20/20, but not as bad as Clorox.

Nikki then proceeded to tell us she was on the main island trying to get a passport for Maryleen, a bright, perky nine-year-old student of hers on Ngatik who had been at the Pohnpei hospital for more than a month before finally being diagnosed with Leukemia. The objective was to get her to Manila where she would receive advanced treatment.

Despite Maryleen's weakening condition, her eyes lit up when we visited that afternoon with Barbie dolls and toys from the kid's closet. Only a week later, however, the light in her eyes began to fade rapidly. We needed to move fast to save her. Our phone rang early one Saturday morning.

"Hello, is this Jeff Martin? This is Jimmy O'Kihn. I am Maryleen's father. We need you to help us. Can you donate blood?"

258

"Of course," I said, still trying to wake up. "When do you need it?"

Before I even finished the question I was banging my head with the phone. Once again, despite what they tell you, there are indeed such things as stupid questions. Within minutes I was at the hospital with a needle in my arm. No disclaimers to read, no papers to sign, no dire warnings about hepatitis, Ebola or AIDS, and no pointed questions asking me if I'd ever been to the bad blood countries around the world. I later went over to Maryleen's bed. She looked worse than I thought. Where only a week ago she was laughing and playing with Devon and Tess, she now just laid on the bed barely moving. Still, she offered a faint smile. "Hang in there kid," I said. "We'll get you out of here."

When I went back out into the waiting room her father jumped up and couldn't thank me enough for the blood I donated. "You are family now," he said grabbing and pumping my hand. "You are like my brother."

We sat back down. Slight in build with smooth facial features, Jimmy looked much younger than his 29 years and was surprisingly talkative for a Pohnpeian, particularly one from the outer islands. He offered that his wife was still on Ngatik with their two other children, both boys, aged eight and two. I asked him what he did back on the island. "Nothing," he said, shrugging his shoulders. After a pause, I quickly went to the island appropriate question I should have asked in the first place – "Do you fish?"

"Oh yes, all of the time," he said, leaning closer. "Back home there is much fishing to be done; lots of fish. Here on Pohnpei, you don't have nearly as much. We use our outrigger canoes and sometimes go out eight, nine miles and catch many, many fish. Here on Pohnpei, they don't believe us. They say we don't go that far, but here they use small canoes." He lowered his hand so that it was only a foot off the ground. "Back on Sapwuahfik, our outriggers are big," he added, raising his hand three feet off the ground. "We can go far."

I nodded. "You use a drop-line?"

"Oh yes, a drop line," he said. "You have to work for the fish." He thrust his hands out and I could see they were covered with scars. He pointed to a particularly long white mark on his left forearm. "This I got from trying to pull in a Marlin … seventy, maybe eighty pounds."

He continued to talk about fishing and his village and spoke highly of Nikki. "We had two other volunteers years ago and they were good, but Nikki, everybody loves Nikki. She's in there helping us with everything."

The conversation then came back to Maryleen. Jimmy spoke of how his father, Lahsiano, a great medicine man known for his healing touch back on the island, massaged her aching joints. For her stomach pains, he mixed "*rempwul*," a local root, with the skin of a red palm leaf and the skin of a lemon. After rubbing them together in a piece of cloth he added one inch of hot water. The medicine was squeezed four times into a cup, which she then drank. Lahsiano tried his best before eventually offering her up to the hospital gods of Pohnpei.

"Now we have to wait until Tuesday to go to Manila," Jimmy said, staring at the floor. "I wish it was sooner, but that's the first plane we can take."

Tuesday, however, would be too late. Jimmy later told me that in the predawn hours on Monday, Maryleen whispered to him, "I'm going." She died shortly after eight a.m.

Bette and I attended the wake held later that day over in Pohnpei's Sapwuahfik community. We were directed to a small plywood room empty of furniture where Maryleen laid on a mattress on the floor, covered up to her neck with a light blue sheet. Plastic flowers were placed on her body and a small basket with dollar bills lay on her legs. Women and children sat on woven mats on the side while several of her aunts and in-laws sat closer, surrounding the body. One aunt massaged her forehead, then her eyelids in an attempt to close them.

In the midst of the crying and praying, two men entered and stood on either side of the mattress. They pulled out a tape measure and stretched it width-wise across the body, then turned and held it down about a foot from her face to measure her length. They exited as quickly as they came.

Though they tried, the children sitting on the side couldn't help quietly giggling and flicking each other. A funeral, even one for someone so young, was nothing out of the ordinary for them. Meanwhile, I noticed the Barbie dolls Devon and Tess gave Maryleen were tucked in on the other side of her body and I felt like crumbling on the spot. Jimmy came out, his eyes bloodshot from crying. Still, he shook my hand, offered us Kool Aid and donuts, and introduced us to his relatives.

The funeral was held the next day amongst the green ferns and palms on the side of a hill. There was no path, so Nikki and I made our way through the brush and under the faded blue tarp where a local priest and an elder from the community presented mass. Dress was typical island casual – shorts and faded T-shirts. One of the men helping to dig the dirt wore a Dallas Cowboy shirt with a photo of Troy Aikman emblazoned on the front. A mandolin played in the background and the women all sang a sweet song in perfect harmony, but it did little to cover the mournful wail of Maryleen's mother who lay over the coffin in an attempt to keep it from going anywhere. Hers were the deep, guttural, heartfelt shrieks one makes when their soul is being ripped away from them; the most unnerving sound you will ever hear. I gritted my teeth and looked off into the jungle.

After the plywood coffin was lowered and a few mounds of earth were thrown onto it, a man jumped into the hole and walked back and forth on the freshly shoveled dirt to pack it down. They then continued covering the coffin.

News of any death on the island spreads swiftly and within hours friends and relatives flock to the house of the deceased, bringing rice, sugar, canned meat and any other food that can be prepared quickly to serve the mourners during the night. Women will continue crying, wailing and moaning even as they prepare the food while the men, of course, begin pounding the *sakau*.

Of all the traditional customs, there are none more frustrating to Pohnpeians than the costs associated with a funeral which often can include entire communities and run thousands of dollars (a year's salary for most on the island). Fortunately, the community responds in kind by contributing baskets and baskets of baked bananas, fish, taro, breadfruit, rice, and drinking coconuts. The pigs are to be supplied by the host and Jimmy made sure to have several on hand. A quick stab to the heart, a few short squeals, and soon they were cutting them open and taking out the gooey, steamy and still beating organs – delicacies, but I was having none of it. The kids, however, grabbed some of the organs, thrust a stick through them, and roasted them like marshmallows over the open fire. They then popped the hot tasty treats into their mouths, waving their hands inches from their lips in a failed attempt to cool them off.

Suddenly the man with the Troy Aikman shirt, who was crouched down low over the pig and helping with the organ transplants, nudged my arm and showed me something golden, wet and round in his pocket. I thought I saw it still beating. "You want?" he asked. I shook my head from side to side and made a face. Ugh. Why would he put one of the pig's organs in his pocket and why on earth would he think that I would want it? A few minutes later, Nikki came up to me and said, "Hey, the guy in the Dallas Cowboy shirt just offered me this Golden Cowrie seashell he had in his pocket for only $10. I know Bette wanted one so I got it for her."

I shook my head at what a dope I had been. Golden Cowrie seashells, prevalent on Sapwuahfik but rare elsewhere in the world, are collector's items with their smooth, shiny, golden exterior and can be worth several hundred dollars outside of Micronesia.

As honored guests, Nikki and I were asked to sit next to the *sakau* rock, a privileged spot, and our names were actually brought up in several of the speeches. Several hours and *sakaus* later we decided to call it a night.

Jimmy came to Pohnpei often during the following year and we became close, "like brothers" he'd say, often drinking sakau on the dirt floor of his mother's *nahs* or beers over at the Rusty Anchor. Like Nikki, he also tried to persuade me to visit the atoll.

"Come to Sapwuahfik," he said. "The most beautiful atoll in all of Micronesia," he said. "It is an easy, relaxing sail," he said. "Three, four hours tops."

Chapter 20

Red Sky in Morning ...

The sea finds out everything you did wrong.
~ Francis Stokes

The trip to Sapwauhfik was doomed from the start.

I knew this when I arrived at the departure time to find no one even in the boat, which really shouldn't have surprised me since the boat was still on the trailer in front of the SDA school a couple of miles from the water. Eleven a.m. sharp they said. HA! Nothing was ever "sharp" on the island. It was all blunt, round, obtuse even, especially anything involving departure times.

My second clue was the amount of rice, Raman, and flour (along with the always essential branches of beetle nut) they were loading into the small storage hold. When that was filled they began piling the sacks onto the deck. It was a lot considering there were only eight local passengers, including Jimmy, scheduled to be aboard the 32-foot boat. John, our young, fearless captain looked, well, fearful. "There's no doubt we're going to end up offloading most of this," he said, shaking his head.

Eleven a.m. dragged past noon, then 1 p.m., which crawled to 2 p.m. and still the heavy sacks of rice, Raman and flour were being heaved aboard. Captain John later estimated the boat was holding a combination of passengers and cargo weighing almost 2,000 pounds. With boat in tow, we finally made our way to get fuel only to find the gas station was out of gas, not an altogether uncommon occurrence on Pohnpei. Fortunately, there were two gas stations in Kolonia. The boat's capacity to hold 260 gallons of gas had us waiting a full 20 minutes before the pump finally clicked off. Unfortunately for those waiting in line and, in retrospect, us, we emptied the gas station's tank, dredging up water, rust and dirt from the bottom of the container.

At 3:30 p.m. we cut loose from the trailer on the causeway and, thank god, were buoyant. The engines revved and we bolted out into the harbor. Actually, waddled would be a more accurate word.

"Too much weight," Captain John said. "We'll have to turn back and offload."

"Bad luck," Beru, reminded me once again later. "The local custom is you never go back. If you go back, even for your favorite lure, the trip is finished and you must stay until the following day."

Back at the causeway we unloaded a few sacks of rice, which the locals were rather unwilling to part with. In fact, while some sacks were being offloaded on the left side of the boat, I saw others being snuck back on the right side of the boat. We plunged out into the lagoon, white foamy waves careening off our sides, but after only about a hundred yards Captain John was once again shaking his head.

"We're still not planing. Let's try this again."

We headed back and more sacks were reluctantly offloaded. Since it was just a weekend trip, I had only a bag containing two T-shirts, one pair of shorts, my guitar (admittedly not the most practical item to be taking out into the ocean), a carton of cigarettes to give away (yes, yes I know, but they're a highly valued commodity out there), and a six-gallon container of gas to go night-fishing on the atoll. Since the gas container was the only real weight I was carrying, I did consider offloading it to save someone a sack of rice, but Jimmy's eyes flashed a vehement "NO" and he motioned for me to keep my mouth shut. Night fishing was way too important.

We were off and got several hundred yards out before turning back, yet again, to offload. This time my gas container went with a few more sacks of flour and rice. If this were a movie, the camera would pan back with cinematic irony to the gas container sitting on the dock.

Although still heavy and sitting rather deep in the water, the boat finally planed and we headed out past Sokeh's rock, the surrounding reef, and into the deep blue ocean – some five hours behind schedule. With all of the cargo there was little room left on the boat, and the passengers began to claim precious level space for sitting and sleeping. I settled on a 3' X 2' cooler in the right rear of the boat next to the engines.

With our late departure and the weight of the cargo it was slow going and soon the evening sky faded into black. Despite the constant bumping of the waves, the sea was no rougher than usual and I soon tucked into a fetal position for some sleep on my 3' X 2' bed. I've always been rather proud of the fact that I can sleep anytime, anywhere. Not caring is an essential component of sleep. Even the oncoming rain didn't dampen my drowsiness as I pulled the blue tarp over me and listened to the pitter-patter on my new plastic enclosed studio apartment.

A short time later I was brought fully awake by a wave crashing over me. In what psychologists call denial, but my wife would call typical, I remained under the tarp and merely tried to go back to sleep. The waves at least were warm and actually brought a small amount of comfort against the

267

cold wind and rain. Surprisingly, though, getting pummeled by 15-foot waves is not at all conducive to sleeping.

It didn't take long to comprehend the impending disaster unfolding before us. Captain John and Mr. Benjamin gripped the wheel in the partially enclosed cabin and peered straight ahead into the darkness. The objective was to steer the boat into the oncoming swells, idle the engine as we rode straight up and plummeted back down again, then gun the engine to the next swell eight seconds away.

Timing the walls of water was important to maintain some semblance of balance, and though no one said a word, you could see everyone counting in their heads. Just when we all thought we had the count down, the dark ocean twisted violently and sent a wave three seconds ahead of schedule. Gasps turned to screams (ok, maybe that was just me) and that's when I smacked my mouth against the railing. Although bleeding, at least there was plenty of salt water for me to swish around and cleanse the wound.

Usually these storms punch through, violently, but rather quickly. This one I could swear stayed put directly over our boat, and only our boat, for the better part of an hour, with the wind and rain growing in intensity. The boat shuddered with each crashing wave and I clung to the rail, now my best friend despite the wrap to the mouth.

After being tossed about for what seemed like an eternity, the storm finally blew past and the waves, no longer having to obey the wind, settled back into a soft, rolling slumber. We continued on our journey through the dark waters; the black line between sea and sky becoming more distinguishable as the stars appeared, first by the hundreds, then by the thousands. Hours later the Sapwuahfik Atoll came into view and, without electricity, appeared as nothing more than a shadowy speck silhouetted against the inked horizon.

I had to hand it to Captain John and Mr. Benjamin who, since the boat's GPS system wasn't working, guided us across the 75 very nautical miles of ocean by compass direction alone. We had arrived, but were still far from being home free – the 30-square mile lagoon was filled with treacherous reef and there was only 0.67 square miles of land to save us. We spent the next hour in the dark looking for the only proper, and very small, opening in the outer reef to pass through, then spent another hour trolling through the inside reef as Jimmy sat on the bow with a flashlight, steering us left and right. Upon reaching the islet of Ngatik, a full 13 hours after our initial departure, we anchored the boat and waited for daybreak when the local boats could ferry us ashore.

The history of Sapwuahfik is not a happy one. According to Pacific Scholar Saul Riesenberg, the atoll's population in 1855 consisted of just seven Gilbertese women, one Pohnpeian man and woman, 15 Sapwuahfik women and four men, and eight children of uncertain parentage. From this tiny number, the present population – about 400 people inhabited the nine islets – came to be. The reason for the small population back in 1855 was due to one of the most tragic incidents in Oceania history.

In 1836, the British cutter *Lambton*, commanded by Captain Charles "Bloody" Hart, came across Sapwuahfik in search of the coveted turtle shell. The crew was treated well and offered food and the atoll's traditional hospitality. That night, however, with a fire roaring and the drink flowing heavily, two of the crew aroused the ire of the elders by being disrespectful and, more than likely, just a little bit randy with the local women. A fight ensued and the two men made their way rather hastily to the boat with an angry mob just behind them. Upon leaving the harbor one of the men told the captain he saw an endless supply of turtle shell in the main hut.

With revenge and riches in mind, in 1837, exactly one year later, the *Lambton* returned. This time a well-armed crew came ashore and slaughtered every male, and most of the women, on the island. The booty – only 20 pounds of turtle shell. Subsequent British admiralty investigations proved worthless and none of the attackers ever paid any penalty for their outrages.

Despite the cruelty of colonization, the atoll grew anew and, free from further western "influence," the people thrived, living a harmonious, peaceful and, I must say, rather immaculately tidy existence.

After the arduous journey over, and passing out on a mat in Jimmy's hut for the entire morning, I awoke to the smell of a wood fire. Ah, rice and fish for lunch, this time without the flies. In fact, I don't think I saw a single fly on the island and there was a very good reason for that. Ngatik was spotless. "We're careful to pick up after ourselves," Jimmy said proudly. Pristine stone-lined paths led around and through the island and even the jungle itself seemed crisper, greener, kind of like Tom Sawyer Island, the one in Disneyland not Disney World.

The turtle shell had long become scarce by the time I had arrived, but that didn't mean the atoll was without its treasures. Besides the celebrated Golden Cowrie, rare spider conch shells could be found on its shores along with exquisite marble cone and abalone shells, naturally polished to a glimmering sheen by the sea. I didn't have to go far to get them; they came to me. As soon as the residents learned I had items to give away they stopped by throughout the afternoon with shells in hand. The women, being the smarter of the genders, eschewed my material offerings for cold, hard, cash.

Captain John and Mr. Benjamin had their own goodies to give away, courtesy of the SDA school. "What's wrong with this picture," John asked me as he opened up a box and held up a crisp 'LA Lakers – 2008 NBA Champions' T-shirt. Answer: the Boston Celtics won that year. Every year, in any championship sporting event, they make T-shirts for both teams so they can be sold immediately after the game. If you ever wondered where all of the "loser" T-shirts went, look no further than your nearest developing country. On the various islands of Micronesia, one could spy a 'New England Patriots – 2007 Super Bowl Champions' T-shirt (the N.Y. Giants won that year), or Tampa Bay Rays – 2008 World Series Champs T-shirt (the Philadelphia Phillies won that year). The islanders didn't seem to mind, but offer them a

'2007 England World Rugby Cup Champions' T-shirt (South Africa won that year), or a '2008 German Euro Soccer Champions' T-shirt (Spain won that year) and you would surely go shell-less.

Determined to make the 24 hours on the atoll a genuine experience, I went spear fishing with Jimmy and Nikki that afternoon near a small reef wall in the lagoon. We swam out holding the six-foot-long homemade wooden spear guns and prepared to catch our dinner. Macho! Well, it would have been if only I could, while treading water … pull … the long rubber hose … back … to spring load the metal spear … dammit! After several failed attempts I realized the only way I would be getting dinner was if a package of Gorton's Fish Sticks came floating by.

Jimmy swam over and, snap, the spear was set. He then took a deep breath and headed down into the dark blue water below. What seemed like 20 minutes later he surfaced holding a good-sized reef fish. Nikki did the same, holding her breath for eternity before surfacing again with a fish. This wasn't going to be easy since the only experience I had holding my breath for any length of time was on the Log Flume, the one at Disneyland, not Disney World.

I hauled in as much oxygen as I could and dove. Sure enough, there was a bright yellow and blue reef fish just below. I swam down, took aim on the little sucker and … JESUS I NEEDED AIR! Panic stricken, I exploded to the surface where my spear gun went off and almost skewered a sea gull. Total down time: 27 seconds. I spent the next hour diving down, getting as close as I could to a fish, then firing and basically ruining yet another reef (oh stop already; like you've never wrecked a reef).

Night arrives quickly and quietly on an atoll and soon the warm glow of wood fires dotted the darkness throughout Ngatik. In the distance, tiny yellow sparks of light also appeared on the jet black horizon as fires roared to life on the nearby outer islets. Jimmy's wife, Morleen, arrived with coconut water along with plates of parrot fish, crab and rice, which we

271

devoured immediately. Suddenly, Nikki stepped out of the darkness and into the radiance of the fire holding a plastic Clorox container.

"Fresh," she said, thrusting it before me. It might have just been the ambiance of the island, but that was easily the sweetest, tastiest coconut toddy I ever had. We watched as the embers of the fire rose up and up until eventually they joined the stars in the night sky. Nikki, who was at the end of her two-year tour, sighed and reflected on her Peace Corps experience.

"The kids and the peace and solitude fit my personality really well," she said. "It was easy. Teaching only played a small part of my stay on the island. I worked but really there was a lot of just hanging out. The real experience was becoming a part of the community and enjoying the people on a personal level. I've never felt more at home."

She thought for a second and then added with a grin, "I'm round tripping my ticket so I'll be back within the year." True to her word, she did come back within the year and, to the best of my knowledge, still remains on the atoll.

Chateau Niki

Soon the bottle of Clorox was empty and Jimmy and I found ourselves by the dying embers of the fire trying to get enough light to compare our scars. In addition to again showing me the multitude of marks caused by hauling in deep sea marlin and tuna, he peeled off his shirt to reveal a series of gashes carefully etched across his heart, each two inches long and a half-inch wide. "These are from when I got mad at an old girlfriend and I wanted to show her how deeply she hurt me." He shook his head. "I was young and stupid."

"Boy, I'll say." I quickly changed the subject as I knew my hernia scar from when I was four would never measure up.

Eventually, a good portion of the case of beer I brought (did I forget to mention that on the initial cargo list?) lay strewn about us and, after several rousing and unique versions of Bye Bye Miss American Pie accompanied by my guitar, we called it a night, or rather the night called it for us.

At the crack of dawn the next morning, Jimmy and a friend took me the length of the lagoon on their boat until finally we reached the S.S. SDA, moored to a buoy at the small opening in the reef. As I climbed aboard, Jimmy stood in his boat and thrust an oar high over his head. "Goodbye Jeff," he yelled. "Remember, you are my brother."

I offered him a solid salute and kept my eyes on him until he faded in the distance.

The return trip was doomed from the start.

I knew this when I boarded and noticed only one of the engines idling. Captain John popped his head up from the second engine and wiped the smudges off his face. "No good," he said. "All that dirt, rust and gunk we drudged up from the bottom of that tank at the gas station. Don't know why the other one is running, but ..." He shrugged his shoulders.

"So, once again, this isn't going to be 'three, four hours tops,'" I said deflated.

"Ahhh, probably not."

I collapsed in my by then familiar corner of the boat, pulled up the faded blue tarp, and once again tried to set up my plastic studio apartment. After a while the clouds gave way and the sun burst into the sky, beating mercilessly down on us. Fortunately, with only six of us heading back to Pohnpei, I was able to crawl into the small hold up front and catch at least some sleep next to the elderly Pohnpeian man who didn't move during the entire trip and may or may not have been dead.

The trip back was in direct contrast to the dark, stormy, crowded and chaotic trip over. Instead of gunning it in between 15-foot swells, the boat now merely inched forward, gently rolling along waves only a few feet high. "We can't strain the engine," Captain John said. "It's the only one we have." Ennui became tedium followed by languor, which begat boredom and still we lolled along without land in sight. Days passed.

"How long have we been out here?" I asked.

Captain John looked at his watch. "About two hours," he said.

I settled in the cargo hold again for another few hours and finally the afternoon came. The monotony and the heat were starting to get to me. Man, what I wouldn't have given for a good trashy People magazine. I'd have even pretended I cared about "Who Wore It Best," Jennifer Aniston (54%) or Mira Sorvino (46%).

"Hey, I know," I finally said. "Let's play the alphabet game. The object is to go through the alphabet by spotting the letters on the signs we pass. License plates don't count."

My boat mates just stared at their fishing lines. Did I really just say that out loud? I had to check.

"How about 'I Spy? I'll start. I spy … NOTHING. NOT A GODDAMN THING!"

274

They continued staring at the water's smooth surface where their hand-held fishing lines remained flaccid. Whew, all in my head, just as I had hoped.

Late afternoon sipped into early evening and that's when the engine began to sputter and Captain John made his blithe announcement that we were out of gas. The blue tarp was then pulled from my studio apartment (I was going to redecorate anyway) and fastened as a sail from the front of the boat to the cabin to at least offer the illusion that we were going somewhere.

The last vestiges of light faded behind us as Captain John, back at the console, continued his distress call through the ship-to-shore radio in a fruitless attempt to reach the mainland. The boat creaked and slowly rocked as the rolling swells picked us up and edged us forward. Mr. Benjamin and the other two passengers seemed bored, sitting on the edge of the boat as if waiting for a bus. The extremely elderly man who, at that point I was certain was dead, continued to lie motionless in the hold of the bow. In front of us, but definitely further to the left than before, Pohnpei disappeared into the night.

Amidst the eerily quiet calm, the enormity of the situation finally overwhelmed me. What began as merely an inconvenience had become the horrifying reality that we were drifting out to sea without any hope of being rescued that night – or quite possibly at all. A sick, nauseous feeling gripped the pit of my stomach, but outwardly I still tried to appear as composed as the others.

"Where are the life jackets?" I asked. "I just want to use one as a pillow."

I tried to stay positive and remembered the line from Frank Herbert's novel *Dune* – "fear is the mind killer." I closed my eyes, relaxed, and sure enough that warm, preternaturally peaceful feeling of resignation came over me, much like the feeling you get just before you freeze to death, but it was oddly reassuring. I decided to count my blessings. At least Bette was safe and the kids were with Uta and Steve who, besides naming their daughter Maggie after the baby on *The Simpsons* and their propensity for going to Rammstein concerts in East Germany, I was completely comfortable with. Also, the stars were out in full force, which meant the clouds had been kept at bay, at least for the time being. I smiled, thinking it could be worse. I mean we could be out of gas on the Beltway in Washington, D.C. where there would be absolutely no chance of anyone helping us.

Ironically, or luckily, take your pick, Bette made me take the Peace Corps EPIRBS (which stands for Emergency Positioning Someone Get The Hell Out Here NOW System), a small device that sends a radio distress beacon to the nearest U.S. Naval station. Since that would have been Guam, several thousand miles away, and I more than likely wouldn't deploy the device until we were already sinking later that night, that meant the planes and ships wouldn't arrive until late morning, in time to salvage our lifeless bodies and give us decent burials. Frankly, the EPIRBS did little to reassure me.

Captain John again tried the ship-to-shore radio to no avail and then leaned over the side of the boat with his cell phone, as if the extra three feet would put him inside the coverage area. Just as I decided on which cooler I was going to cling to in the dark, black water, John's cell phone crackled with a faint voice. It was Nahlap, the small island nearest us just off Pohnpei. A loud cheer erupted within the boat, although it would have been louder if only someone else cheered besides me. Coordinates were given, or at least the best we could come up with ("we are directly under Orion's belt ... right ... NOW"), and they promised a boat would be arriving as soon as possible. Another hour-and-a-half went by and we approached midnight, still peering into the darkness for the faint light of a boat. Nothing. The proverbial needle in a haystack in the middle of the Pacific Ocean, 20 miles off the coast of Pohnpei.

276

A few times we thought we saw a light in the distance appear then disappear with the waves, but it turned out to be just another star on the horizon. Suddenly, that same light remained constant and grew larger until we were assured it was the rescue boat. This time Captain John and I hugged and patted each other on the back. Mr. Benjamin and the other locals merely threw their fishing lines back in the water in hopes of catching a fish before the boat arrived. Pohnpeian right to the end. Also, I watched in amazement as, with a deep yawn, the dead man finally exited the hold in the bow.

The rescue boat was small, but it had several containers of gas and that was all we needed. Once on Nahlap, even though it was almost midnight, they offered us fried chicken and sushi left over from a feast given earlier and our ordeal was officially over. Another boat trip from Nahlap to the main island, a 40-minute ride in the back of a pickup truck, and I was finally walking along our front path where I was attacked by Buddy and the wild dog pack. The house was empty as Bette was still away and the kids were sleeping over at the Finnen's, but it was a welcome sight nonetheless. Funny how a stable bed in your home can roll back and forth and up and down after 16 hours at sea.

The next morning, I dropped the kids off at school and, on the way home, noticed Bette left the car well below "E." The engine sputtered. Oh good god! You've got to be kidding me. I spied the blue tarp we kept in the back of the car. Hmmmm....

Chapter 21

Death Takes a Holiday ... Here.

In nature there are no rewards nor punishments;
there are only consequences.
                                        ~ Robert B. Ingersoll

"Stabbing Death in Chuuk May Have resulted from a dispute over bananas" read the headline from the *Kaselehlie Press.*

Lois, the banana lady, would have been appalled ... and probably more than just a little bit curious as to what type of banana it was. I, too, questioned the rationale for such an act. I mean if someone were to take my banana, I would go over and squeeze their hand real hard so it would squish the banana and maybe mess up their shirt, but I don't think I would stab them to death.

Chuuk, however, was the wild west out there – the bad boy brother of Pohnpei, akin to Oklahoma's "Texas" problem. In fact, if anything went wrong on any of the islands in the FSM, it was the Chuukese who were to blame, even if there wasn't a Chuukese on the island. Aggressive by nature, the Chuukese were known to rely on the machete to settle scores, apparently even if it only involved a ripe banana.

Wanton acts of rage weren't confined to Chuuk, however. In fact, they happened on Pohnpei with some regularity. News got out every now and then regarding someone being hacked to death during an argument. One particularly gruesome incident involved a son taking a machete to his father and severing his head. Not sure if the local forgiveness contract custom or any amount of *sakau* could have gotten him out of that. Yes, they were still the friendliest and most mellow people on the planet but, alas, they were also human. There were even times when forgiveness, the unspoken law of the land, wasn't truly kept within one's heart. I was told with the wink of an eye that sometimes, even years after an incident, a perpetrator would be invited out fishing by relatives of the victim and just never come back. South Pacific justice, Soprano style.

With that in mind, I picked up Gibson, a 43-year-old Pohnpeian whom I met through Peter and who had helped me work on my boat. Gibson had the look of a middle-weight boxer from Brooklyn; a beat up "palooka" with cauliflower ears and a nose that spread across his face – the result of it being broken "four, I don't know, maybe five times." The obligatory tattoos were everywhere, including a marijuana leaf covering his right bicep, an eagle covering his left, and a small apple on his neck. "I got this one in a prison in Guam," he said taking his shirt off and proudly displaying a crudely inked spider web sprawled across his entire back.

The never-ending fights, he told me, were because, despite being a born-and-raised Pohnpeian, he was white, the result of having a *men wai* father who left when he was just three. "And, perhaps, because you can sometimes be an asshole?" I offered.

"Yeah, well that too," he said with a smile. The fact was, while being a conscientious worker and always extremely courteous and friendly to me, he drank most nights and transformed into Mr. Hyde. In the car, as he

Gibson

was updating me on his financial situation ("So instead of cash, Peter gives
me an old air conditioner, only the fucking thing don't work..."), I reminded
him that he said he'd help me with the boat that Thursday. "Not a problem,"
he said. "It'll have to be after my court date in the morning, though."

"Court date?"

"It's nothing. I almost stabbed some guy to death," he said. In an
attempt to emphasize the 'it's nothing' part, he added, "He didn't die,
though."

The car was silent for about a full minute, and just as I was
contemplating jumping out while I still could, he unloaded.

"See, I took my car to a shop owned by some guy named Sesario.
Well, Sesario takes my engine out and puts this crap piece of shit engine in
thinking I wouldn't notice. While I'm arguing with him, his friend, some big
guy about 6'2", says 'why are you arguing with Sesario?' Then he slaps me
and throws me across a table full of stinking fish. That's embarrassing, am I
right? Yeah, but that table also had a big fish knife on it. I grabbed it and
stabbed him. I aimed for his heart cause I meant to kill the motherfucker."

"Couldn't you have just squished a banana in his hand," I asked?

He continued. "Later, the detectives pounded on my door but I never
answered and they went away."

Clever, I thought. I'll bet there are a lot of criminals behind bars who
are thinking, "If only I just didn't answer the door."

Fortunately for Mr. 6'2", Gibson missed his heart by a fraction of an inch. While he was convalescing, Gibson went into high gear, gathering pigs, *sakau* and several hundred dollars from relatives, then paid him a visit with the Pohnpeian forgiveness contract in hand.

"You know what?" Gibson asked smiling. "He admitted he started it and we were laughing right there in the hospital. He signed the forgiveness contract, but I knew it wouldn't matter cause this one detective is always out to get me. So I bought a half-gallon of vodka and just went home and waited. Sure enough, that night about 10 cops showed up and this time they didn't knock."

After spending two nights in jail and posting $500 bail, Gibson remained a free man pending a trial, which had already been postponed for more than a year. He smiled and, with a wave of his hand, told me what we both already knew. "There ain't gonna be no trial."

A few weeks later, Gibson showed up at my house with a half-gallon of Lone Wolf vodka and his three "uncles." They swayed menacingly in the doorway.

"We want to take you out fishing ... on your boat," he said grinning.

This had bad vibes written all over it, however I had previously promised him we'd go fishing and, what the hell, should the boat come back without me in it, it had been a good life. Out on the boat, Gibson, his uncles and I downed the vodka, chased only by bottles of water. They then showed me how to string several lures onto the bottom of the hand line so that you could catch two, sometimes three fish at a time and soon we were hoisting reef fish, trevally and small grouper into the coolers by the dozen. Gibson kept us entertained through various out-of-tune songs and reenactments of his fights, some with the uncles on the boat.

"I kicked his ass," one of the uncles boasted.

"Fuck you, you did," Gibson said standing up in the back of the boat. The uncle, steely eyed, stood up in the front with the fishing knife in his hand.

They were drunk –and dead serious. Suddenly, the reenactments weren't so entertaining.

"Ok, as captain of this ship I order you both to stand down," I said. They looked at me, and then back at each other. "Captain of the ship?" Gibson laughingly roared pointing at me. The uncles howled. Just like that the lines were back in the water and the banter continued. Every so often, someone would mumble, "captain of the ship," and the boat would again erupt with laughter.

Back at the dock, Gibson and his uncles gathered in a circle, held hands and bowed their heads as they thanked God for the bountiful fish, the beautiful day, and for me taking them fishing. It was touching; a little bizarre, perhaps, but touching. After they had gone, I said my own prayer of thanks and vowed … never again.

I found it interesting that death and danger could come calling in paradise anytime they felt like it. How tacky. I mean, how are you supposed to enjoy yourself with them hanging around? It just didn't fit. Death, danger, paradise – one of these things is not like the other. When I thought about it, however, it made a lot of sense in a place where machetes and alcohol were abundant and advanced medical care wasn't. Living on a tropical island in the middle of nowhere was like swinging high up on a trapeze – it felt wonderful and the view was gorgeous, but every now and then it hit you that, far below, there was no safety net. You could purchase Tylenol, though.

The fact that we were surrounded by water should have been our first hint. Death and danger just love water. Precautions were usually taken, but accidents happened and people either went missing or drowned. Even the most experienced expats and locals weren't immune. Through her many travels to Yap, Bette had befriended a dive master there who always gave her and her Peace Corps volunteers cut rates to go scuba diving. Only a few weeks after I had met him, he was teaching another diver how to "deep dive" at 300 feet. At that depth, an insane depth I might add, the air goes quickly, requiring spare air tanks to be hung about 150 feet from the surface. They began to ascend but an unusually strong current picked up and prevented them from reaching the spare tanks. A second attempt got them closer to the spare tanks, but not close enough. They ran out of air, forcing them to shoot straight up to the top without decompressing. Miraculously the other diver survived. The dive master didn't.

Soon after, a young man whom Simon introduced to us at a party of ours and whom we met at a few other social gatherings went spear fishing for snaggletooth tuna. An experienced spear fisherman, he'd free-dive, heaving in a huge gulp of air before going down as far as 60 feet where, heavily weighted and wearing camouflage to hide him from the fish, he waited for the tuna. This time, however, he suffered what is known as a deep-water blackout, a loss of consciousness caused by cerebral hypoxia on ascending from a deep freedive or breath-hold dive. Unconscious, he sank to about 90 feet. Because of the camouflage he was wearing they had trouble finding him and when they did, it was simply too late. A year later, the same fate would befall another young man visiting his girlfriend serving in the Peace Corps.

While danger hid in the shadows of the jungle and the depths of the water, death was bolder and one day simply strode right up our front path. Clairie, the Mallarme's dog, was on her way over to our porch where Devon and Tess were wrestling with Doggie and Buddy when a loud "CRACK" filled the air. Clairie yelped in pain and the kids turned to see her, not more than 15 yards away, limping toward them with Maxson close behind holding a .22 caliber rifle. Apparently Clairie was to be a part of that night's high school graduation feast. Maxson laid the rifle down, then picked up a club and proceeded to beat the dog senseless; blood splattering everywhere. I was later told this was to increase the adrenaline level within the dog which many believed produced a more tender, tastier meat.

With presence of mind, Devon grabbed Buddy and ran inside screaming, "they're killing Clairie, they're killing Clairie." She then ran back outside, grabbed Doggie and locked her with Buddy in the kid's bedroom. Calvin, a friend of Devon and Tess, simply jumped in our car and locked the doors crying. Tess, obviously in a state of shock and unable to move, just stood there watching about 10 feet away with her mouth open. Bette, who could actually hear the "thump, thump, thump," from the club in our kitchen, ran out and pulled Tess away. As she was doing so, Maxson merely looked up with the club over his head, smiled and said, "Oh, hi Bette," then continued to pound away.

By the time I got home the kids were still shaking and Doggie and Buddy remained locked in the kid's bedroom. I assured them they could let the dogs out and that they wouldn't be eaten (at least not that night), then walked over to the Mallarme's yard, where a group of people sat preparing food for the night's feast. Maxson sheepishly smiled as I approached, also smiling, but shaking my head and with my outstretched palms facing upward with an unstated question.

"I might have scared your kids," he said.

"Ya think?" I asked, still shaking my head.

"Sorry about that," he said, then offered me sakau. Ah, yes, sakau, that mind-numbing nullifier of anger, the ultimate ingredient in conflict resolution that resolves everything ... except this.

I took a drink from the coconut cup and continued, "Maxson, you can't shoot your dog, 15 yards away from my kids I might add, then club it to death with them watching. It's just not something we do in the United States, except in Georgia, Alabama, and certain parts of South Jersey." I paused to make my point. "I understand it's your culture and you have to do what you have to do, but next time could you do it just a little more privately and away from my kids?"

He nodded his head in agreement, then waved his hand in the air, signifying that the incident, and all conversation concerning it, was over.

Death also left its calling card in Rat's motel room right next to his unconscious body. He had suffered a major stroke and laid there for the better part of a day before Ron, my new country music friend from Rusty's, found him. A few days later, Gibson and I went to the hospital to visit him and all I could think of were his first words to me when I first met him in the dark recesses of Peter's garage. No, not "What the fuck's it to you?" After that. "I came here to die."

But he didn't die and instead, thinly clung to life. Gibson had been extremely good, stopping by every day to feed Rat and keep him company. "I have to," he said, "because those fucking nurses just leave the tray of food by his bed. He can't even raise his head to feed himself, but they don't care. The man in the next bed said the nurses argue over who is going to change him and most times they just don't. When I heard that, I went upstairs and let those fucking nurses have it.'

After hooking him up to an IV for nutritional purposes, the hospital discharged him only a few days later without, to my knowledge, confirming that it was indeed a stroke or offering any other diagnosis.

Gibson and I later found Rat lying on a bed in the back room of Peter Shirkey's place. The sweat poured off him as he lay there emaciated, weighing maybe 80 pounds, if that. At times he sounded somewhat coherent, but mostly he was disoriented with absolutely no idea of where he was. Peter took care of Rat for a few months before finally reaching his son back in the States. Eventually, Rat boarded a plane, still suffering from the effects of the stroke, and that was the last we heard of him. Death's calling card wasn't for him. It was for someone else.

Only a week after our *King of the Road* drinks at Rusty's, Ron came home to find his son, long since troubled with alcohol and drugs, waiting for him with a machete and a club. An argument ensued and the son attacked, leaving Ron in a pool of blood. The regulars at Rusty's took it especially hard.

It appeared death and danger weren't leaving paradise anytime soon but, then again, neither were the Mallarmes. Melyann gave birth to a girl, Kaiatia, and the yin and yang rhythm of life on the island continued.

> "A child who gives you the most grief early in life
> will be the one closest to you later in life."
> ~ Pohnpeian belief

The birth of a child is by far the most important occasion in island life. In the days of old, special considerations were to be shown by the husband, who was expected to live and sleep separate from his wife during the pregnancy. He was not allowed to cut his hair during those nine months as well, for to do so might cause death, or the birth of a frail newborn. It was also forbidden to have sex with his wife for several months after the birth of the child. Only women attended to the expectant mother, who received magic each morning, stayed out of the sun, and wore a banana leaf over her head if she ever ventured outside. Disobeying these requirements surely meant a difficult childbirth.

While I'm sure modern medicines were involved, I do know that Melyann adhered to many of the traditional spiritualisms and customs, including absolute silence during the birth. You heard right. On Pohnpei, it is considered quite shameful for the expectant mother to show pain by crying out during labor or the actual birth (let's just say Bette was somewhat less traditional during the births of our daughters). Consequently, we didn't hear a sound until Mrs. Mallarme emerged with the good news.

In times past, a piece of the umbilical cord was placed in a mussel shell and presented to the father who would then place it atop a breadfruit or coconut tree. The tree then became the "tree of the child" – their first possession. The infants first nourishment after birth was coconut juice with squeezed ginger root. Only after that did they consume the mother's milk. Banana was fed to the infant after only ten days. Foods donated and gifts presented in those days were called *pilen dihdi* or "watery breast," although this usually only referred to gifts that could be consumed. We gave her a waffle maker.

Despite the birth of Kaiatia, or maybe because of it, death decided to linger just a little longer outside our front door. As usual, the call came in the middle of the night. It was Bette who was visiting the volunteers out in Palau.

"I just got off the phone with one of my contacts in Washington and had to call you," she said excitedly. "They were awarded a huge five-year USAID project and they want me to come back to D.C. and help manage it."

So now death was after my irresponsible lifestyle and trying to kill the dream I had worked so hard to not work hard for. That bastard! The air was sucked out of the room and I felt dizzy. We were reaching the end of our two-and-a-half-year stint with the Peace Corps, and really only expecting to finish one tour before heading back anyway. Still, the news hit me like a ton of coconuts, the large brown ones, not the small green kind.

"Hello ... Jeff ... are you still there?"

In a state of shock, I offered her congratulations and hung up the phone. The dream was dissipating right before my very eyes. Paradise lost. Oh, the finality of it all. Death, that irrevocable journey to eternal sleep in an office where the copier in service center #1 never works.

The next day the sun rose in a beautiful blue sky and, looking out over the water, I realized I had journeyed through the night and awakened in the final stage of acceptance. Who the hell was I to complain?

Funny how fate can feign one way, then juke another. As soon as we accepted the inevitable, life threw us off course. Or, as far as I was concerned, back on course. The door to Bette's USAID-related opportunity in DC unexpectedly slammed shut due to a number of unforeseen "devil in the details" difficulties, but another phone call and another interview within the Peace Corps led to her being offered a second two-and-a-half-year tour as the deputy director in St. Lucia. Should we take it or were we just being selfish and avoiding going back the grind in DC? We did promise the kids we'd only

288

spend two-and-a-half years overseas. Then again, we promised the kids a lot of things that never came about. It's important to pass down parental guidance and wisdom from one generation to the next, and this taught the kids a crucial lesson – never trust anyone.

Selfish avoidance it was. We were heading to the Caribbean.

That night, I laid down with the girls to get them to go to sleep. We listened for a while to the high-pitched, staccato clicking of the geckos hidden in the shadows of the room before I filled their heads with tales of Noved and Sset in the land of the Keeblers and the Kobblers, accompanied with pictures drawn by my fingers on their backs.

I stroked Devon's hair. A faint smile drew her lips upward and she almost purred. Bette came in and cuddled with Tess who had already fallen asleep. The family was warm, whole, and complete. The dream continued, at least for the time being, and death and danger remained far, far away … so long as we stayed away from the bananas in Chuuk.

Chapter 22

Yap Dance

*This is the land that suites me. Where the natives go nearly
naked and appear to enjoy life as well as the fashionables
of New York, where the earth produces all that is required
to sustain life without labor, and where although it is
sometimes warm there is never any cold to freeze a person,
where that fruit is always in season and is free to all.*
~ Capt. Crayton Philo Holcomb
(in a letter to his sister, 1874)

Bette always liked to pretend she was culturally sensitive, but she really wasn't. "For the last time, NO!" she said, holding her hand up and walking away.

"Oh, come on," I implored. "It's the custom there."

It was no use. She refused to go topless around our house to practice for our trip to Yap, an island which, I'd like to point out, took its customs quite seriously.

Historians disagree, but I believe *that* is exactly why Capt. Crayton Philo Holcomb left his wife back in New England while he traveled about. Actually, Ms. Holcomb would count herself lucky not to be with the captain when, in 1885, he attempted to barter for mother-of-pearl shell just off the shore of Trench, a tiny island in the northern province of New Ireland in Papua New Guinea. The shell was a precious commodity on Yap and he planned on bringing it back to the island. According to *A Yankee Trader in Yap*, a book by Father Francis Hezel, an elderly priest on Pohnpei with whom we became friends and who, I might add, throws vicious elbows while rebounding in "friendly" pickup basketball games (just saying), as Holcomb was standing in a row boat showing the islanders some cloth that he proposed to give them they let loose a salvo of spears from the beach. Struck by one of the spears, Holcomb fell over the gunwale and into the shallow water of the bay. The Yapese crew in the boat, almost all of them wounded, paddled furiously back to the ship, but not before turning to see Holcomb's body lifted on a spear point and carried away to the interior of the island.

I was pretty sure spears wouldn't be flying, but just to be safe, I had Bette and the kids go out the cabin door first when we landed. Actually, for some reason we always found it was better if people met Bette and the kids first before they met me.

We had time for one last trip before we left and there was little doubt it would be to Yap, one of the most beautiful and culturally colorful islands in Micronesia.

After we settled in to our hotel, Regina, the Peace Corps' rep for the island, took us to her house and it wasn't long before Rhea, her nine-year-old daughter, Devon and Tess were doing cartwheels in the soft summer grass. Larry, her husband, was cooking unicorn fish, so named for the small horn that protrudes from its forehead, and parrot fish, named for its odd beak, on a grill over an open fire. Later, we sat beside the thatch *nahs* illuminated by the firelight and ate the funny looking fish with our hands while watching the star filled sky slowly turn above us. Larry and I pulled out our guitars and together we played Van Morrison's 'Brown Eyed Girl' and the surreal feeling of being in two worlds at the same time continued on into the night.

Larry and Regina were the future of Micronesia; fully embracing the ancient customs of the Yapese way of life while also maintaining a perfectly manicured front lawn which may or may not have been cut by a rider mower. Armed with a degree in psychology from the University of San Francisco, Larry, 41, had risen up the ranks of the Yapese government to become the director for the Department of Youth and Civic Affairs. He was asked to be the FSM representative to the United Nations and, later, the liaison to China but turned both offers down so that Rhea could stay on the island and learn the Yapese culture before moving off on her own.

Regina, whose grandfather was the last traditional paramount chief on the outer island of Fais, attended school in Japan before transferring to middle school in Maryland, St. Mary's Academy high school in Virginia and, eventually, setting off again for Oxford to study international relations.

Even with a strong western influence, however, the Yapese beliefs remained pervasive. It was interesting to hear Regina talk about international politics in one breath and how Larry's cousin could call the thunder down in

Unicorn fish

another. Sorcery, though a dying art form, was still practiced on the islands, a fact reinforced with Regina when she was bitten by a centipede at 10 p.m. one night, the exact time Larry's grandfather died.

"It was him," she said. "He was a sorcerer and could control the centipedes. It was horribly painful and I couldn't sleep at all that night. The whole family said he was just saying goodbye to me and I was like 'well, that was one painful goodbye.'"

"We're proud of our culture," Larry said. "We can act western but we'll always be Yapese through and through."

Located on the western end of the FSM, the islands of Yap spread across 625 miles of ocean but consist of only seven square miles of land in total. Yap proper, also known as Wa'ab by locals, is actually made up of three islands interconnected by bridges – Yap, Gagil-Tomil, and Ma'ap. The nearby island of Rumung is only a stone's throw away, and 15 outer atolls dot the horizon, including Ulithi and Woleai, which I quickly found out, weren't made up names from a Star Trek episode. The serene, peaceful waters of the vast Ulithi lagoon made it hard to imagine 700 U.S. warships assembling there in early 1945 just before the historical landings on Iwo Jima and Okinawa. Evidently they left a few historical artifacts behind as a U.S. Navy Explosive Ordinance Disposal (EOD) team from Guam safely detonated a World War II naval mine in the Yap harbor only a month before we arrived.

Yap was the picture postcard of the South Pacific with a reputation for good government that, get this, actually lived within its budget. Its roads were well maintained and the residents made a point of picking up any and all litter. A system of ancient stone pathways led past villages and centuries-old taro patches still in existence and ended with stunning views of the ocean beyond fields of pandanus and dry scrub grass.

The island was known for being the most traditional state in the FSM. Bette scored big when instead of sitting up on the stage with all of the male island big shots during an official outdoor ceremony, she instead settled down on the ground next to the stage with all of the women. Traditional society drew sharp distinctions between those from the main island and outer islands (of lower caste) and, especially, between men and women. Each village had a traditional *pebai* or meeting house – a huge bamboo structure with high thatched roofs – for the men, while the outer island women could expect to be placed in the *pal*, or women's house, during menstruation. As a visiting official, Bette could have sat onstage. The fact that she instead chose to sit with the women brought overwhelmingly positive remarks from both genders for her knowledge and observance of traditional customs.

Tattooing is a serious art form on Yap with traditional tools – a small, smooth wooden spear-like instrument tapped with an ornately carved hammer – and ink from local plants being used. There are three different types of tattooing; *Yol*, which covers the upper part of the body and is the mark of a high rank; *Zalbachag*, which covers the legs and is the mark of a man who is an expert fighter during wars between villages; and *Gachow*, which anyone can have, man or woman, high or low caste.

One of the more comical scenes on the island was watching the men, also known for their ear and nose piercings, walking from village to village carrying a small basket made of woven palm fronds (think of heavily tattooed bikers carrying purses). The basket held more than just their betel nut, which they chewed incessantly. "There is wisdom in the basket," Regina told me. "Wisdom and respect." Its main purpose, however, was to signify to other villagers that the visitor's intentions were honorable. "A man walking without a basket is up to no good," she added. The practice came from the old days when a visitor entering another village would hold a green branch in one hand as a sign of peace.

I was talking with Luke, a Yapese tattoo artist whose unique sea turtle design I chose as the logo for the Micronesia Challenge, when it dawned on me; why not get a tattoo to go along with my mid-life crisis? It would be cheaper than buying a 1977 Pontiac Trans Am with the gold firebird painted on the hood and definitely a lot safer than having an affair. I wanted the *Zalbachag* tattoo that showed I was an expert fighter in wars between villages, so when I spied a man prancing by with his basket I thought about going over and kicking him. No, that wouldn't do, Luke told me. A *Gachow* it was.   I was also disappointed when Luke eschewed the traditional tools and instead brought out a modern tattoo gun. "The original way is too long and too painful," he said. "This is quicker and easier, believe me." A few hours later, I had an aquamarine sea turtle –a fierce, war-like creature if ever there was one – on my upper right arm with "Devon" arcing over the top of it and "Tess" arcing underneath.

Speaking of fierce war-like creatures, Bette claimed I stole her thunder. "Hey," she snapped, "that was my idea to get a tattoo while out here."

"I don't recall that," I replied.

"You don't recall anything I say," she said examining the artwork. "Devon, Tess, very nice…where am I?"

"Ummm, you could be the turtle," I said thinking quickly. SLAP, right on my sore arm. "OW, careful, it's still wet," I said grimacing. "Besides, the kids are forever – you I'm not so sure about." SLAP! Again with the sore arm. One day later, Bette showed me a small, tasteful design on her hip that depicted dolphins jumping out of the water. I do want it noted that at no point did I even think of asking, "Where am I?" regarding her tattoo.

Tattoos of leaping dolphins and fierce aquamarine sea turtles cost money, which led to yet another enlightening fact about the island's financial transactions. While *Yar*, or shell money, is still used as currency, Yap is especially notable for its stone money. Known as *Rai*, the large doughnut-shaped, carved stone can measure as much as 12 feet in diameter and take a dozen or more men to carry (done so by placing a pole through a hole cut in the middle). Smaller stones, some as little as 1½ inches, were also used and, I'm guessing, easier to get out of ATM machines.

While size mattered, the age and history of the stones were more valuable since none were originally from the island. In ancient times, some of the stones came from nearby islands like Papua New Guinea, but most were crystalline calcite mined from the limestone caves of Palau. The hardships of the 250-mile journey from Palau to Yap in tiny canoes gave the stone its real value. Even with the best weather, the trip took a week or more and the conditions were far from ideal. Sometimes, entire expeditions were lost at sea. In 1929, the Japanese counted more than 13,000 pieces of stone money on Yap, but only about half that number survive today.

Rocks as money. Ah, the simpler things in life; it's funny how we sometimes can take them for granted. Take the air that we breathe for instance. It turns out that oxygen is a bigger deal than we usually give it credit for. I found this out 60 feet under water. Being a highly trained professional diver, I made sure I checked my air thingy on a regular basis, or maybe it was the depth doohickey. Either way I was satisfied I had enough oxygen until the know-it-all dive master looked at my gage and began making wild arm gestures while, rather theatrically I might add, slashing his finger across his throat. You'd think by now there'd be a more subtle way of letting someone know they're out of air. He then thrust his air regulator into my mouth while taking mine into his. "Really?" I thought. "On the first date?" I must say his air was way better than mine. The fact that he had next to no air from my tank didn't matter to him since, being a seasoned local diver, it seemed he could go hours without drawing a breath.

We quickly made our way up to the dive stop 15 feet below the surface to decompress. The fact was, that guy saved my life. I put my hand over my chest to illustrate a heartfelt thank you, but apparently that was the international Divers Advisory Network sign for "I'm having a heart attack at the dive stop 15 feet below the surface." He quickly motioned for a second dive master to come over so I gave a thumbs up to let them know I was ok but apparently that meant I needed to get to the surface immediately. I'll tell you, there's more sign language in scuba diving than the entrance exam to Gallaudet University for the deaf. Finally, I gave the universal "ok" sign which everyone understood. The second dive master had me breathe from his regulator and eventually we reached the surface. Chagrined, I climbed into the boat and did the sign of the cross, which is the international Divers Advisory Network sign for "holy shit."

On an earlier trip to Yap, Bette experienced even more dive drama than me. After completing two normal 60-foot dives earlier in the day, she took a hot shower and discovered her hands and feet tingled. Then her left arm went numb. She quickly called a dive specialist and a doctor who both cautioned she could be experiencing a form of decompression sickness, something that happens when a diver doesn't acclimate to the decreasing water pressure as they surface causing an excessive amount of nitrogen to remain in the body. In short, that can lead to a lethal case of nitrogen narcosis or decompression sickness. They said it was probably a mild case, but just to be safe they recommended she get herself into a decompression chamber – a small compartment where atmospheric pressure can be raised or lowered gradually, allowing the diver to readjust to normal atmospheric pressure. Bette was lucky that Yap had one (and I believe the only one in the FSM).

The decompression chamber in Yap was no place for the claustrophobic (Bette) as it only had space inside for barely two people and required a minimum stay of at least five hours. A trained professional was also required to be in the chamber to observe Bette for the entire five hours. It was the "observe her" part that bothered me as the "observer" was both young and male. "He was cute," Bette later told me, but added that spending that amount of time sealed in a small container with no way of getting out wasn't exactly romantic. "Mostly I was thinking PANIC ATTACK!" she said. Wisely, she waited a few weeks before also letting me know the cost for the procedure was $4,000. I felt like I needed the decompression chamber after hearing that. No I didn't. Bette's wellbeing was paramount. "Your health and safety is all that matters," I assured her, and of course money was no object. Did I mention that it cost $4,000?

The first night Bette got home from that trip I pulled her close after we got into bed, but she said she was tired and thought she still might have a few nitrogen bubbles inside her bloodstream which, and I give her credit, was easily the most creative excuse for not having sex that she's ever come up with.

The highlight of our trip was Yap Days, an annual celebration of the island's culture with a colorful and sensorial display of local food, costume, dance, music and breasts. I raised my camera. Bette lowered my camera. She was starting to become a real culture killer. Spread over two days, the festival offered a number of activities and competitions between islands, including conch shell blowing, copra husking, spear throwing, thatch roof making, and fire starting.

Among all of the items on the program, the most keenly anticipated events by both islanders and overseas guests alike were the *churuu*; highly developed and complex traditional dances that were the envy of the islands in Micronesia. The dances and chants that accompany them were once used to pass stories from one generation to another and were taught with great care. Some of the dances still practiced today are so ancient that the present generation cannot translate their meaning, but the chants and the movements are the same as in the past. Performances are considered a community-based activity and all villagers are required by tradition to participate in one form or another. The caste system is especially noticeable as outer islanders can only perform with permission from the Yapese mainlanders. Also, men and women are to be kept separated, with the men performing the standing dance and the women performing the sitting dance. Stick dancing, introduced from the outer islands east of Yap, had recently allowed the commingling of the two sexes, but even then it was only for young boys and girls. The stick or bamboo dance is particularly festive, some might say violent, with lots of shouting and choreographed bamboo collisions done while the dancers twirl high in the air.

The Stick Dance

Controversy struck when members from one village performed what Regina designated to be an R-rated dance which only men were allowed to do. "It's a sexual dance and that is why it is forbidden for women," she said shaking her head.

For the life of me, I couldn't see what was so sexual about it as they mostly just slapped their thighs and shouted, "Hoy, hoy, hoy," a lot. Still, Regina assured me the men were trying to attract the women as if they were at a bar.

All of the dancers in the festival made considerable effort to decorate themselves in extremely elaborate attire. Bodies were greased and painted with vibrant blue, red and yellow designs. Men and young boys were required to wear a *thu*, a long, colorful cloth wrapped under the crotch and tied around the waist. The colors of the *thu* were important; red meant they were warlike, white meant they came in peace, and blue, the most popular color and culturally appropriate, I'm guessing served as formal wear. The women wore decorative *lava lavas*, grass skirts of hibiscus and banana fibers whose woven designs often depicted their island of origin.

The festival came to a close all too soon but the unique tradition and the overall exuberant, unique culture of Yap would stay with me forever. In fact, the first night we got back home on Pohnpei I stood at the foot of our bed wearing only a pillow case as a *thu* and hovered over Bette while slapping my thighs and shouting "Hoy, hoy, hoy," and you know what? It worked. Just a little tip from me to you guys out there. Those Yapese know what they're doing.

Youths, wearing the traditional *thu*, pass by the meeting house

I've come to kill your monkey.
~ Konrad Englberger

"I never said that," Konrad protested.

"Well, he said you did," I said provokingly.

"Yeah, well, I'm sure he said a lot of things," Konrad replied.

In addition to plant protection and helping to prevent invasive species from entering Micronesia, Konrad was also the quarantine specialist for the islands. Tall, lean, and sporting a full, grey goatee, he cut an imposing figure and maintained a no-nonsense attitude regarding his job. He meant business; he had to. It was a matter of survival.

The "he" we were referring to was Bill, himself a tall, imposing Texas cowboy with wavy white hair and a thick grey mustache that drooped down the sides of his mouth. He also was not a man to be trifled with.

It should be noted that both men were normally extremely affable, just not with each other. Bill had the monkey. Konrad said it had to go, not just off the island but, well, to a more celestial place. It was a showdown. The streets cleared and a tumbleweed rolled past as they faced each other out on the dirt road.

"There's no love lost between us," Bill later told me in his low, gravelly voice.

Bill came to Yap as a Peace Corps volunteer in 1976 and never left. "There's not a lot I miss," he said. "I never carry money and haven't tied a tie in more than 30 years. This is home for sure. I'll die here." He then paused and added, "I do miss Texas football, though."

In 2001 he brought the *Mnuw* ("sea hawk" in Yapese), an old wooden cargo ship built in 1898, over from Bali and turned it into a highly successful restaurant and bar. Bill was almost always buying a round of whiskey and, if you were good, he let you jump off the main mast into the water below.

Just before coming over from Bali, the *Mnuw* was tied up alongside another Indonesian cargo ship where the crew, Bill alleged, was mistreating its mascot monkey. His brother-in-law bought it, saved it, and gave it to Bill's son as a present and that's how it ended up aboard the Mnuw in Yap. While the monkey may not have been the viral, but cute, mascot in *Pirates of the Caribbean*, I'm guessing he was no Curious George either.

"That's when our buddy Konrad went nuts," Bill said. "He's a control freak and doesn't trust other people."

"Trust?" Konrad later said. "What trust? That monkey lived on an Indonesian cargo ship and more than likely had a number of infectious diseases. That's my job, to keep those diseases out of Micronesia."

Konrad flew out to Yap and, with the law on his side, soon had the monkey on a gurney. Monkey's rarely go quietly, though, and this one broke free, swinging from the lights and sending test tubes and beakers flying everywhere. Mayhem ensued. When they did get it back down on the gurney, the nurse couldn't get the needle in the right place and finally gave up, walking out of the room. Finally, Konrad administered the lethal dose himself.

"Of course he did," Bill said. "He probably loved it."

"I certainly wasn't happy about it," Konrad later replied.

Far from being over, the scrap in Yap lingers to this day. I'm not saying you need to weigh in on it or anything … just something to think about the next time you find yourself docking in Yap with an Indonesian monkey on your shoulder.

It was 1 a.m. and I was standing on the edge of the Earth looking up at the constellations with Larry and his father-in-law, Peter, who earlier said his age was "I don't know, 66 maybe." We'll put it as sixty something. Age wasn't important in Micronesia. Knowledge was. You were either old and wise or young and stupid. Larry and I woke him up so he could show me the stars they navigate by, which illustrated that both Larry and I were young, drunk and stupid. "He won't mind. He loves this stuff," Larry said.

Sure enough, Peter sprang from his sleeping mat and within seconds he was pointing and explaining how the stars mapped the sky. "There's *Tegal mailapal fang*," he said, spotting a faint, blinking light far to the north before moving his finger down to the right. "And over there is *Paiyor*." He turned to me and asked, "Are you familiar with the sky?"

"Vaguely," I replied. Actually, my knowledge was limited to the Big Dipper and that small light you see moving slowly high across the sky every now and then but you don't know if it's a satellite or a plane. I also saw the Pink Floyd Laserium at the Hayden Planetarium in New York City a couple of times.

He continued. "There are 32 stars we navigate by, starting with *Welewel fas magut* ..."

"The north star," Larry interjected.

"... and ending with *Welwelel up*."

"The Southern Cross," Larry said. "Sixteen stars to the right, north to south, sixteen stars to the left, north to south." Larry then laid out 32 pieces of coral in a circle to form a star compass. The positions of the stars form a system of reference points that Yapese navigators used for organizing information about winds, wave patterns, and currents as well as the positions of the islands, reefs and other sea marks. Peter called out the names and Larry translated; *Yeluyel* – Orion, *Welego* – the Big Dipper, and so on until the coral on the ground were situated like the stars in the sky.

I was actually starting to get it, or at least thought I was until they ventured further into the sky, calling out stars not on my little coral chart and warning of the consequences of the celestial movements.

"Look," Peter exclaimed. "*Sota* and *Lag* are falling. When you see this a storm is coming and there will be rough seas."

"You also need to watch for *Metarue* and *Mon* rising in the east in the early morning," Larry added. My head spun with the stars above.

Yap is one of the last locations on Earth where "master navigators" use the traditional art of reading the wind, sea and stars to find safe passage, sometimes thousands of miles across the ocean. For 4,000 years the secrets of the sea had been passed down from generation to generation until, one by one, the navigators died and those that remained stopped training their replacements. The tradition was nearly lost until Mau Piailug (pronounced

Pee-eye-lug), one of the last master navigators, decided to break tradition and share his knowledge with people outside his family, and even with cultures outside of Yap.

Mau made headlines in 1978 when, using only the lessons learned from his grandfather, he guided a traditional canoe from Hawaii to Tahiti, more than 3,000 miles across the Pacific Ocean. The journey proved to scientists, once and for all, that the islands scattered across the Pacific were not populated by accident.

The next day I met with Leo Racheilug, 55, the chief of Satawal, the outer island where Mau lived, and Bruno Tharngan, 58, the chief of Ma'ap. Leo, a master navigator, wore only the traditional blue *thu* while Bruno was more conventional, wearing shorts, a T-shirt and a Mnuw Restaurant baseball cap. I decided not to bring up the monkey. Both had short grey hair and large bellies that shook whenever they laughed which was often. They plopped down and popped a wad of betel nut into their mouths.

Leo began by telling me his father, older brother, and even his mom all learned the secret ways of navigating the sea. Women learn it, he said, so that it can stay in the family but they are not allowed to travel at sea.

"I started at five-years-old," he continued. "At first it was easy; counting the stars and such, but then you had to learn by going out to sea, often by yourself and, let me tell you, that's where it can become difficult."

"Some people come back, some don't," Bruno added. Oh sure, easy for him to say since he had the power to call down rain whenever he wanted. "I learned the power from my uncle," he said. "It's happened lots of times. It's a secret, though, and I can't tell you how it's done. It's like black magic."

Leo himself only became a "master" at 54. He claimed he could navigate by feeling the movement of the Earth within the universe. I was curious.

"Ok," I said, "Suppose you're out on a canoe in the middle of the ocean and it's night. Where are you going to start?"

"I always start with *Mailap*, the eastern star," he said. "The points in the sky guide me. The Northern Star never moves, but the Southern Cross will hit five positions during the course of the night."

"Suppose you're out on a canoe and it's cloudy so there are no stars," I pressed.

"We can tell by the location of the islands in the distance," he said.

"Suppose there's a storm and you can't see the islands."

"Then we know by the fish in the water," he replied. "Certain fish are found near certain islands. Also, the birds. For instance, if we see the *Yepak* we know we are near Satawal."

"Alright," I said, drawing in a long breath. "Suppose it's night, the storm is all around you and you can't see the stars, the islands, the fish or the birds. Then what?"

"Well," he said. "Then I'd pull out my GPS." At this, both he and Bruno roared and slapped their knees. Then Leo leaned in close as if to reveal a secret. "The waves always move east to west," he whispered. "The water in the bottom of the boat will move in the same direction as the waves, east to west."

Ah, so that would explain "feeling" the movement of the Earth. "Not entirely," he said. "There's a lot more to it than that."

While he certainly knew a lot about navigation, Bruno instead studied to become a master builder. "You have to see the canoe in the tree," he said. "That's where it all starts." In the old days, they would touch the tree and say a specific chant before cutting it down but, unfortunately, the words were lost through the ages, apparently along with the ancient tools. Shells and stones gave way to modern chisels and hammers, and sails of woven pandanas were replaced by canvas or plastic. While it used to take years to build even a small canoe, the process today takes about seven months to complete. As usual, women are forbidden during this time.

"It's bad luck for the canoe," Bruno added. "I take hold of my students and tell them to stay away from the women, but they're young and I know they still sneak off. It's kind of hard to do."

"No relations with women for seventh months?" I asked.

"You can't even masturbate," Leo said. "A wet dream is ok, though, because you have no control over that." Bruno emphatically nodded his head in agreement.

The next day we boarded the *Munmoownga Maday*, which meant 'the water between Yap and the moon' and, with its sails set high, soon found ourselves moving swiftly over the water. Larry, looking smart in his white *thu*, was at the helm. "In the old days they thought they could sail to the moon," he said explaining the name of the outrigger. His first mate had a blue *thu* and looked more like a pirate with his matching blue head scarf. "Pain is Love" was tattooed over his heart.

Painted a war-like red with black trim, the *Munmoownga Maday* was the typical size of a canoe built by Bruno, measuring six fathoms (30 ft.) in length and over one fathom (5 ft.) across. The attached wooden outrigger sprawled several more feet off to one side. The crew yanked on the ropes and adjusted the sail as we tacked back and forth. One young boy, obviously showing off, stood on the wooden rudder in the back while helping to steer the canoe. Suddenly he slipped and fell into the water but managed to hang on while the other boys, laughing hysterically, hauled him back in. Larry looked at me and just shook his head; so much for being noted as masters of the sea.

We sailed out across the waves; just me, the crew of *thu's*, and the open sea before us. Behind us, Yap faded in the distance, becoming a small ridge of rolling green jungle with only the occasional thatch hut and the smoke from an evening fire dotting the shoreline. I asked Larry if the culture and customs of Yap could withstand the Western influences descending upon it. He assured me it would.

"Just remember the basic navigational mainstay," he said with a wink. "You must have your point of origin in sight before you can determine your point of destination."

Chapter 23

Wave ... Bye-Bye

Go strip off your clothes that are a nuisance in this mellow clime.
Get in and wrestle with the sea; wing your heels with the skill
and power that reside in you, hit the sea's breakers, master them,
and ride upon their backs as a king should.

~ Jack London

Surf now, apocalypse later.
~ Beachside graffiti in California

"Look at this, look at THIS," Allois said, tapping the computer screen. He pointed to a storm off Japan almost 3,000 miles away. "We're right here at 160 degrees. As the wind gets sucked around the back end of the storm, we're gonna have as good a wind force as you're ever going to get for surfing in Pohnpei. The waves could hit 13 – 19 feet tomorrow."

The surf forecasting companies had pinpointed Allois's "virtual buoy" coordinates just off the island and were sending information on the surge activity scheduled for Pohnpei. Surf of that magnitude only happen there once a year – some years it didn't happen at all – so Allois had been tracking the storm since, well, before it even was a storm. "Weather that happens a week earlier will generate swells 10 days away," he said. "Often you're looking at storms that don't even exist yet."

In addition to Pohnpei, this North Pacific low-pressure system – some 5,000 miles wide – had sent swells across the Pacific, from the Philippines all the way up to Alaska and down to South America.

The world-elite surfers gathered around the computer in anticipation and finally pro surfer Ian Walsh nudged Allois aside and called up the surfing forecast. When it popped up the dialogue erupted in surf lingo.

"10 feet, 14 seconds (the height and distance between the waves), that's radical!"

"Backdoor is going to be firing, dude."

"Screaming rights and lefts."

"Yeah, but it could be all lefts. You don't want to get barreled backside."

The decision then was whether to fly out in the afternoon to compete in the upcoming Pipeline Masters in Hawaii, one of the sport's premier events, or stay and catch some of the best surf Pohnpei had seen in years. The group had already been on the island for a few days with great surf.

"The biggest waves weren't the best ones, but the big ones we caught were crazy," said Reef Macintosh, another pro surfer in the group and, with a name like that, one destined to surf from birth.

Both the waves and the pro surfers were news to me. Earlier, I had taken Devon and Tess on our boat to snorkel over at Palikir Pass when Noel, a friend of ours, arrived with his kids and pulled his boat alongside ours. "Do you know who that is out there?" Noel's teenaged son asked. "It's Kelly Slater."

I shielded my eyes from the sun and glanced over at the waves. Seeing surfers was a regular occurrence, however this bunch did seem awfully good. I vaguely recognized the name Kelly Slater and decided to bluff my way through this reality show quiz.

"Oh yeah," I said, still shielding my eyes. "Didn't she win American Idol or something like that?"

There was a palpable silence and even the waves stopped for a brief second. "DUDE," our friend's son screamed. "You are such a loser!"

Thus, you can imagine my surprise when nine-time World Surfing Champion Kelly Slater, who wasn't at all a girl, walked into the "should I stay or should I go now" debate and stood next to me in Allois's room just as Walsh switched over to the Pipeline website. "We need an excuse," Walsh said, flipping through the site. "We'll tell them we couldn't get off the island."

They all looked to see if the waves scheduled to arrive at the Pipeline the next day were small in the off chance they would postpone the first day of the tournament. Evan Slater (no relation to Kelly), editor of *Surfing Magazine*, started a chant, "stay, stay, stay, stay," then added, "Oh, come on Kelly, they won't start without you and Andy (three-time World Champion Andy Irons who also was on Pohnpei)."

Kelly Slater shook his head. "Yeah, but there's gonna be, like, 50 guys going 'forget them. Who cares about those four guys?' Nah, even if there are four to six-foot waves they're starting tomorrow."

He threw his hands up. "I think it's gonna be really good here and … I think they're gonna hold the competition."

Walsh continued to scroll down the page looking at the photos of the surfers selected for the first round. "I'm not even in this round. Hell, I'm not going anywhere." He turned to Slater. "Have a good flight, man." One last click to the next page, however, revealed his smiling face. "Damn!"

To no one's surprise, Slater found out he and Irons had a pass for the first round and so a decision was made. *Surfing Magazine's* Evan Slater confirmed it. "I love it here. I've seen so many photos in our magazine but I didn't realize how tucked away it was; the dense jungle, the amazing waves. We're staying."

Like a high stakes game of surf poker, both Walsh and Macintosh went 'all in,' gambling that the tournament would be delayed as the forecast predicted smaller than normal waves in Hawaii, and larger than normal waves in Pohnpei.

Later, I went back to check on Allois who continued to survey the storm activity in his room at the PCR. The crowd had left, but our old laidback pal Mitch was still stretched out on Allois' bed reading, natch, a surfing magazine.

"You know to really hone your Mitcheconomics, you should be reading Fortune magazine," I said as I flopped down on the end of the bed.

"Fuck Fortune," he replied without looking up.

Allois ignored us. I have to admit, despite the surfing royalty on the island and all that was at stake regarding the storm swells that would either make or break the entire visit, he kept his cool and detached surfing Zen while remaining ever focused on the tasks at hand. This was a critical week. Even a letter-to-the-editor criticizing him in the latest *Waves* magazine for all to see didn't faze him.

> "I nearly shat myself when I read *Waves'* write up of P-Pass. 'Discovered in 2000 by Allois Malifantani' (sic) ... What the fuck? ... I have friends who surfed that wave long before that Brazzo douche bag ever set foot on Pohnpei ... there is nothing courageous, bold or valiant about a no talent ass clown like Malifantani (sic) exploiting a wave and the people of Pohnpei. All that stupid cunt has done is rape another people's treasure. You're fluff piece of journalism/propaganda has perpetuated Allois's myth of discovery and sharing to a new level that makes me want to vomit."

The editor merely replied: "You're taking wave discovery way too seriously. Is there a freezer nearby? Jump in it, chill out and harden the fuck up."

Allois passed it off with a wave of his hand.

"Hey," I said, turning to Mitch, "your Jason Mraz 'I'm Yours' video is still playing on MTV."

"No shit?" he asked suddenly energized and sitting up. He explained that the director had previously shot a documentary on him and his friends skateboarding the empty swimming pools of LA. When they needed a Californian stereotype for the Mraz video, they knew exactly where to go. "Dude," Mitch said raising his hand to high-five me, "I got to hang out for the day, plus I got paid, like, $500." In his financial scheme that kind of money would last him half a year.

"Oh, and I guess congratulations goes out to you too," I said to Allois. His girlfriend, Haley, had been pregnant and was about to give birth. Allois stopped typing. Evidently, this was the one topic that could break his Zen-like focus.

"What's that supposed to mean?" he said turning towards me.

"Nothing," I said. "Just congratulations."

"I know where you're headed with this; all your talk about you and your kids," he said waving his arms in the air. "Well, it's not gonna change my life."

I let out a derisive laugh.

"No, I'm serious," he said, turning around in his chair to address me. "Haley will take care of the kid."

"And what happens when Haley is sick or has something of great importance to do and she shows up at the dock holding the kid with outstretched arms for you to take care of?"

Allois thought for a moment and then, smiling, turned to Mitch. "He's fucking with me, isn't he," he said waving his hand at me. Mitch just shrugged his shoulders and continued reading his magazine. Allois went back to his storm system. "Haley's problem. I won't have life jackets small enough for the kid."

Early the next morning, thanks to being granted a reporting assignment for the *Kaselehlie Press* from Bill Jaynes, and Allois graciously bestowing his blessings upon me ("Just don't be a fucking pain in the ass"), I found myself on one of the boats along with Slater, Irons, and a host of photographers and videographers documenting the trip. There were also a few on board who were just plain fanatics, including Mark Ryun, 41, a self-described "C League" surfer who ran a flooring business on the North Shore of Oahu. According to Ryan, a key aspect of being a true devotee is the ability to drop everything and get to where the surf is (he and his wife, Laila, had planned their trip only a few days earlier). "Like everybody else," he said, "you gotta come to the swell."

The swell he spoke of had become thunderous walls of water pounding the reef all across the north side of Pohnpei. We skimmed past Sokehs Rock and already the surf off in the distance at Palikir Pass was easily visible as it exploded, sending funnels of spray some 30 feet in the air.

Even Beru, the veteran Pohnpeian captain who was driving our boat, shook his head and added, "this is easily the roughest I've seen it in a long time."

Pohnpei's best surf was about to meet the world's best surfers.

Described as one of the most exciting surfers to come along in the past decade, Andy Irons won the Pipeline Masters, the Triple Crown and his first ASP World Title in 2002, a feat he then repeated in 2003 and 2004. The 2005 season was a non-stop fight to the finish with Kelly Slater and at the end, Irons finished just 45 points short as Slater won his seventh World Title.

A shade over six-feet, Irons was taller and slightly heavier than today's average surfer, which could also explain his aggressive style of surfing. According to *Surfing Magazine*, Irons had "the miraculous combination of big-wave craziness and small wave ripping down better than any surfer in the world right now. It's a horrifying skill range."

314

But while Irons had achieved greatness, Slater had attained God-like status, not just among surfers but throughout the entire sporting world as well. "The planet's greatest surfer deserves to be mentioned in the same breath as Michael Schumacher, Lance Armstrong and Tiger Woods," exclaimed an article in *The Guardian*.

Slater's record nine world titles included five consecutive titles from 1994-98. In May 2005, in the final heat of the Billabong Tahiti Pro contest at Teahupoo, Slater became the first surfer ever to be awarded two perfect scores for a total 20 out of 20 points. He also was the youngest (at age 20) to win the world title and the oldest, having shored up the 2008 world title at the Billabong Pro Mundaka, in northern Spain, at the age of 36.

The subject of countless surfing documentaries, Slater also played the recurring character Jimmy Slade on several episodes of Baywatch in the early 1990s. An avid guitar player, he played with friends Ben Harper, Jack Johnson and Pearl Jam's Eddie Vetter. His shaved head, piercing eyes, and rugged good looks didn't hurt him either as at one point or another he had been romantically linked to Pamela Anderson, Brazilian supermodel Gisele Bündchen, Sports Illustrated swimsuit model Bar Rafaeli, and Cameron Diaz (after her split from Justin Timberlake).

Ever the journalist, I remained professionally unimpressed. I mean, I won "most congenial" in ninth grade and once went on a date with baseball legend Joe Garagiola's daughter, Gina Maria Angelina Garagiola, but you won't see that splashed all over Wikipedia. I also noticed, by the way, that there was no mention of him ever winning American Idol.

Our fame and fortune aside, on that day both Slater and Irons had assumed the Pohnpei mellow, laid-back style as they chatted about the waves; their long-time rivalry miles, and years, away.

The surfers waxed and prepped their boards and moments later everyone was in the water. Well, almost everyone. Slater was particular if nothing else. While the other surfers were out carving the waves, he worked his board, intently focused on waxing one specific square-inch of the front tip. Stroke, stroke, stroke. He stopped, examined it, and then ran his finger across it. No good. Stroke, stroke, stroke. Still no good. This examination process took over a half an hour. At one point, Beru offered him a bar of *Sex Wax Quick Humps* surf wax. Slater just smiled. "No thanks, got my own." Finally, he was in the water.

The waves weren't as big as predicted, but they were certainly daunting enough, cresting at 10 feet and roaring menacingly past the boats and onto the reef. The curls were perfect as the surfers skimmed through the aqua-green tunnels of water, creating that spectacular "barrel" poster shot you see on the surfing magazine covers. Swilly, the professional surf photographer, was once again on hand and shooting away with his cannon-like camera. "Where's your camera?" he yelled over from one of the other boats. "You're not going to get many opportunities like this, I can tell ya that, mate."

Just then Allois splashed over on his new jet ski. "Hop on. I'll get you even closer to the action." I straddled the back of the jet ski and put my hands on the sides of his waist to hold on.

"What the fuck are you doing?" he yelled, pulling away from me.

"I'm just holding on," I said.

He shook his head. "No, no, no. I'm from Brazil and in Brazil a man NEVER touches another man, not even as a hug from your father or brother. NEVER! You hold on to the straps on the side."

My head jerked back as we zoomed toward the waves. Well, not just toward the waves, but over and sometimes through them.

"You know how to swim?" he yelled over the roar of the engine.

"Sure," I said.

"No, I mean really swim. If we flip over, which is likely, the waves and the current out here will really fuck you up."

316

Ok, that's an important safety tip, I thought. Finally, we settled down just off to the side and watched Reef Macintosh catch a breaking wave, nonchalantly slide to the bottom of it, then quickly shoot to the top and cut back across the lip before angling back down again.

Slater saw a huge wave breaking late and flipped his board around to catch it. With a powerful stroke he was up and flying down the side of it, making cuts and turns with ease. Suddenly he shot straight to the top, hung for a moment, then twisted the board around in a perfect 180-degree turn. Just as the wave broke onto the reef he swung back up and over the crest, flying off the board and raising his hands into the air in a "ta-da" finale.

Irons came down into a barrel surrounded by water, his right hand playfully skimming the backside of the wave until he was overtaken and completely disappeared in a wall of white foam. A moment later he punched through, still in the barrel and gave the "V for victory" sign with both hands. The surfers back on the boat let out a roar of approval.

"They're on a completely different level – they're aliens," Dave Ward, later said with a laugh. Although Ward, 50, had spent the past 40 years surfing the North Shore in Oahu, he was content to just watch as the waves rocked the Pohnpei Surf Club boat only 30 yards away from the action. "I'm not even going out when it's like that. These guys have no fear."

"We're not in their league," added Ryun. "Nobody is."

Later, however, during a break in the action, I learned that even the greatest surfer in the world can be intimidated, maybe just a little.

"Heck yeah, man," Slater said, "the adrenaline is still there. It's a wave … it'll still light you up."

Irons, who had also previously surfed Pohnpei in 2005, was equally impressed. "The waves were more hollow for sure; top to bottom, real powerful," he said. "They didn't get as big as we hoped, but when they did they were amazing, great waves. It was quality over quantity which is cool."

317

The sun began to fade and cast an orange glow around the boat as it plowed through the water back to Kolonia. In less than 24 hours the surfers would be back in the water at the Pipeline Masters where yet another Kelly Slater-Andy Irons showdown awaited. And though it wouldn't decide a world champion – Slater clinched the title in early October – it would provide compelling theater for those on hand.

Sitting back in the boat, Slater seemed ready for the showdown but, at 36, one had to wonder how much he had left in him. I asked him about retirement and the Neil Young line, "It's better to burn out than to fade away." He just shrugged.

"I don't know. Maybe it's good to burn bright, and then just give it up." He looked down and added, "I'm still having fun, though." When he looked up again a wide grin spread across his face. "Maybe I'll just keep going and fade away."

[Note: The gamble taken by Ian Walsh and Reef Macintosh proved unlucky as the Pipeline Masters held its first round the next day without them. Slater, however, arrived on a 2 a.m. flight and within hours was gliding his way through the second round. The next day he breezed past the quarter finals and finally, inevitably, to the 2008 Pipeline Masters championship.]

"Why am I here?" I asked myself. It wasn't some existential, cosmic question involving, say, theology or intelligent design or standing in line at the Division of Motor Vehicles. It was a legitimate question rooted in practicality. My mind and my body pondered the question and agreed with each other (a first by the way) unlike the last time I was where I was. "No, we really shouldn't be here," they warned. Even the karma surrounding me seemed to indicate that my being at that exact location precisely at that moment in time was an aberration.

Suddenly the sun disappeared and I looked up at the wave looming behind me. I could hear the water thundering to my left and to my right. Far more frightening, however, was the fact that I could also hear it roaring directly above me. I instinctively jumped up on the surfboard and planted my feet. I mean, that's what you're supposed to do, right? Just keep your hands up, bend your knees, stick your butt out and listen to the theme from *Hawaii Five-O* play in your head as you float godlike across the water.

Still on my board, I felt the force of the ocean surge through me and for one brief, exhilarating moment I was lifted high into the heavens and experienced that speedball of adrenaline and dopamine surfers talk about getting just before they're dropped into the maelstrom below. It didn't take long, however, before I was reminded of my insignificance and banished to the churning depths. The land, air and sea, those are the rulers of the Earth and don't let any Roman tell you otherwise. Gasping for air, I ascended only to find yet another monster wave hovering over me like a giant fist. BAM! Down it came, sending me back into the foamy oblivion. A guy by the name of Paul Strauch once said, "Surfing is like making love. It feels good every time you do it." Well, if that's so, then it must be a weird, kinky, and extremely painful sado-masochistic love, I thought to myself as I tumbled head over heels underwater, dangerously close to the sharp coral.

"Tell me again why we are here?" my mind asked, trying to reach me one last time as I struggled to the surface.

The answer wasn't easy to come by. Even Kelly Slater had joined the chorus of surfing sages warning me against learning to surf at P-Pass. "Don't do it, dude," he said. "This isn't the place for you. Start with some nice easy waves somewhere else." He looked out at the walls of water crashing down and then back at me. "I'm serious."

I didn't listen, I couldn't. Bad decisions make for great stories. Once again, however, that saying got stuck in my throat as I stood on the dock of the Pohnpei Surf Club earlier in the day. Chris Groark, Allois's business partner and, I might mention, a 6'5", 27-year-old sculpted stud, walked up to me, or maybe it was his identical twin, Tom. If there's anything that will make you feel insignificant, besides a 1,000-foot wave, it's standing between two 6'5", 27-year-old sculpted studs. I looked up at their smooth pecs and wondered whatever happened to the day when women fell for us guys with the hairy chests? You know, the sexy Sean Connery hairy chests of 40 years ago? Never mind, I just answered my own question.

"Be careful out there," Chris, or Tom, said with a strange grin.

Be careful? No shit. "What's that supposed to mean?" I said. Could he be any more vague? He shrugged his shoulders and said nothing. Later, as we boarded the boat, he added, "Keep your head, dude, and be aware of the reef."

Again, no shit. "Why did you just say that?" I asked. "What's the best way to avoid the reef?"

He just shook his head. "Can't really tell ya. You just gotta watch us."

I gave him an "I gotcha, dude" look, but as I turned and walked to the back of the boat I was thinking, "fuck, fuck, FUCK!"

Man, this is not good, NOT good, I thought. I rolled my head to loosen my neck, then bounced just a little of the tips of my toes like a boxer before stepping into the ring. This is not good at all.

Suddenly the boat engines roared to life and Beru thrust us out and into the great blue beyond. I wasn't about to leave Pohnpei without having at least attempting to surf. This was it, my last chance at romance; my final stab at gaining a spiritual and (mostly) physical understanding of exactly how "surfing is like making love."

We moored the boat and, once again, a full year after my first attempt, I found myself rising up and over the huge swells. However, this time it was different. This time I was actually psyched and ready to do battle with the waves. Just me and the water, mano y droplets. The ocean rose as another set rolled in and, frankly, there were a lot more droplets than I thought there'd be. Still, I remained determined. You can't go halfway and there is no easy way. In fact, you really don't ease into it in any way, shape or form. You go all the way or you go home. I turned my board and raced to catch the first wave.

The swell picked me up and then, suddenly, with adrenalin and confidence coursing through my veins, the unthinkable happened. I was drowning. You know all of those inspirational sayings you're always telling your kids; adages like "Dreams can come true if you have the courage to pursue them," by Walt Disney; or "I've got to formulate a plot or I end up in jail or shot. Success is my only mothafuckin option, failure's not," by Eminem? Well, frankly, they're not really all that inspirational when you're ten feet underwater.

Here's another saying I'd like to see on the burn list, "practice makes perfect." Time and again I jumped onto the board. Time and again I fell backwards into the water after standing upright for about as long as one of those fraction-seconds they use to determine the winners of Olympic swimming events. Deja-vu; rinse, shampoo, repeat. After being pummeled for an hour, one of the longest hours of my life I might add, I'd had enough and decided to make my way back to the boat. That's when Tom, or maybe it was Chris, swam up to me as calm and cool as could be. "Ok, Jeff, we gotta get you up on one of those," he said, pointing to the next heaving, surging, crashing, crushing wave.

"Well, to be honest, I already caught my share of waaay...." Before I could finish he shoved the back of my board so that I was in the vortex of yet another huge waaay.

Rinse, shampoo, repeat. Chris or Tom swam over shaking his head. "If you were anywhere else, ANYWHERE else, they'd be ragging you big time," he said. He figured out I was jumping up too soon. Apparently, the trick is to wait a few seconds more until it catches you and rockets you

321

forward. Then, against all sense of self-preservation, you have to lean slightly forward on your board ahead of the wave and into the direction of where this powerful surge of nature is about to explode. Logic and a sound mind will tell you not to do this. Disregard them both and you will attain the Zen of surfing.

For the next hour I tried. Lord knows I tried, but to no avail. I fell forward, I fell backward and many times, defying the laws of gravity, I actually fell upward, each time getting absolutely wrecked. Practice makes perfect my ass. After the 147th attempt it finally dawned on me – you know what, this really isn't fun. In fact, this isn't like making love at all.

Later that night over beers at the Pohnpei Surf Club, I apologized to the other surfers for getting in their way out on the water.

"Nah, it was fun watching you get smashed," one of them said.

"Glad you found it entertaining," I said.

"Dude, no one in their right mind would have tried that," another surfer added shaking his head. "No one, I mean NO ONE starts off at P-Pass. Next time you're in Kauai I'll take you to a place where the waves are soft and just roll in with a sandy bottom, not this razor blade coral."

I finished my last beer and headed home. Soft sand and slow rolling waves in Kauai are for wussies, I thought. Then I started planning my trip to Hawaii.

Chapter 24

Living The Low Hand

Yeah, well sometimes nothing can be a real cool hand.
~ Paul Newman, *Cool Hand Luke*

     Knots are an essential part of boating. All good sailors should have an arsenal of knots they can pull from memory at a moment's notice. The six basic knots that every boat owner should know how to tie are: the overhand or thumb knot, the square knot, the figure eight, the clove hitch, the double half hitch, and the king of knots – the bowline ("The rabbit comes out of the hole, runs around the tree, and goes back down the hole."). These versatile knots can be used for any one of a number of maritime activities, including controlling the sails, docking, mooring, and anchoring.

     The common everyday bow that you use to tie the kid's shoes should not – and I can't stress this enough – be used to secure a boat to a buoy to prevent it from once again going under the dock and sinking.

Ok, so I wasn't a good sailor. That much had already been established. In my case, the rabbit always ran the wrong way around the tree or never stayed down the hole for long. Most times, the rabbit just died, leaving me with an amazing rope trick that made the knot pop back into, well, just a plain piece of rope. I also tried the double mocha latte half hitch and the herb hitch or whatever the hell they're called, but they always came out looking more like a Rorschach test than an actually knot; thus, the bow tie, which wasn't always effective. Come to think of it, the common everyday bow tie isn't even good enough for the kid's shoes. Ask any teacher, who inevitably has to retie the shoes with double knots to the dismay of parents who have to undo them. By the way, a double knot should never be used to secure a boat either.

Our stay on Pohnpei would end the same way it began – with the QE VI at the bottom of the Nett River and it appeared that no amount of salt water, neither sweat nor tears (of which there were plenty) and especially not the sea, could ever keep it afloat for long.

There was a certain symmetry to it all, though – the rising and setting sun, our coming and going, the ebb and flow of the tide, and the sinking, raising, sinking² of our boat. After two-and-a-half wonderful years everything seemed to be coming full circle on the island, and all for the better I might add. When their post in Mauritania didn't work out, Damian and Mary returned with a new addition – a beautiful baby girl named Luna, and Allois could be seen showing off Mila, the adorable baby he had with Haley.

"Hasn't changed my life a bit," he said, holding a diaper bag.

Even Wayne from the Rusty Anchor had come about, although I don't know if you could say it was full circle; maybe semi-circle. "It's the new and improved Wayne," he said smiling. "I've decided I'm going to start being nice to everyone." He did a quick scan of the regulars around the bar. "Well, almost everyone."

We were nearing the end of our farewell tour – a three-month process of teary, beery goodbyes with Pohnpeians, Brits, Germans, Australians, and alcohol-laden coolers filling our *nahs* every other night which, come to think of it, wasn't any different than the rest of our time on the island. Indeed, though, the end was at hand. One of the toughest tasks was telling the kids that Buddy wouldn't be making the trip with us. Though we fed him and the girls played with him endlessly, he still maintained a wild streak and rather enjoyed running with the packs of Pohnpei. While the kids found this difficult, surprisingly they accepted it quite well. The island really was his home and so we decided he'd stay with Peter. There, Buddy would spend the rest of his days until he grew old – or was eaten.

The finality of it all really hit home when Konrad, known for the competitive nature of his fishing and the fact that he usually sailed alone, asked me to join him on one last trip as a goodbye gesture.

After rising and readying our gear in the wee dark hours, we made our way to the causeway where the fiery pink and red early morning sky seemed to cast its rosy glow directly upon two young female joggers bouncing along the road in tight running shorts.

"DON'T LOOK AT THEM," Konrad commanded. "Bad luck."

Silly fishing superstition? Konrad thought not. He let me on his boat, the *Bavarian*, only after I promised I didn't have bananas or money on me. I also assured him that I definitely didn't have sex the night before … or the night before that, or the night before that, or … "Alright, alright, I get it," he said pulling me aboard. He immediately cracked open two beers, despite the early hour of the day.

Soon we were far out to sea, lolling for hours on end with nothing but the light blue sky above and the deep blue water below. Ah, to loll. I loll, we lolled, they are lolling, we all lolli (plural possessive) … I was snapped out of my lolliness as the fishing line went taught and began to whir out into the sea.

"Skip Jack," Konrad announced pulling back the throttle.

Suddenly, THWACK, the pole in the gunnel bent ferociously downward. I looked up in time to see a huge blue, black and silver beast explode out of the water in a shower of white foam.

"MARLIN," Konrad shouted. "Hang onto him!"

The fish wriggled high in the air before plunging back into the depths, causing the line to again go taught and speed out into the churning water below. Fizzzzzzzzzzz! My mind was in complete chaos. Do I yank him back in or do I continue to let the line unreel? Dereel? Disreel? FUCK!

"Let it out, let it out," Konrad yelled. "Let the line out!" After several seconds I was then told to start reeling him back in. As I did so, he again burst out of the water to perform a beautiful slow motion pirouette in the air. Gorgeous, absolutely gorgeous, I thought. Suddenly there was a loud SNAP and the line went limp.

"Gone," Konrad said, stating the obvious. "Bad luck."

It was bad luck. Damn those young female joggers in their tight running shorts!

On the way back we rounded the bend by Madolenihmw (pronounced ... oh never mind) and, instead of heading straight home, decided to slowly circle the entire island. The trip revealed only a lush, verdant jungle stretching from the center peak of *Nahna Laud* straight down to the coastline below with little more than a brown thatch hut poking through here and there. It was an island untouched by time and I marveled at the fact that Pohnpei still looked almost exactly the same as it did thousands of years ago. It was surreal. Our life was surreal.

The island had been especially good to us during our time there and, it seemed, everything always worked out for the best. I often wondered why that was. Not that things didn't work out back in DC, they did. They just seemed to be more complex and, thus, take a bit longer. Without its supplement of stress, complexity withered in the sun and slow pace of

Pohnpei. Island time and island rules applied, forcing us to slow down and we found, surprise, the more we slowed down, the less complicated things got. Intricate problems were fixed with simple solutions; feuds were forgotten, fences were mended, and holes were patched, which brings me back to the boat, our boat, the one at the bottom of the Nett River.

I roused Peter and headed back to our dock where, to my surprise, Johnny was already waiting. "Looks like you could use a little help mate," he said smiling before jumping into the water, clothes and all. Peter and I followed him in. Word spread quickly and within minutes Steve and Paul from the Aussie compound next to the Mallarmes arrived which meant I had Pohnpei's entire Royal Australian Navy working the rescue. Bette called down to say that Simon and Konrad were on their way and when I turned around Steve Finnen was already in the water. I was humbled by the response, to say the least.

There we all stood, chest deep in leptospirosis, hauling the boat as close to the surface as possible so that Johnny, cigarette affixed to his lip and dangling just a quarter inch above the water, could get to the engine. He felt his way around, loosening the bolts one by one with his ratchet. Not all of them complied, however. Every now and then he'd have to take a huge gulp of air and dive down, only to re-emerged with a bolt in hand. I'd then hand him his cigarette back. Once unhinged, the oily, wet and rather heavy engine was hauled up using a heavy rope thrown over the beam that supported the small tin roof covering the dock. Johnny and Peter went to work on it, flushing out the seawater, deluging the insides with WD-40 and replacing the spark plugs, while the rest of us bailed the boat out as it rose above the surface of the water. After a few false starts, the engine roared to life.

The Yamaha 40 pulled through yet again. With a little patchwork and a little touch-up paint, the QE VI became the QE VII and, ironically, the property of Damian and Mary, the ones who suggested I buy the boat in the first place. The circle of life on the island continued.

After showering the leptospirosis, dengue, malaria and Ebola from the river off their bodies, everyone came back that evening to celebrate the resurrection of our boat. Uta and Bette prepared a freezer feast (whatever was in the freezer they cooked, including our special steaks from Guam and lobster from the previous full moon); Susan, the Australian ambassador, arrived with bottles of wine, and Jade, Johnny's partner, created exotic shots. The party was on.

Bette and I raised a toast, several toasts in fact, to the many dear friends we made on the island; friends who dropped everything and came running when we needed them. Not once, not twice, but many times, every time. It was a sentimental moment, for sure. Music played, alcohol flowed and, as usual, a poker game broke out and took us well into the early morning hours.

Often, we had both the high and low hands split the pot, meaning an ace, two, three, four and six of different suits, the lowest possible hand, was just as good as a royal flush. Since I'm normally dealt the worst hand possible, I actually was able to win, or co-win, a number of games. Imagine that, low hand won; an anomaly in the winner-take-all world I was used to. With much of the material world missing (and 24/7 news, I might add), we were living the low hand on Pohnpei and couldn't have been happier. No matter where they were, what they were dining on, or whoever they were firing, the richest people in the world weren't having a better time than we were playing poker and eating freezer burned steaks from Guam out on a spit of sand in the middle of the Pacific Ocean.

Pohnpei adhered to the two basics rules of an old saying: "Rule #1: Don't sweat the small stuff. Rule #2: It's all small stuff. And if you can't fight or flee, float." So that's exactly what I did, I floated, except for an occasional tussle with the kids and, from time to time, Bette and, of course, the boat. The boat definitely didn't float. Then there were the cockroaches and the dogs and, you know what, forget the floating part. Instead, I managed to cope, which is like floating except in a panicked, holding on for dear life kind of way.

Coping is an important part of parenting. It is the only weapon we have against chaos, that cosmic constant in our lives. We may try to achieve order, but order is a universal anomaly like quasars and alternate side of the street parking. We may tell our children to move the glass of milk from the edge of the table, but in doing so they will inevitably spill it the other way. Coping helps us accept this. Coping is surrendering with dignity.

But I did more, oh so much more than just learn how to cope. Sink or swim is an apropos idiom on an island, and on the open seas of parenthood I learned to swim and swim fast. Despite the Vegas odds on me sinking, I managed to cook and clean, cajole and console, correct and, perhaps most importantly, connect with the kids. They say that in bringing up children spend on them half as much money and twice as much time. On Pohnpei, for the first time in my adult life, that's exactly what I was able to do and I quickly understood the simplistic genius of that saying.

On one occasion, this included surprising Devon and Tess by letting them stay home from school one rainy day. The perfect start of any day is waking up, then going back to sleep with the rain beating against the windows. Eventually, they jumped onto my bed. We wrestled and I playfully slammed them with flying elbows, eye gauges and face rakes. We ate breakfast at 10 a.m. and then watched *Pirates of the Caribbean* for the 18th time. For lunch, we used huge green banana leaves as umbrellas and walked in the pouring rain down to the PCR for the rotating counter filled with all-you-can-eat sashimi, sushi, rice, soup and, for Tess, fried chicken. Seven plates and a pile of chicken bones later, we flopped on the hammock in our *nahs* and continued watching the downpour; a lifetime of memories in a single day. Does it get any better than that?

As a Home Daddy I was afforded the opportunity to be a real part of our kid's lives and, in the end, I couldn't have been happier taking care of them (and complaining about taking care of them). One of the greatest gifts I've been giving in my life. Sure, I may have lost my composure once in a while and yes, I once threw a hot dog so hard it stuck to the wall, but the kids were still alive, and that meant I could declare victory. For a man, even a modern-day man, that was saying a lot (idea for a bumper sticker: "My Heroes Have Always Been Home Daddies").

A quiet, orderly calm had settled over the good ship *Neason Martin* as we prepared to leave the South Seas bound for the distant shores of the Caribbean. It would be different, it would be exciting, but it wouldn't be Pohnpei. I missed the place already, but also knew that a small part of the island, or more specifically, the sea, would remain with us. The movers made sure of that when they packed our Tupperware, including my lunch of tuna fish, in a box with our pillows and sheets, where it would remain in the hull of a cargo ship until it arrived in St. Lucia three months later.

The tuna surprise notwithstanding, I stood in the empty house and suddenly had the feeling that something was missing; something of vague importance but you can't quite put your finger on it, like where you left your beer and you just know you had one last gulp left. And then I remembered, "Oh yeah, my career."

What would it take to be fully integrated back into the honest employment of public relations? Surely I was missing out on important developments taking place in the hi-tech world of marketing and communications, and what about the latest advances in social media? I checked the important "chatter" taking place at my former organization.

FROM: HR
TO: All Staff
SUBJECT: Refrigerator cleaning schedule

All – attached is the refrigerator cleaning schedule for the remainder the year. We will be cleaning one refrigerator each week on Friday afternoon between 5 – 5:30 pm. Any items left in the appliance will be tossed (even if labeled "save" or "do not throw away").

Nope, wasn't missing a thing.

That evening, the crew gathered one last time to say goodbye, including the Mallarmes who brought a basket woven from palm leaves and filled with breadfruit and coconut shavings, just as they had the day we first arrived. For their part, the Aussies offered a host of recommendations regarding the month we'd spend in Australia before flying to St. Lucia, but the best advice came from Eddie.

"No Fosters. Got it, mate?"

At one point the crew decided to review our departure checklist one last time. Everything all set, they asked? Boxes (and tuna fish) stored in the cargo ship? Check. Peace Corps paperwork completed? Check. Visas obtained for Australia? Check ... wait, WHAT?

Susan Cox, the Australian ambassador, pushed me aside and grabbed Bette. "Come on, honey, we have some paperwork to fill out," she said as they headed out the door and over to the embassy ... at 10 o'clock at night. Sure enough, calls were made, paperwork was completed, and they were back by 11 p.m. In case of emergency, I highly recommend getting to know the Australian ambassador nearest you.

Eventually it was time for our final farewell. The hugs and tears flowed freely. This was goodbye. "No, no," Konrad said waving his hand in the air. "In Germany, we don't say goodbye, we say *aufwiedersehen*, which means see you again." We all agreed, but for a split second, Bette and I looked at each other and there was that aching realization that that might not be so.

The morning of our departure, in the final hours of my dream, I went down to the river and stood in the QE VII one last time. Damian would be coming by that afternoon to bring it over to a dock closer to his new house, so I still had time for one last excursion. Instead, I simply put my hands behind my head and leaned back in the boat smiling. The voyage wasn't over; in fact, it was just beginning with yet another adventure already lined up on the horizon. You know; that distant point where the sky and Earth meet that we never seem to

reach?

The wind picked up and I closed my eyes and smelled the salt in the air. I didn't have to imagine it, I really was there; the Saint Somewhere Jimmy Buffet sings about, the screensaver image on the computer in my office that puts me in a wooden boat on water so clear the boat appears to be suspended in mid-air somewhere between the yellow and green coral reef below and the sinewy white clouds that dot the baby blue sky above.

"DAD," Tess suddenly screamed over the railing high above. "Devon put a huge bug in my Lucky Charms and I almost ate it. I HATE HER!"

Shit!

Disclaimer

I would like to humbly apologize to the good people of Micronesia and the expats therein for any and all misrepresentations, misperceptions, falsehoods, innuendos, deceits, fabrications and outright lies found in the preceding chapters. While I did conduct research and checked as many facts as I could, alas, research and fact checking requires due diligence and frankly, I didn't come to an island paradise in the South Pacific to, I shudder at the mere mention of the word, "work." (Point of fact: Micronesia is not officially in the South Pacific but I went ahead and said it because she is unquestionably more seductive than her older brother, the cold North Pacific, and considerably more alluring than her older sister, the Western Pacific, where Micronesia does lie and, honestly, who's going to quibble over six lousy degrees of longitude? Second point of fact: distance measured east and west of the International Dateline is actually latitude, not longitude.)

See what a pain due diligence is?

Author's Note

Among the books I researched, three stood out and proved to be especially useful, *Pohnpei: An Island Argosy* by Gene Ashby, and *First Taint of Civilization* and *A Yankee Trader In Yap* by Francis X. Hezel, a Jesuit priest who has lived and worked in Micronesia for 45 years and is easily one of the most authoritative figures regarding the island's history and culture. Forgive me father for I have sinned and possibly "borrowed" from all three books.

Also, thanks to Pacific scholar Saul Riesenberg for his research on Sapwauhfik.

Lastly, *Phantastica: A Classic Survey on the Use and Abuse of Mind-Altering Plants* by Louis Lewin, which was useful in more ways than one.

A former journalist and public affairs specialist, JJ Martin has won awards from the Public Relations Society of America and the New Jersey Press Association, and has had articles featured in several publications, including *Travel & Leisure, Cineaste, American Cowboy*, and the *Denver Post*. He currently resides in Silver Spring, Maryland.

Made in the USA
Middletown, DE
23 July 2021